To Myra,
   Love, your sister
        Alice

INTERNATIONAL FIRMS
AND LABOUR IN KENYA: 1945-70

INTERNATIONAL FIRMS AND LABOUR IN KENYA: 1945-70

Alice Hoffenberg Amsden

Lecturer in Economics, The London School of
Economics and Political Science, and
Goldsmith's College, London

FRANK CASS & CO LTD
1971

First published in 1971 by
FRANK CASS AND COMPANY LIMITED
67 Great Russell Street, London WCIB 3BT

ISBN 0 7146 2581 7

Printed in Great Britain by
Clarke, Doble & Brendon Ltd.
Plymouth

Table of Contents

ACKNOWLEDGMENTS

Research in Kenya was made possible by a grant from the Central Research Fund of the University of London. Further study was aided by a Leverhulme Research Grant from the London School of Economics. I am indebted to the following people for assisting in the preparation of this study at its various stages: B. C. Roberts, C. H. Allen, E. M. Hyde-Clarke, Shiela Ogilvie, G. J. M. Grey, Adam Kutahi, Miriam Auma Bwana, the staff of the Federation of Kenya Employers, and numerous members of Kenya's Trade Union movement. My parents deserve very special thanks for their encouragement and aid. My husband was of such great help that surely some of the errors which undoubtedly appear in the text are his.

November, 1970   A.H.A.

INTRODUCTION

In a symposium on wages policy and economic growth, the head of Shell-BP's Industrial Relations Department in Lagos made the following remarks:

> . . . while the union movement in Nigeria is not yet really very strong, it derives considerable power from its division into unions which adhere to the West and those leaning to the East. For employers are prepared to concede considerable wage rises to 'western' unions in their attempts to support them.[1]

Mr. Ofurum's remarks are unusual for their frankness. They are also unusual for their description of an employer strategy less subtle than most. But they suggest that employers have a calculated influence on the personality and practice of labour relations in an underdeveloped country. If such a suggestion is unusual, such influence is not.

The study that follows is concerned with just such influence, particularly as it is exercised by the big corporation. Kenya provides the case study precisely because the big corporation has exercised such decisive influence there.

The emphasis is placed on how the Federation of Kenya Employers influences labour relations, rather than on how labour relations are influenced by the FKE. The fine distinction rests on the fuller coverage accorded the employer movement rather than the total intricacies of labour relations. The disadvantage of such an approach is that treatment of trade union affairs and the government's role in industrial life is short-circuited. The advantage is a greater familiarity with the activities of international firms overseas and the avenues through which these activities are pursued, allowing those interested in underdeveloped countries other than Kenya to draw parallels.

Corporations acting in an individual capacity always constitute a significant force behind the scene. But in Kenya, a centralised network of associations projects the voice of corporations more forcefully on it. The historical explanation lies in the 'Mau Mau' revolt. Lurid accounts of the Emergency, spanning from 1952–60, have been discredited by scholarly accounts of injustice. The white European settler community rendered the Kikuyu tribe in particular short of land, in possession of inadequately paid jobs, subject to a colour bar, and denied practical access to channels of protest. Some of these causes of the nationalist struggle are described in Chapters One, Two, and Three. Their effects are central to all subsequent Chapters. The 'Mau Mau' revolt, however, does not necessarily set Kenya apart from other British colonies where African Government came easier. Rather, it makes for a magnified case study of the frustrations and change evolving more gradually throughout the Continent. Then, too, the behaviour of international firms in Kenya may be perceived for purposes of comparison as a sharpened version of the behaviour of international firms in neighbouring states.

The Emergency redoubled African opposition to colonial rule and reinforced a conviction of the right to self-government and the rewards of industrialisation. Independence came to Kenya in 1963, only three years after the Emergency ended. The turn of events also moulded the nationalist movement. Its politics were conditioned by the British presence. Its goal was to control as the British had controlled rather more than to create a new political economy. This provides the underlying theme in Chapters Six to Nine.

The Emergency made no less an impact on the Colonial Administration. However much 'Mau Mau' was initially viewed as tribal mania, measures of atonement proliferated. They promised to put an end to the settlers' land privileges, a low wage economy, and racial discrimination in employment.

The effect on private employers was profound. Government legislation grew costly to management and 'Mau Mau' made investors uneasy. The big corporations energetically set about organising themselves to meet the challenge. Their objective was two-fold: to maximise political stability and to minimise labour costs. The Association of Commercial and Industrial Employers, later re-christened the Federation of Kenya Employers, seized upon a policy first advocated by the Colonial Office and made it work: bread and butter trade unions were widely encouraged to pre-empt radical unrest. Built into bargaining procedures of the FKE's design, however, were mechanisms to hold the line on wage increases. The corporations were not of the same vintage as the self-made tycoons of an earlier heroic age. But neither did they view their profits with the tolerance the myth sometimes exploits.

The coming of Independence created surprisingly less impact than 'Mau Mau'. To be sure, Kenyatta's Administration has been no slacker than other African Administrations in exerting its control over economic and political affairs. Many analyses, however, fail to look behind this control in an effort to convey its breadth. They then miss the entrenched sources of power other than the State. Continuity between old and new is understated as well. The single-minded Africanisation exercise of the ruling party has left the economic structure unchanged. The Western model of industrial relations, born in the image of the Western corporation, has also endured. Legislation and police tactics have largely been designed to close the loopholes. Over thirty industry-wide unions have survived the transfer of government. They continue to distinguish themselves for their 'pork chop mentality' rather than their use of labour power to effect political change. Collective bargaining has reached impressive proportions and it is vigorous and ordered. The Federation of Kenya Employers has done its job well. The implications for the well-being of Kenya and other underdeveloped countries that extend a welcome to international firms are summarised in a concluding note.

II

The philosophy intended to guide the parties which act out their lives in Kenya bears the title of Democratic African Socialism. It may be as much a misnomer as the Holy Roman Empire. All the brave ideals are there but as one critic observes:

> If well-paid foreign experts, incentives to overseas firms, loans to the most progressive farmers, investment in the most fertile provinces, and a tax structure which enables the enterprising to enjoy the reward of their efforts will best promote the development of the country, then the paper [setting out the philosophy of Democratic African Socialism] is single-minded in endorsing them. But would this not mean that social justice and human dignity are, after all, to be compromised for material ends, in the faint hope of reinstating them more fully in some distant future? Does the paper, in applying its principles, forget its own warning?[2]

Democratic African Socialism of the Kenya variety is not incompatible with private ownership of the means of production. President Kenyatta stated in 1964:

> We consider that nationalisation will not serve to advance the cause of African Socialism. . . . I believe it must now be clear to everyone that my Government actively wishes to encourage more and more investment from all countries.[3]

Such clear encouragement has given the Federation of Kenya Employers the confidence to act unselfconsciously: more so, perhaps, than other employer movements in Africa where greater stigma attaches to foreign investment.

Democratic African Socialism of the Kenya variety nominally rejects the harsh Western capitalist system as well as the class warfare of Marxist theory. It seeks to build on what is claimed to be a tradition of pre-colonial Africa: classlessness. The logical implication would seem to be:

> The growth of an entrepreneurial African class is not looked upon with favor. . . . There appear to be many advantages in permitting and encouraging foreign private investment while inhibiting the development of indigenous capitalists.[4]

Not so in Kenya, however, where indigenous capitalists have received an official fillip. President Kenyatta conveyed his enthusiasm shortly after Independence:

> I was very proud when . . . my attention was drawn to a radio manufacturing company . . . wholly owned and run by Africans . . . we plan to expand . . . such . . . industries to a total . . . of three or four hundred.[5]

The employer community, both foreign and local, is treated as an accepted pillar of society. This, too, affords the FKE freer licence to act in labour affairs.

The paper on Democratic African Socialism is reputedly the work of the late Tom Mboya. It is the philosophy of the Kenya African National Union (KANU), which has governed Kenya since 1963. At the time of Independence, KANU was opposed by the Kenya African Democratic Union (KADU). KADU advocated *majimbo*, or regional government, and wooed the small tribes fearful of the tenuous axis of the more numerous Kikuyus and Luos in KANU. In 1964, however, KADU M.P.s joined the majority party. A united front prevailed until 1966, when the supporters of Oginga Odinga were purged from KANU and reassembled as the Kenya Peoples' Union (KPU). They allegedly stood for a socialist society, but not for long. In 1969, the KPU was outlawed, discredited by the government for stirring up tribal hatreds. Many of the KPU's followers are Luo. The discreditors, however, mostly Kikuyu, may be playing on the very tribalism they deplore in order to shroud real issues. A former headmaster of many of today's leading politicians once remarked:

> The tribes in Kenya are as different as the nations of Europe and get on with one another about as badly.[6]

Tribalism may seem as irrational to the European as nationalism to the Kenyan, yet the real tragedy is surely this: poverty incites tribalism (and nationalism). The uneven horizontal distribution of wealth amongst tribes intensifies it. But the uneven vertical distribution of economic, political, and social resources is obscured by it.

Kenya's most pressing problems and those of *all* poor Africans may be articulated in three demands: more land, more education, and more jobs. The already critical scarcity of land, however, will worsen as the population grows at its alarming rate of over 3 per cent *per annum*. The dispossessed will need jobs; so will the children of Africans rich enough to afford even primary school fees; and so will the children of the less fortunate. Yet in the past few years, employment has stagnated. The hardcore jobless are now said to number one-third of recorded employment. Salaried personnel account for 7 per cent of recorded employment but account for 44 per cent of the wage bill.[7] The income differential between wage earners and the mass of peasants has been described as large but the income differential between unskilled operatives and capitalists has been described as enormous. It is against this background that the activities of international firms in Kenya are best understood.

REFERENCES

1 *Wage Policy Issues in Economic Development*, ed. by Anthony D. Smith, The Proceedings of a Symposium held by the International Institute for Labour Studies at Egelund, Denmark, 23–27 October 1967, under the Chairmanship of Clark Kerr (London: Macmillan, 1969), p. 61.

2 Peter Marris, 'Economics is Not Enough', *East Africa Journal*, Vol. 3, No. 11 (February 1967), p. 15.

3 Jomo Kenyatta, *Harambee!: The Prime Minister of Kenya's Speeches, 1963–64* (Nairobi: Oxford University Press, 1964), pp. 79; 75–76.

4 W. H. Friedland and C. G. Rosberg, Jr., 'The Anatomy of African Socialism', in *African Socialism*, ed. by the same authors (Stanford: Stanford University Press, 1964), p. 7.

5 Kenyatta, *Harambee!*, p. 76.

6 E. Carey Francis, 'Kenya's Problems', *African Affairs*, Vol. 54, No. 216 (July 1955), p. 187.

7 R. H. Green, 'Wage Levels, Employment, Productivity and Consumption', in *Education, Employment and Rural Development*, ed. by James R. Sheffield (Nairobi: East Africa Publishing House, 1967), Tables I & II. Referred to by Dharam P. Ghai, 'Incomes Policy in Kenya: Need, Criteria and Machinery', *East Africa Economic Review*, Vol. 4 (N.S.), No. 1 (June 1968).

SECTION I

THE HISTORICAL SETTING: 1945-56

THE COLONIAL OFFICE

Three policy measures have been singled out for study in the following chapters because they capture several essential equations in Kenya's labour history during the post-war period. Their adoption by the Colonial Office in the early 'forties indicated an awareness of the mounting pressures and frustrations throughout Black Africa. Their shortcomings as safety valves for discontent found graphic expression in the 'Mau Mau' revolt a few years later. Their repair during the Emergency signalled a new brand of colonialism—taken to a far conclusion by a new-styled class of expatriate managers. Their legacy at Independence opened to question the ideology and practices of Kenya's nationalist movement and its European mentors.

Thus, as a prologue to developments not only in Kenya but elsewhere in Africa, there follows a discussion of the Colonial Office's directives on labour: the important catalyst for events abroad.

British Labour Policy in the World War II Period

It seems that the colonies were never forgotten during the war even at the worst of times, for in the year of the London blitz, Parliament passed the Colonial Development and Welfare Act. It is generally acknowledged that the purpose of the 1940 Act was as officially stated: 'to promote the prosperity and happiness of the peoples in the Colonial Empire'.[1] The presumption seems to have been that the Empire no longer existed exclusively to serve the mother country. Lord Hailey, however, points out that the Act recognised that to promote Britain's war interests, more investment overseas was wanted from London.[2] In any event, under the terms of the Act, funds were to be made available to finance development in the colonies.

Apparently, the government believed that legalising trade unions would further promote the 'prosperity and happiness' of colonial peoples. For on the insistence of a group of Labour Members of Parliament, the Colonial Development and Welfare Act made aid to a colony contingent on the passage of protective trade union legislation.[3] This provision for the first time armed the Colonial Office with coercive powers over trade union policy. Previously, Circular

Dispatches to Colonial Governors had merely urged the passage of protective trade union legislation and had met with little compliance.[4] The first of such Dispatches, issued by the Labour Government as early as in 1930 (when Sidney Webb was Secretary of State for the Colonies) pointed out that trade unions were a therapeutic safety valve for the expression of grievances.[5] Another dispatch, issued by the Conservatives in 1937, cautioned that if trade unions remained illegal, extremist organisations would fester.[6]

'Safety valve' and 'best alternative' theories along with 'prosperity and happiness' ones boiled down to a recipe for the gradual demise of paternalism and the introduction of joint determination of employment standards in the post-war years. The Labour Adviser to the Secretary of State for the Colonies, for example, recommended the application in East Africa of 'The well-tried principles of collective bargaining and negotiation. . . .'[7]

The Atlantic Charter, and the momentary burst of idealism accompanying it, spread a nimbus over the Colonial world. In this spirit, the International Labour Organisation issued its own Charter in 1944. The Philadelphia Charter of the ILO held that 'The improvement in living standards shall be regarded as the principal objective in the planning of economic development'.[8] To improve living standards, a system of industrial relations was envisaged which also featured collective bargaining. This found expression in an ILO Convention of 1947. Other Conventions based on the Philadelphia Charter amounted to a fairly comprehensive labour code for the underdeveloped countries.

In compliance with this code and ILO first-principles which are evidently themselves anglo-saxon in origin, Britain fastened on a system of industrial relations for her colonies based on the home model.

Britain's post-war labour policy has been criticised on a number of counts, some of which are raised again shortly.

First, a recurrent indictment is that trade unions are inimical to the quality of African society. Mr Guy Hunter maintains:

> The insistence of the British Government that trade unions must be established in Africa has always seemed to me one of its most unimaginative decisions. It took a hundred years of strife, suffering, waste, and bitterness to . . . create the powerful organisations which in most of Europe, and in the United States, are still among the most illiberal and conservative of all major social institutions . . . there were other traditions that could have been used. . . .[9]

Yet, traditions more radical than trade unions, if regarded at all, were judged 'extremist' in London. Traditions less radical than trade unions were greeted with suspicion in Africa.

Second, anything short of crash measures to benefit African

labourers before Independence was viewed as indefensible. Now it is a growing conviction that voluntary collective bargaining and the strike weapon are vestiges of colonialism, no longer sacrosanct or desirable. They are unjust for they further the interests of an urban elite relative to a peasant majority. They are insupportable, for they retard economic growth. The imprudence of colonial policy, however, is less the argument than that of imposing checks on the demands of labourers in African states still clinging to a Western model of economic organisation.

Finally, the 'safety valve' theory of Britain's post-war labour policy has come under attack. On the one hand, some observers have perceived that, in the political field especially, Britain failed to permit trade unions to become mechanisms for the expression of discontent. On the other hand, the complaint commonly heard since Independence is that rather than acting as 'safety valves' intended for the ventilation of grievances, trade unions increase rather than institutionalise opposition.

Mr. Guy Hunter implies that the British Government's ethno-centricity fixed on less than ideal institutions for export. Some have used a harsher word than ethnocentricity, others a kinder one. Constraints on the political activities of colonial trade unions, however, imply that exported institutions were not infrequently depreciated versions of the home product (at closer or further remove from the ideal). British trade unionists, for example, were free to engage in politics whereas African trade unionists, particularly in Kenya, were not.

The country of import was in part responsible, not usually caring for the home product in full strength. It has been suggested:

> . . . the position of a British Secretary of State for the Colonies in relation to his Colonial Governors resembles that of a medieval king in relation to his great feudatories.[10]

It is hardly surprising, then, that the labour directives of the Colonial Office underwent significant local adaptations. We thus leave the London prologue for the African sequel.

In Kenya, the way in which the general directives from London were applied was mainly influenced by contemporary politics. For political skirmishes in Kenya after the war had an extra dimension which was absent in British colonies where few Europeans had permanently settled: the 'great feudatory' in Nairobi had to contend with thoughts of divine right to rule amongst some of his white subjects. This is evinced in the history of the first policy measure of the post-war period to be examined: the introduction of a protective labour code or practices of fair employment.

REFERENCES

1 Great Britain, *Statement of Policy on Colonial Development and Welfare*, Cmd. 6175, 1940, p. 8.
2 Lord Hailey, *An African Survey* (Rev. 1956; London: Oxford University Press, 1957), pp. 1323–24.
3 B. C. Roberts, *Labour in the Tropical Territories of the Commonwealth* (London: G. Bell and Sons Ltd. for the London School of Economics and Political Science, 1964), pp. 187–88.
4 Great Britain, Colonial Office, *Labour Supervision in the Colonial Empire, 1937–43*, Colonial No. 185 (London: HMSO, 1943), pp. 11–12.
5 Roberts, *Labour in the Tropical Territories of the Commonwealth*, pp 177–78.
6 Great Britain, *The Colonial Empire in 1937–38*, Cmd. 5760, 1938, Appendix II, p. 79.
7 Great Britain, Colonial Office, *Labour Conditions in East Africa*, Colonial No. 193, by G. St. J. Orde Browne (London: HMSO, 1946), p. 30.
8 International Labour Office, *Social Policy in Dependent Territories*, Studies and Reports, Series B (Economic Conditions), no. 38 (Montreal: ILO, 1944), p. 173.
9 Guy Hunter, *The Best of Both Worlds? A Challenge on Development Policies in Africa* (London: Oxford University Press for the Institute of Race Relations, London, 1967), pp. 88–89.
10 Thomas Hodgkin, *Nationalism in Colonial Africa* (London: Frederick Muller Ltd., 1956), p. 43.

CHAPTER ONE

A PROTECTIVE LABOUR CODE

Beginning in 1946, the Labour Department in Nairobi supervised the enactment of a protective labour code for the African worker. The more egregious abuses of employment were ended and those dark satanic mills were less likely to appear. When trade unions emerged, they could set their targets higher than the very barest minimum standards of employment, for these had already been legislated. The experience of politicking for legal safeguards in the factory, common to Western labour movements, was by-passed. The political development of African trade unions may reflect this.

The government's code was suggestive of a new status relationship between workers and employers. After 1949, Kenya's catch-all Employment Ordinance was no longer administered on a racial basis. Previously, it had been applied to Africans only. Its nomenclature was also modified. The word 'employee' was substituted for the term 'servant', a change in terminology identical to that effected in Britain nearly a century earlier. Such a legal admission in Kenya may have prepared the most paternalistic of employers for less authoritarian personnel practices.

In accordance with Convention No. 65 of the International Labour Organisation, Kenya's Employment Ordinance was recast so that penal sanctions for breach of contract were abolished, with the exception of the offence of 'desertion', for which such sanctions were reduced. Labour recruitment was made subject to stricter government surveillance. Recommended standards of medical treatment, housing, and rations were improved. Protection was afforded to women in nightwork and children in municipal employment. A ceiling was imposed on the hours worked by juveniles in agriculture. In 1946, a Workman's Compensation Ordinance was passed. In 1950, a comprehensive factories ordinance was enacted. Labour inspection was tightened and, to some extent, helped ensure that the measures incorporated in Kenya's labour code met with compliance.

The positive side of the balance sheet is thus impressive. The negative side, however, tends to cancel it out. Two employment practices for which Africans entertained the greatest dislike were not put right until after 'Mau Mau'. The first concerned the *kipande*.

The Kipande

The *kipande* was a work certificate which all African males were required to carry. It contained their fingerprints. Its original purpose, as conceived in 1920, was to ensure that Africans under compulsion to labour for the government in fact did so for a given number of days each year. It has been alleged, however, that the *kipande* also helped locate the deserted labour of settlers, and breach of contract was punishable by imprisonment.[1] The *kipande* was the crowning symbol of racialism in Kenya, for whites were exempt from its provisions and pitted their political power against that of blacks to keep the *kipande* in effect.

The *kipande* provided the focal point in 1922 for what amounted to a general strike and mass rally in Nairobi, which ended in the death of at least 21 Africans.[2] The *kipande* again became a burning issue in the 'forties. In fact, riding the crest of the liberal wave of the immediate post-war years, Kenya's one African on the Legislative Council, Eliud Mathu, succeeded in extending the *kipande* to members of all races in 1948: a 'personal triumph' for Mathu, as hailed by the Native Commissioner.[3] A storm of protest, however, soon arose in settler quarters. The *kipande*, it was said, made Europeans feel like criminals and smacked of totalitarianism. The government was accused of appeasing the Africans and as a result, reneged on the issue. In 1949, the Legislative Council moved to keep finger-printing in effect only for men (that is, African men) who could not fill in and sign a work card in English unaided.

Only after the coming of 'Mau Mau', did the *kipande* fall into disuse. Whilst it would be unwarranted to overstate the lessons taught to management by the *kipande* incident, international firms may have sensed the need to dissociate themselves from the older rough-shod type of colonialism. It was proving a bad risk.

Payment by Race

The second employment practice to escape the round of immediate post-war labour reforms also countenanced racial discrimination. It concerned the payment of wages on the basis of colour, both by public and private employers. In 1948, the Holmes Commission was instructed to review conditions in the civil services of Kenya, Uganda, Tanganyika, and Zanzibar. It recommended that a racial structure of payment be retained: differential rates being attached to jobs in the middle ranges of the civil service and three-fifths European salaries being the rule for Africans holding higher posts.

The Commission posed several arguments in support of its proposals. The first rested on the belief that common rates of pay promised economic disaster:

> . . . it would be wrong for any Government, in pursuit of this or that ideology, to disrupt the economy of its territory. . . .[4]

The second argument fixed on the alleged inequality of work performance distinguishing the communities:

> It has to be remembered that the indigenous peoples of the three mainland territories are removed by little more than fifty years from a state of society far more primitive than that of Britain at the beginning of the Christian era . . . ignorant of the wheel, the plough, and the loom, a society in which the only rule was the rule of the spear or of the sorcerer.
>
> With such antecedents it would be idle to expect to find in the African of today those qualities of mind and character which go to making a good civil servant developed in any marked degree.[5]

As a third argument, it was noted that:

> The disadvantages of so remunerating any class of Africans [on a par with Europeans] as to create a Mandarin caste, divorced in income and interests from their fellows, would not be confined to the economic field.[6]

It was only in 1954, during the height of 'Mau Mau' that salary scales in the public services became 'essentially non-racial in character'.[7] This followed the report of a commission under Sir David Lidbury, which a European field officer in the Labour Department claimed 'did as much to defeat "Mau Mau" as the British army'.[8] Equal pay for equal work was accepted in principle by the commission. The three-fifths rule was abolished and local Europeans, Asians, and Africans came to receive the same salary for the same job. Expatriates were given a special allowance.[9]

Since Independence, this formula has been advanced as a solution to the problem of expatriate remuneration in very poor countries.[10] But paradoxically, the situation in Kenya may be less satisfactory than elsewhere, for whilst Africans are paid on a par with local Europeans (and expatriates, minus their special allowance), locally born Europeons are typically more numerous than elsewhere, and salaries have come to be geared to the style of life to which this historically privileged minority became accustomed. Thus,

> . . . a huge gap appears between African managers and African workmen or supervisors; so that the whole wage level, from the labourer upwards, comes into question.[11]

In Kenya today, it is questioned with growing disbelief whether equal pay for equal work signifies a distribution of income such that starting salaries for college graduates (regardless of colour) are almost seven times as great as prevailing wages for experienced subordinate staff.[12] Nor are the problems of a Mandarin caste confined to the economic field. If nationalist leaders fought in the struggle for equal pay under colonialism, few have been as valiant in the equalising struggle since then. As for employers, one of their interpretations of equal pay is equality under the labour law for expatriate and African entrepreneurs, regardless of 'ability to pay'.

Conclusion

The questioning and dislocations attendant upon the Lidbury proposals were felt almost immediately. As Africans in the upper echelons of employment began to earn a more handsome salary, the sights of the unskilled were raised accordingly. Less than two years after the Lidbury proposals were published, leading employers met to discuss how they could rationalise Kenya's wage structure: i.e. put a lid on the pot. Yet another report published in the same year as that of the Lidbury Commission set the pot on the boil for employers, as the next chapter relates.

REFERENCES

1 John Middleton, 'Kenya: Administrative Changes in African Life, 1912–45', in History of East Africa, Vol. 2, ed. by Vincent Harlow and E. M. Chilver (Oxford: At the Clarendon Press, 1965), p. 356.

2 Carl Rosberg, Jr. and John Nottingham, The Myth of "Mau Mau": Nationalism in Kenya (New York: Frederick A. Praeger for the Hoover Institution on War, Revolution, and Peace, Stanford University, Stanford California, 1966), p. 45.

3 George Bennett, Kenya: A Political History; The Colonial Period (London: Oxford University Press, 1963), p. 122.

4 Great Britain, Colonial Office, Report of the Commission on the Commission on the Civil Services of Kenya, Tanganyika, Uganda, and Zanzibar, 1947–48, Colonial No. 223 (London: HMSO, 1948), p. 24.

5 Ibid., pp. 24–25.

6 Ibid., p. 27.

7 Colony and Protectorate of Kenya, Labour Department Annual Report, 1954, Nairobi, p. 13.

8 Interview, Mr. Anthony Clayton, London, Autumn 1967.

9 East Africa High Commission and others, Commission on the Civil Services of the East African Territories and the East Africa High Commission Report, 1953–54 (2 Vols.; Nairobi, 1954).

10 Anthony D. Smith, ed., *Wage Policy Issues in Economic Development*. The Proceedings of a Symposium held by the International Iinstitute for Labour Studies at Egelund, Denmark, 23–27 October 1967, under the Chairmanship of Clark Kerr (London: Macmillan, 1969), pp. 110; 125; and 156.

11 Guy Hunter, *The New Societies of Tropical Africa* (London: Oxford University Press for the Institute of Race Relations, London, 1962), pp. 229–31.

12 D. P. Ghai, 'Incomes Policy in Kenya: Need, Criteria and Machinery', *East African Economic Review*, Vol. 4 (NS), No. 1 (June 1968), p. 21.

CHAPTER TWO

MINIMUM WAGES

Following the passage of the Colonial Development and Welfare Act, a dispatch was circularised from London charging colonial governments with the 'imperative duty' to raise living standards amongst Africans, 'alike for humanitarian, political . . . and economic reasons.'[1] Hence the Kenya Government's second major post-war policy: the improvement of African wages through the device of statutory minima.

The see-saws which subsequently characterised the government's wage policy merit close consideration, for the lead taken by Kenya in the field has often been followed elsewhere. One writer laments this and notes that the important Kenya Committee on African Wages (1954) resisted the services of economists on the 'extraordinary grounds' that contradictory advice amongst them would arise in any event. 'There is a need for controversy in this area, for there has been too little of it in the past.'[2]

Post-War Regulation

Humanitarian and political arguments for raising African wages were amply supplied in Kenya during the war. Labour disturbances throughout the 'forties evinced the abysmally low level of African earnings and standards of housing. Two boards of inquiry paid eloquent testimony to depressed conditions.[3] The economic considerations behind statutory regulation were of special importance. The Labour Department in Nairobi stated in 1946:

> Long-term policy is directed towards the maintenance of stability between the agricultural and industrial areas. This means the development of an independent wage worker without subsidy from the native land unit. . . . The position in the native land units which are faced by over population and a deterioration of soil fertility . . . is such that [a reliance by the wage earner on subsidisation from subsistence agriculture] must now cease. The first step towards stability is the general adoption of a 'living wage' standard for an African divorced from his native land unit.[4]

As a first step in raising wages, Kenya passed a Minimum Wage Ordinance in 1946. Initially this statute was applied only to Nairobi, then to Mombasa and Kisumu, but it later came to cover six other industrial towns. Today, its provisions are limited to thirteen urban areas.

The formula adopted for calculating the minimum wage in 1946 was based on two conceptions: the Poverty Datum Line (PDL) and the Effective Minimum Level (EML).[5] The Central Minimum Wages Advisory Board used Professor Edward Batson's formula for assessing the PDL. Writing about this formula, Batson states:

> Such a standard is perhaps more remarkable for what it omits than for what it includes. . . . It is not a 'human' standard of living. It thus admirably fulfils its purpose of stating the barest minimum upon which subsistence and health can theoretically be achieved.[6]

Since a margin of income was needed above the PDL, Professor Batson devised the Effective Minimum Level. He defined the EML as 'the income level at which the competition of other wants slackens sufficiently to permit the purchase of a budget equivalent to that allowed for in the Poverty Datum Line'.[7] Batson believed that the EML was most appropriately set at 150 per cent of the PDL.

Three points about the minimum wages established in Kenya before 'Mau Mau' deserve emphasis.

First, such minima were geared to the needs of a bachelor occupying a single bed-space. This was in spite of the Labour Department's claim that a stable work force demanded a minimum wage sufficient to support a family.

Second, grave doubts were expressed as to whether or not post-war minimum wages were adequate to provide for the barest needs even of a bachelor. These misgivings were advanced in a study carried out by the East African Statistical Department in 1950.[8] The study disclosed that nearly all employees earning the statutory minimum wage in Nairobi spent the greatest part of their earnings on food and other basic requirements. Almost nothing was spent on luxuries. Nevertheless, even for single workers, expenditures on essential items frequently exceeded income. Employees were forced to borrow at high rates of interest and were under the compulsion to engage in shady manoeuvres to make ends meet. The percentage of income spent on food was approximately 150 per cent of that allowed for in the minimum wage formula. A large proportion of workers had little or nothing to eat for the last few days of each month.

Third, whereas the Batson formula recommended the assessment of the Effective Minimum Level at 150 per cent of the Poverty Datum Line, the Kenya Government chose to implement the less generous figure of 133⅓ per cent.

After the 'Mau Mau' rebellion erupted in 1952, a post-mortem was made on the government's seemingly disastrous pre-Emergency wage policy. The inadequacy of bachelor wages was written off as an error of assessment. The failure of the government to implement a 'family' wage structure was subject to more intensive scrutiny.

Post-War Arguments Against
A 'Family' Minimum Wage

Sir Philip Mitchell, Governor of Kenya from 1944–52, devotes a number of pages in his *African Afterthoughts* to the problem of wages in the post-war period. He states that in the matters of agricultural prices, rents and wages,

> I now think we took the wrong decisions, which amounted in effect to a prolonged—and fruitless—struggled to hold prices and rents down to what in fact was an excessively low wage level.[9]

Thus, rather than raising wages so that Africans could afford to pay uncontrolled farm prices and free market rentals, the government chose the costly subsidisation path instead. What resulted, to the great disadvantage of the African labourer, was that prices and rents continued to rise, controls on them proving 'fruitless', whilst wages remained at 'an excessively low' level (Mitchell's words). Two additional points are noteworthy. First, in a report made in 1954, it was estimated that African wages had done little more than keep up with price increases: 'Throughout most of that period [from 1944–1953], the *real* value of the worker's wage, as represented by its purchasing power, has remained approximately the same.'[10] Second, in a report by a cost of living commission in 1950, one essential equation in the matter of inflation in Kenya was clarified: 'It is to be noted that in Great Britain the tendency is normally for wages to take the upward initiative. In Kenya, the initiative is with prices.'[11]

Governor Mitchell goes on to say, however, that the level of African wages after the war presented a problem

> much easier to state than to solve. It can be solved if we can find the economic key to a substantial rise in the general level of wages; but this is bound to involve, for a time at least, a serious consequential problem of unemployment. For if the Africans in Nairobi all did a full day's work . . . there would certainly not be enough work to go round.[12]

What was criticised as a government supported supply of cheap African labour was not really cheap since African productivity was appallingly low. Retrenchments would follow if African workers began putting in a full day's work and if employers were forced to pay higher wages, they would certainly demand more output. In effect, Mitchell argued that the minimum wage which would have been required to sustain a worker and his family would have been in excess of what post-war economic circumstance could bear. As indicated in Chapter Four, private industry could not have expressed more agreement.

Invariably, any major policy in effect in Kenya after the war is partly traceable to the behaviour of the settlers. It appears that minimum wages are no exception.

Many employers have emphasised that the interests of Kenya's agricultural community had to be taken into consideration when minimum rates were being formulated. Whilst the lure of city life (both material and financial) usually ensured the existence of a plentiful urban labour supply throughout the post-war years, there were occasionally shortages of labour in certain agricultural pursuits well into the Emergency—although not nearly to the extent prevailing before the war. Therefore, it was presumed that if wages were raised unduly in the urban areas, labour shortages for rural employers would become more acute or alternatively, labour costs would be forced up. It was certainly in the best interests of the settlers to keep statutory urban minima as low as possible.

Conventional wisdom of the early 'fifties held that the nature of the African labour force precluded the passage of higher minimum rates. There was little disagreement that most Africans were migrants. A distinction, however, was increasingly drawn between two different types of migrant, of equal proportions in the labour force. One was a 'target' migrant who left the reserves to work for a period of six months or less. The other was a migrant who stayed in wage employment for a longer period of time but who still maintained close contact with the native land unit.[13] It was advanced that if 'target' migrants earned higher wages, they would remain in remunerative employment for even shorter periods of time thus making the labour force still less productive and permanent.

Finally, and perhaps most important, one writer lends a perspective to these arguments when he states:

> [The migrant system in Kenya] . . . certainly accorded with the inclinations of the ruling classes, who were enabled to postpone serious consideration of the formidable social and economic problems which would be posed by the emergence of an urban proletariat. This development, in the view of the Administration, would have disrupted the whole existing social and political order—as, indeed, it was to do, throughout Africa, in the 1950's.[14]

The Minimum Wage Ordinance of 1946 was not the embodiment of the government's wage policy. It was intended only to provide a floor

on the level of employment conditions. The Central Minimum Wage
Board's stated objective in 1946 was to devise a wage which '. . .
while covering the cost of living of a single adult male employee working at
unskilled labour would not give him that feeling of complacent
satisfaction in which he would make no effort at self-improvement'.[15]
The government envisaged three methods besides statutory minima
for raising African wages in the post-war period.

The first concerned awards of boards of inquiry or arbitration
tribunals arising out of labour disputes. A most noteworthy tribunal
in this regard investigated a strike in Mombasa in 1947.[16] The strike
involved 15,000 African workers, almost the entire labour force in
the area. True enough, the tribunal's award, besides increasing the
payrolls of employers directly concerned, had the spillover effect of
pressuring other companies to fall in line. But the award was
exceptional in post-war experience.

The second means by which the government hoped to bolster the
level of earnings concerned the establishment of wages councils. The
Regulation of Wages and Conditions of Employment Ordinance was
passed in 1951. The principles upon which it was based bore a strong
resemblance to those prevailing in Britain. Wage councils were to be
introduced as a first step in the development of collective bargaining.
They were most suitable where trade unions and employer associations
had been unable to represent the entirety of firms within one industry.
Yet few industries in Kenya around 1951 had even the embryo of
labour or employer organisations. By 1955, only two wages councils
were functioning.[17]

Third, the government hoped to manipulate post-war pay rates
through the policy it pursued in the public services. Such a policy was
a powerful tool insofar as the government was the largest single
employer and its wage scales served as a yardstick for rates in the
private sector. In 1950, the Labour Department stated:

> . . . minimum wages form the platform upon which the wage structure in
> urban areas is based. It is really an engagement rate for unskilled labour.
> Government, for instance, in the case of employees in Nairobi and
> Mombasa, takes on unskilled labour at the current rate which, in practice,
> coincides with the minimum wage. After three months, a rise is given and
> after a further period of nine months . . . the employee is regarded as a
> minor employee and enters a segment in an appropriate wage scale. The
> Department has persuaded a large number of employers to take up the
> same attitude.[18]

But to what effect?

In 1952, the Labour Department carried out a survey of African
wage earners in Nairobi and found that only 10 or 11 per cent earned

the barest statutory minimum. But the Department went on to say that 'though the wages of the remainder could be said to provide something better than the subsistence standard of living for bachelor labourers, the general level of wages must be described as low'.[19] A committee on African wages in 1954 was more emphatic. It emphasised that legal minima largely governed the wages paid to unskilled labour in the towns. Rather than acting like a 'social safety net', as the government intended, post-war statutory minima had, in fact, 'acted like a magnet to hold wages down'.[20] The East Africa Royal Commission noted this as well. Whilst it expressed appreciation for the government's efforts to devise minimum rates which would not give a worker 'that feeling of complacent satisfaction in which he would make no effort at self improvement', it concluded, 'there is little doubt that the avoidance of "complacent satisfaction" was effectively achieved'.[21]

The Emergency and the Adoption of a 'Family' Minimum Wage

It was not until 1954 that the government accepted the policy of establishing appreciably higher minimum wages for bachelors and minimum rates calculated to enable a worker to maintain himself and his family near his place of work. This followed the publication of the *Report of the Committee on African Wages*, commonly called the Carpenter Report. Not unlike the fight for equal pay for equal work, Africans only won their battle for a higher minimum scale when the violence of 'Mau Mau' had registered its effect.

The Carpenter Committee championed the cause of labour stability. It was moved by 'a growing recognition of the social evils (overcrowding, malnutrition, prostitution, venereal disease, juvenile delinquency, etc.) which are seen to result from the employment of migrant labour in towns'.[22] It argued with unabashed ethnocentricism:

We cannot *hope* to produce an effective African labour force until we have first removed the African from the enervating and retarding influences of his economic and cultural background.[23]

The Committee devoted most of its Report to the economic benefits likely to accrue from a stabilised labour force. As Africans remained in employment for longer periods of time, production would increase as labour turnover and absenteeism rates fell. Consequently, employers would find it more to their advantage to train their workers, increasing production still further. A more stable workforce also implied a more efficient workforce in the long run. Africans would have the wherewithal to make expenditure on more nutritious foods and more amenable housing. Rising productivity would be the complement.

To achieve labour stability, the Carpenter Committee advocated 'the payment of a wage sufficient to provide for the needs of the worker and his family'.[24] A dual minimum wage system was recommended. A 'family' minimum wage would be paid to male workers over 21 years of age with a service qualification of 36 months of continuous employment outside the native land unit. A 'bachelor' minimum— calculated on a more liberal scale than that obtaining before 1954 —would be paid to all other workers.

Agricultural workers were exempted. With something of a double standard, the Committee fell back on the belief that higher wages would prompt agricultural workers to put in a shorter day. Thus commenced the distortion in income distribution between town and country labourer which is critical today. The legal urban starting scale is now 300 per cent greater than the rural one. So too, distortions were introduced by the *ad hoc* arbitration tribunals appointed by the government in the wake of unrest. The Mombasa awards of 1939 and 1947 started the ascent of dockers' wages far above those of other unskilled operatives.

The government in Kenya accepted without reserve the main principles of the Carpenter Report but significantly altered some of its more specific proposals.[25] The government determined that a dual minimum wage should be established on the basis of an 'adult' wage (instead of a 'family' wage with a service qualification) and a 'youth' wage (instead of a 'bachelor' wage). The government proposed initially to calculate the 'adult' wage in accordance with the needs of a man and wife with no children (the Carpenter Committee assessed its 'family' rate on the basis of a man and wife with two children). The government's ultimate aim, however, was to tailor an 'adult' scale to the needs of a family with three children (the average family in Kenya appears to have six children). The government also refused to be bound by the Carpenter Committee's time-table for the full implementation of a 'family' rate (the Committee recommended that the transition from a 'bachelor' to a 'family' rate for eligible workers be accomplished over a ten year period). Instead, the government preferred a measure of leeway and took full advantage of this escape clause in the next decade.

Nevertheless, in little more than two years after the Carpenter Report's publication, the statutory minimum wage for adult workers in Nairobi increased by 68 per cent whilst other workers secured a rise of nearly 50 per cent.[26]

The Arguments Revisited

From a recent perspective, the arguments surrounding minimum wage policy during the 'fifties, and the refinements to which they gave rise in the 'sixties, can be more clearly evaluated. It is important to emphasise that, in the interim years, the most liberal statutory minima of the Carpenter Report were not nearly approached.[27] Average African earnings, however, rose precipitously and maintained themselves at a wide margin above the legal floor.[28] This in itself should be of interest to underdeveloped countries entertaining a dual policy of 'family' minimum wages and auxiliary practices such as collective bargaining. But even in cases where average earnings hold a comfortable lead over stautory minima, statutory minima may influence average earnings. In the United States, where the lead is more than comfortable and where data are available, the relationship is said to be significant.[29]

In Africa, reliable data are often unavailable for fundamental developments which have overtaken minimum wage fixing since the 'fifties. To avoid being repetitious, all conclusions to be drawn later warrant more than the usual amount of caution. Nor, usually, can hypotheses about relationships of crucial concern to wage policy be validated statistically. Unhappily, discussion too frequently takes the form of *a priori* reasoning.

A Sequel on Unemployment

The spectre of hardcore unemployment evoked by Governor Mitchell as a counter-argument to a 'family' minimum wage in the early 'fifties has proved all too real,[30] and it is argued with little dissent in the relevant literature that there is a cause and effect between the two. In the past, rising wages led employers to cut back on the use of labour. More efficient and/or capital-intensive techniques were introduced.[31] At present, attractive wages in town lure an excessive supply of underemployed labour from the countryside. The political inexpedience of empirically confirming the degree of urban joblessness precludes even a sobering of employment expectations. In the future, higher wages are predicted to discourage investment altogether or to encourage labour-saving production biases. It has been asserted that 'modernisation is a generator of unemployment'.[32] The demand for labour increases at a slower rate than output because productivity rises. Labour requirements per unit of product fall through more efficient management. As workers become more efficient, the labour

c

coefficient is reduced. That modernisation may proceed erratically also takes its toll. A Kenya Government report in 1960 suggested that, apart from relatives, severe population pressure on the land and agricultural stagnation forced some job hunters to the towns.[33] That an increase in the number of primary school graduates outstrips the number of jobs created means that Africans with little taste for agriculture, modest schooling, and over-modest employment ambitions swell the number of job applicants (whilst pay rates rising faster than farm incomes hasten the metropolitan inflow).

Labour Stability

Running parallel with rising wage and unemployment rates in the late 'fifties in Kenya was the advent of labour stability: and not coincidentally. But if substantial evidence for labour stability is wanting, so is a consensus as to what precisely is meant by the term. Most expatriate firms in Kenya anticipate that a large percentage of their present employees will reach their retirement age before stopping work. In some cases, however, the wife and children of a worker may still live in the Reserve. They will be paid a visit as often as time, money, and inclination permit. An annual paid leave allowance, typically of three weeks, in addition to paid public holidays are common features in collective agreements today. In other cases, even if a worker brings his family with him to the site of his industrial employment (and population figures for Nairobi suggest this to be the trend), he will in all probability still retain his tribal land rights.[34] 'Circular migration', that is, the movement of workers to industry and back to agriculture, seems not an inaccurate description of a large segment of the labour force in Kenya today.[35] The interval spent in remunerative employment has simply grown much longer.

If, however, a long-term migrant is labelled unstable, then so, in the extreme, should a lathe operator in England with an allotment. Commitment to a factory way of life eludes easy definition. Therefore a stable labour force may be taken to mean one with a low turnover rate: low being a rate comparable to or lower than that existing in most Western industrial societies, occupation and product corresponding. The Kenya Labour Department's unpublished annual figures for the engagement rate in the private sector suggest that labour turnover today is appreciably lower than before the late 'fifties. Officers of the Federation of Kenya Employers would go much farther. From unofficial surveys undertaken, they contend that the quit rate in the large expatriate companies is now less than one per cent for African manual workers and slightly higher (because of a scarcity factor) for technical and managerial staff. The quit rate in smaller companies and commercial agriculture is probably much higher.[36]

The causes of labour stability are most easily sorted out through a review of selected arguments for and against 'high' and 'low' wage policies in underdeveloped countries. This is the fundamental debate. In principle, the arguments for and against 'high' and 'low' wage policies are as relevant to setting minimum rates as to regulating average terms of service. In scale, however, allowance must be made for the expected differential between the two. Quantitative differences may become so great as to become qualitative for minimum wage fixing. Terminology is once again ambiguous. By a 'high' wage policy is meant one which has lower turnover as its specific objective and by a 'low' wage policy, for the time being, is meant one which does not. This allows for continuity, for lower turnover was also the over-riding objective of the Carpenter Report.

A 'High' Wage Policy

In a study on migrant labour in Uganda in the 'fifties, Walter Elkan attacked the Carpenter Committee's major assumption, that better pay promised more stability.[37] Elkan argued that so long as positive income attached to remaining on one's farm, the labour force would remain unstable. Elkan's argument, however, suffers from one-sidedness.[38] In general, the higher the wage in urban employment relative to rural income, the lower the turnover. Since World War II, a backward bending supply curve of African labour (convenient gospel during the 'fifties), appears to be of little validity.[39] As a simple test, Mr. S. Kannappan draws attention to cross-section data (from India) which indicate that turnover rates are higher in smaller than larger firms, with wage levels just the reverse. The same is true of Kenya. 'The wage paid thus plays a critical role in attracting a stable labour force or in inducing greater stability.'[40]

One thesis in favour of a 'high' wage policy which does not have stability as its guiding objective is that of the Senegalese economist, S. Amin. Mr. Amin argues that all must be subordinated to economic growth. The most efficient (profitable) techniques of production must be adopted. These tend to be capital intensive. Hence, a wage sufficiently high to guide the proper choice of technique is warranted. Income and productivity disparities between modern industry and subsistence agriculture will widen, but it is pointless to narrow these differences 'in the name of a moralising principle'. Progress, according to Mr. Amin, must after all be marked by 'the gradual contraction and final disappearance of the relatively stagnant traditional sector'.[41]

One criticism to be levelled against Mr. Amin's thesis is that instruments other than high wages could better serve to stimulate capital-biased production (if any stimulants are, in fact, required).[42] A second criticism has much more significance. If growth is the uncompromising goal, it must be assured that greater profits from more efficient technology will be earmarked for fruitful development purposes. Yet, the consensus of a recent symposium on wage policy was that 'the conditions which would ensure this are not often found in developing countries'.[43] So, too, are seriously weakened arguments in favour of austere wage restraint to allow the accumulation of surplus which, it is held, will be reinvested. The qualification, however, is rarely put. Finally, Mr. Amin has been criticised for his cavalier attitude towards the unemployment predicted to accompany his proposals in the 'short' run. Yet the political intensity of the unemployment problem has made such proposals most untenable.

One implication for minimum wage setting is as follows: labour stability may be seen to arise from unemployment (both hardcore and disguised). The job-hungry in front of factory gates suggest that living standards in the towns are pulling far ahead of those in the countryside. Thus, workers fortunate enough to hold jobs and unfortunate enough to need them remain tenaciously with one employer. It has been argued that the margin above real incomes in the traditional sector necessary to induce even lower labour turnover rates than those in advanced economies appears comparatively small. Consequently:

> as a means of encouraging 'commitment', the difference between a high-wage policy and a low wage policy is more apparent than real.[44]

With respect to minimum wage fixing in particular, it may be infinitesimal: a point on which the Carpenter Committee has been taken to task.

A 'Low' Wage Policy

The problem of unemployment features prominently in arguments favouring a 'low' wage policy (which may still be theoretically distinguished from a 'high' one). An essay by Mr. Elliot Berg recognises that lower turnover can be bought with higher wages. But Berg suggests that minimum wages should be set with a definite view towards a continuation of migrant employment.[45] The meagre wage packet could then be subsidised with subsistence income. Anything but wage restraint will worsen unemployment and job creation, inhibit investment, adversely affect balance of payments, raise taxes, and reduce public development expenditure; if only because the government is generally the largest single employer. Anything but wage restraint is also inequitable, since industrial workers are an elite by comparison with the mass of subsistence peasants. (Mr. Amin also claims to have equity on his side: higher wages are a due reward for the more productive labour of the modern sector.)

One assumption of Mr. Berg's argument is crucial. It is that 'Most African countries are thinly populated' and that '. . . land remains relatively abundant in most areas'.[46] In Kenya, however (and in a growing number of other African countries), this is hardly the case. In a 1963 survey of middle-income African employees in Nairobi, of the 324 respondents sampled, 46 per cent claimed to own some land whilst 54 per cent claimed to own none.[47] Under a crash programme to create jobs in 1964, 106,300 registrants were classified as hardcore unemployed: landless and in search of work through a labour exchange for at least 12 months. Two years later the hardcore were estimated to number 200,000 (recorded employment in Kenya is roughly 600,000).[48] How then, are landless workers to support themselves and their families on a 'migrant's' wage?

Mr. Berg takes a hard line and reminds us:

> That most African wage earners are poor, and many desperately poor, is not in question. Almost all Africans are poor. It is relative positions that are of importance in considering wage policy. . . .[49]

This is also the basic tenet of proposals submitted on the subject by H. A. Turner. Whilst minimum wages need not be fixed with the migrant in mind, they should be fixed, according to Mr. Turner, with the actual living standards of the subsistence peasant as a reference.

Turner stresses the important role to be played by the economic expert. He emphasises that minimum wages should be fixed according to objective economic criteria. To assess a worker's needs, as the Carpenter Committee attempted to do, is pseudo-scientific guesswork at best. Also, by setting 'low' minimum wages (income in the traditional sector being the yardstick, with a margin thrown in for '. . . the minimal extra costs of town life'), the real purpose of a legal floor is satisfied.[50] It is to prevent exploitation and to permit room for the reward of skill. Thus, an important distinction is drawn between setting minimum rates and influencing take-home pay. Despite an emphasis on objectivity, however, Mr. Turner fails to define 'exploitation'.

Other observers have also raised the problems of objectivity in Turner's proposals.[51] Not only may the extra costs of town life be more than minimal, they may be immeasurable except as pseudo-scientific guesswork. It is also both conceptually and technically difficult to convert subsistence income into monetary terms, to define the dependency denominator of rural households, and to make allowance for intra-family transfers of goods between town and country.

Minimum Wages Since Independence

It is interesting to note the criterion selected by a committee in Kenya for a 17 per cent increase in the minimum wage in 1967. The rise was awarded on the grounds that the old rate did not provide a living wage.[52] The arguments in the literature against such a move were amply supported by economic circumstances. Most unskilled town labourers in Kenya earned far in excess of the minimum even before 1967. Their average wage appeared double the average peasant's household income.[53] The new scales put the urban statutory floor at a 300 per cent advantage over the rural one (known, however, to be evaded by small farmers). Nevertheless the landless manual worker quite possibly was unable to support a family on the old rate short of manoeuvres of questionable legality; his extra costs in town were more than minimal (denied the peasant's easy access to home-grown foods and crude accommodation); his family size did mean a lower standard of living than the peasant's; and he was being exploited prior to the new award (and perhaps after it).

The Kenya wage committee was tripartite in scope. The government's concession to the 17 per cent increase may be seen as a political gesture (representatives from the Ministry of Economic Planning and Development voiced a dissenting opinion, and no attempt was made to assess a worker's needs or a 'living' wage). The motives of the trade unionists for supporting the 17 per cent rise are obvious, those of the Federation of Kenya Employers perhaps most interesting. From minutes of the FKE spanning a number of years, it appears that the Federation was acceptive of a rise in the minimum to protect its smaller firms from non-FKE competitors. Whilst most FKE companies pay well in excess of the statutory floor, some pay close enough to it. By increasing that floor, the competitive edge enjoyed by non-FKE firms was reduced.

Wages and Productivity

Employer policy towards wage increases may be examined briefly from within another context: that of wages and productivity. The relationship between wages and productivity reappears continually in the debate on high versus low wage policy.

The Carpenter Committee claimed that higher wages would tend to increase productivity through (1) a fall in turnover, and (2) a rise in efficiency by means of better consumption. A study of Tanganyika purports to confirm the first argument (although the high unemployment that followed also fulfilled expectations).[54] Since, however, lower turnover now generally follows unemployment, this argument in support of paying high has lost much of its appeal. On the relationship between higher wages and better consumption there is even less evidence. It has been held that higher wages do not guarantee expenditure on goods likely to improve productivity. Whilst such a contention may be unduly static, it has been recognised that other instruments (i.e. in-kind benefits) may achieve the desired productivity gain more assuredly and without the harmful side-effect of unemployment.

The same criticism has been directed against the use of the wage mechanism to stimulate employers to become more efficient (although such a stimulus was found very effective—and very costly in terms of unemployment—in Puerto Rico).[55] More to the point is to question whether employers in underdeveloped countries willingly pay high to get high productivity. It is almost conventional wisdom that they do: to ensure low turnover and to recruit the best available manpower; and not, allegedly, at great expense, as labour costs are a low percentage of total costs and marginal tax rates are high.[56] Given, however, an excess supply of labour and the automatic stability to which it often gives rise, it appears that employers do not have to pay high unless forced to do so or motivated to do so politically. Evidence might show, for example, that to recruit the cream of the unskilled labour force, employers do not deliberately offer higher-than-average wages but make their selection techniques finer. Statements to the effect that employers take the initiative 'in raising wages to increase their profits' may misplace the emphasis.[57] When the Carpenter Committee was in session, there was already a suggestion that hardship was making for lower turnover. Management did not necessarily have to buy stability. It is significant that the employer representative on the Carpenter Committee appended a dissenting opinion to the majority recommendation for a 'family' minimum wage. A 'bachelor' rate was preferable to him. On economic grounds, there may be a tendency to exaggerate management's inclination to pay high in poor countries.

Conclusion

The publication of the Carpenter Report and the gradual emergence of a more stable working population were landmarks in Kenya's labour history. The advent of labour stability in the face of rising wages made it difficult for employers to fall back on the excuse that higher wages promised even less stability and lower productivity. The wage increments specified in the Carpenter Report led many firms to re-examine their practices of industrial relations. An attempt was made to adopt the most efficient personnel policies to minimise expensive labour disturbances. Rising labour costs led many firms to pay closer regard to their methods of remuneration. Once the end to a cheap supply of labour seemed inevitable, employers banded together to tailor a system of remuneration most in keeping with their own specifications. The government's acceptance of a 'family' wage policy made collective bargaining a more realistic possibility. Previously, the low level of minimum wages had acted as a barrier to bargaining. Workers' representatives in the early 'fifties on statutory wage councils held out for a 'living wage'. To them a living wage implied a 'family' wage. Consequently, there was little hope of reaching a voluntary settlement. It was only after the Carpenter proposals came into effect that employers and union leaders began to speak the same language. Finally, the gradual appearance of stability had a most favourable effect on the growth of trade unions. It secured them a more permanent membership. Workers had a greater stake in their jobs and were more prepared to support trade unions in the fight for better terms of service. The fight was legitimised by 'Mau Mau'. Thus, conditions were becoming riper for a policy which the government has been endeavouring to promote since the end of World War II and which eventually awakened employers to the changing times most decisively: the growth of trade unions.

REFERENCES

1 Colonial Office Circular Dispatch of 5th June, 1941, cited by P. G. Powesland, *Economic Policy and Labour: A Study in Uganda's Economic History*, East African Studies No. 10, ed. by Walter Elkan (Kampala: East African Institute of Social Research, 1957), p.73.

2 Elliot J. Berg, 'Major Issues of Wage Policy in Africa', in *Industrial Relations and Economic Development*, ed. by Arthur M. Ross (London: Macmillan for the International Institute for Labour Studies, 1966), p. 185.

3 Colony and Protectorate of Kenya (hereinafter referred to as Kenya), *Report of the Commission of Inquiry Appointed to Examine the Labour Conditions in Mombasa* (Nairobi, 1939); Kenya, *Report of the Committee on African Wages* (Nairobi, 1954), p. 15, makes reference to the Phillips Commission Report of 1945.

4 Kenya, *Labour Department Annual Report*, 1946 (hereinafter referred to as *LDAR*), Nairobi, pp. 9 and 14.

5 Kenya, *Report of the Committee on African Wages*, p. 50.
6 *Ibid.*, p. 52.
7 *Ibid.*
8 Kenya, *The Pattern of Income and Consumption of African Labourers in Nairobi, October–November 1950* (Nairobi, 1951).
9 Philip E. Mitchell, *African Afterthoughts* (London: Hutchinson, 1954), p. 233.
10 Kenya, *Report of the Committee on African Wages*, p. 22.
11 Kenya, *Report of the Cost of Living Commission* (Nairobi, 1950), p. 12.
12 Mitchell, *African Afterthoughts*, p. 237.
13 Kenya, *Report of the Committee on African Wages*, p. 13.
14 C. C. Wrigley, 'Kenya: The Patterns of Economic Life, 1902–45', in *History of East Africa*, Vol. 2, ed. by Vincent Harlow and E. M. Chilver (Oxford: At the Clarendon Press, 1965), Vol. 2, p. 262.
15 Kenya, *Report of the Committee on African Wages*, p. 54.
16 Kenya, *Report on the Economic and Social Background of Mombasa Labour Disputes*, by H. S. Booker and N. M. Deverall (Nairobi, 1947), (mimeographed); Kenya, *Official Gazette*, 4 February, 1947, Official Gazette Supplement No. 13, 18 March, 1947, 'Mombasa Island Final Award'.
17 J. I. Husband, 'Wages Councils', in *East African Economic Review*, Vol. 2, No. 5 (January 1955).
18 Kenya, *LDAR*, 1950, p. 7.
19 Kenya, *LDAR*, 1952, p. 8.
20 Kenya, *Report of the Committee on African Wages*, p. 55.
21 Great Britain, *The East Africa Royal Commission Report 1953–55*, Cmd. 9475 (London: HMSO, 1955), p. 156.
22 Kenya, *Report of the Committee on African Wages*, p. 15.
23 *Ibid.*, p. 11.
24 *Ibid.*, p. 16. The Committee also stressed that a permanent labour force demanded family housing arrangements, security for old age, incentive systems of wage payment, opportunities for training, and thoughtful supervision. These necessary but costly services, however, were not allowed to excuse the failure to implement a family wage as the first step towards stability.
25 Kenya, *Sessional Paper No. 21 of 1954: Implementation of the Recommendations of the Report of the Committee on African Wages* (Nairobi, 1954).
26 Great Britain, Colonial Office, *The Colonial Territories 1955–56*. Cmd. 9769 (London: HMSO, 1956), p. 111.
27 The Carpenter Committee's most liberal proposals would have meant an 'adult' minimum wage of at least 250sh. a month in January 1965. In that month, the consolidated minimum wage for 'adults' was 150sh.
28 Although Africanisation of high paying posts was a contributory factor, it has been estimated that wage rates for lower-paid workers also increased at 'a very rapid rate. . . .' Kenya, *Report of the Salaries Review Commission, 1967* (Nairobi, 1967), p. 15. The divide between the going rate for unskilled labour and legal minima are discussed in Chapter Ten.
29 C. S. J. O'Herlihy, 'Minimum Wage Effects in the United States', (ILO, Geneva, D.16/1967), roneod. Referred to by N. N. Franklin, 'Minimum Wage Fixing and Economic Development', in *Wage Policy Issues in Economic Development*, The Proceedings of a Symposium held by the International Institute for Labour Studies at Egelund, Denmark, 23–27 October 1967. Under the Chairmanship of Clark Kerr, ed. by Anthony D. Smith (London: Macmillan, 1969), p. 339.

30   The category of hardcore unemployment is taken to mean the landless and jobless who have no seasonal employment opportunities and who are in search of work.

31   See, for example, Azarias Baryaruha, *Factors Affecting Industrial Employment: A Study of Ugandan Experience, 1954–64.* Occasional Paper 1 (Nairobi: Oxford University Press for the East African Institute of Social Research, 1967).

32   Frederick H. Harbison, 'The Generation of Employment in Newly Developing Countries', in *Education, Employment and Rural Development*, the Proceedings of a Conference held at Kericho, Kenya, in September 1966, ed. by James R. Sheffield (Nairobi: East African Publishing House, 1967), p. 174.

33   Kenya, *Survey of Unemployment*, by A. G. Dalgleish (Nairobi, 1960), pp. 6–7.

34   D. M. Etherington, 'Projected Changes in Urban and Rural Population in Kenya and the Implications for Development Policy', *East African Economic Review*, Vol. 1, (NS), No. 2 (June 1965), p. 68.

35   Walter Elkan, 'Circular Migration and the Growth of Towns in East Africa', *International Labour Review*, Vol. 96, No. 6 (December 1967).

36   A study of one factory in Uganda shows a lower quit rate for middle income employees than unskilled operatives. UN, Economic Commission for Africa, *Social Factors Affecting Labour Stability in Uganda* (Document E/CN, 14SDP/20, 8th October, 1963). The FKE suggests that middle income employees have a higher quit rate than unskilled operatives because their services are at a premium and they change jobs frequently in search of the best-paying employer. The pressure for unskilled jobs may also be greater in Kenya than in Uganda.

37   Walter Elkan, *Migrants and Proletarians: Urban Labour in the Economic Development of Uganda* (London: Oxford University Press for the East African Institute of Social Research, 1960).

38   Emil Rado, 'A Review of Walter Elkan, *Migrants and Proletarians—Urban Labour in the Economic Development of Uganda*', *East African Economic Review*, Vol. 1 (NS), (1964).

39   See, for example, Elliot J. Berg, 'Backward Sloping Labor Supply Function in Dual Economies—the African Case', *Quarterly Journal of Economics*, Vol. 75, No. 3 (August 1961). The implications of the once-common belief in the backward bending supply curve of labour are discussed by H. Myint, *The Economics of Developing Countries* (London: Hutchinson University Library, 1967), pp. 54–57; 63–66.

40   Subbiah Kannappan, 'The Economics of Structuring an Industrial Labour Force: Some Reflections on the Commitment Problem', *British Journal of Industrial Relations*, Vol. 4, No. 3 (November 1966), p. 390.

41   Samir Amin, 'Levels of Remuneration, Factor Proportions and Income Differentials with Special Reference to Developing Countries', in *Wage Policy Issues in Economic Development*, ed. by Anthony D. Smith, p. 277.

42   Capital-intensive production techniques may be adopted in underdeveloped countries even if labour is relatively inexpensive because such techniques have been tested in the West and are familiar, the managers needed to supervise labour are at a premium, and local workers represent an 'unknown' to the overseas firm.

43   *Wage Policy Issues in Economic Development*, ed. by Anthony D. Smith, p. 179.

44   *Ibid.*, p. 183.

45   Berg, 'Major Issues of Wage Policy in Africa', pp. 185–208 and 'The Economics

of the Migrant Labour System', in *Urbanization and Migration in West Africa*, ed. by Hilda Kuper (Berkeley: The University of California Press, 1965), pp. 160–81.

46 Berg, 'Major Issues of Wage Policy in Africa', p. 188.

47 Kenya, *The Pattern of Income, Expenditure, and Consumption of African Middle Income Workers in Nairobi*, July 1963 (Nairobi, 1964).

48 *Education, Employment and Rural Development*, ed. by James R. Sheffield, p. 15.

49 Berg, 'Major Issues of Wage Policy in Africa', p. 189. More recently, however, Mr Berg has argued against reducing the income of the Africal salariat since it mixes with the wealthy European. See p. 155.

50 H. A. Turner, *Wage Trends, Wage Policies and Collective Bargaining: The Problems for Underdeveloped Countries*, Occasional Papers 6 (Cambridge: At the University Press for the Department of Applied Economics, 1965), p. 58.

51 *Wage Policy Issues in Economic Development*, ed. by Anthony D. Smith, pp. 81–83.

52 [Kenya], 'Report of the National Wages Policy Advisory Committee', [Nairobi, *circa* 1965]. (Unpublished.)

53 Kenya, *Report of the Salaries Review Commission, 1967*, p. 15.

54 D. Chesworth, 'Statutory Minimum Wage Fixing in Tanganyika', *International Labour Review*, Vol. 96, No. 1 (July 1967).

55 Lloyd G. Reynolds and Peter Gregory, *Wages, Productivity, and Industrialization in Puerto Rico* (Homewood, Illinois: Richard D. Irwin, Inc., 1965).

56 *Wage Policy Issues in Economic Development*, ed. by Anthony D. Smith, p. 88.

57 J. B. Knight, 'The Determination of Wages and Salaries in Uganda', *Bulletin of the Oxford University Institute of Economics and Statistics*, Vol. 29, No. 3 (1967), p. 263.

CHAPTER THREE

TRADE UNIONS

The establishment of trade unions became little less than a crusade in Kenya after World War II. The Labour Government in Britain, the British TUC, the American AFL and CIO, the International Confederation of Free Trade Unions, and the World Federation of Trade Unions all took the interests of the African labourer to heart and fastened on trade unions as his salvation. To conclude that trade unionism was inspired from above, however, is misleading. To do so implies either an absence of grievances on the part of African workers or an ineptitude at expressing them. Neither was the case, for before and immediately after the war, Kenya witnessed a series of arresting and spontaneous labour protests. Their political character suggests that the Colonial Office preached a-political and 'responsible' trade unionism, which was slow in coalescing, to channel the outbursts of informal workers' organisations or workers acting on an informal basis. Now, even the wisdom of encouraging the formal structure is being questioned, by some who perhaps misrepresent past labour history and by others who perhaps misunderstand it.

The Early Phase

In 1943, the government in Kenya passed an ordinance to legalise trade unions. Its passage smoothed relations with several M.P.s in London who had expressed anxiety over the use of conscripted labour in Kenya during the war. It will also be remembered that a colony's eligibility for financial assistance under the terms of the 1940 Colonial Welfare and Development Act was contingent upon the legalisation of trade unions. The European leader on the Legislative Council commented in the Press that the settler community had accepted the Ordinance only by *force majeure*.[1] Soon, relations between the government and the white farmers worsened on this score. The Labour Commissioner's efforts to build model unions were discredited as nothing less than Stalinist.[2]

For a short while, the '43 Ordinance was a sterile document, for no new African trade union presented itself. The Labour Department behaved like a mother awaiting the birth of a child. It consulted the most likely gynaecologist, the British TUC, in an effort to achieve a painless birth. In 1947, the TUC sent a representative with many years' experience of trade union organisation to Kenya. The Labour Department noted that the adviser spent most of his time.

> bringing home to would-be organisers of Trade Unions the concepts and principles upon which Trade Unions operate. The African found it difficult to grasp that a Trade Union was not a political weapon.[3]

To dispel this illusion, a primer devised by the TUC's adviser, and distributed to interested workers, began with the cardinal ABC: 'A Trade Union is not an organisation with political aims. . . .'[4]

Despite this pre-natal care, when the first major African child of the trade union movement was born in January 1947, the Labour Department regarded it as a monster. In that year, the second mass strike in Mombasa erupted, involving 15,000 workers. Out of it grew the African Workers' Federation, under the leadership of Chege Kebachia. According to the union, the strike was waged over the government's 'indifference' to payment by race, the disrespect shown to African workers, and the 'indirect slavery' bred by a low wage economy.[5]

The strike gave rise to a new militancy, which complemented that of the Kenya African Union (KAU), a political party under the leadership of Jomo Kenyatta. Strikes became more numerous and strike demands grew more radical. The climax came with the activities of the East African Trade Unions Congress (EATUC), whose impact was far more significant than its membership figures would suggest. In strength, the EATUC embraced only six industrial unions, none of which enjoyed a comfortable following in terms of dues-paying affiliates.[6] The EATUC was presided over by Fred Kubai, a close friend of Kenyatta and an activist in the Kenya African Union. Its general secretary was Makham Singh, an avowed Communist (a Party Member? of which country?). Registration for the union was never forthcoming from the government, who judged the real object of the EATUC to be 'the disruption of industry'.[7]

In 1950, the EATUC spearheaded a campaign against the granting of a Royal Charter to Nairobi. It called for a boycott of the Charter celebrations. It was feared by the Kikuyus that the city would swallow up more of their lands.[8] Other grievances underlying the boycott were expressed in a statement reproduced in Makham Singh's book on Kenya's early labour history:

> How can the workers feel the pleasure of expansion and 'progress' of Nairobi, which has been built by exploiting the toil and sweat of hundreds of thousands of workers by a handful of moneylords, and in which progress the workers have no voice.

The workers cannot be pleased by the Nairobi of the rich.

By their boycott they wish to demonstrate that the so-called 'progress' is not the progress of the millions of toiling people but of a handful of capitalists.

It is therefore the duty of the workers of all races to make the boycott a complete success and show the world that 'all that glitters is not gold'.[9]

This anti-capitalist analysis, rather than the usual limited attack on racial discrimination, may have heightened working-class consciousness, if it did not reflect it. Should the terminology and analysis be Singh's alone, he no doubt made the issues more cut and dry for employers as well. Their efforts in later years to build business unions may have sprung more directly from their fear of the otherwise inarticulated and unmentionable class conflict.

The boycott's success is suggested by an editorial in the European press entitled 'Wicked Mischief'. Those who did attend the celebrations were said to have lacked 'enthusiasm'.[10] Shortly after the protest, Fred Kubai and Singh were arrested on charges of being officers of an unregistered trade union. The result was a general strike.

The general strike of 1950 began on May 16th and ended nine days later. If the strike was not entirely general, it was the biggest Nairobi had ever seen. Unofficial evidence suggests that other towns experienced walkouts as well: a spirit of militancy may not have gripped the Kikuyus alone. Some of the demands put forward by the EATUC were not new: the release of strike leaders (Chege Kebachia had been detained after a strike some years earlier); an increase in the minimum wage; an end to payment by race; and the abolition of the *kipande*. One demand, however, was new: self-government for the East African territories. Such a demand climaxed a meeting convened earlier by the Kenya African Union and the East African Indian National Congress. According to Singh, he moved the crucial resolution at the meeting, seconded by Kubai, which stated:

. . . the real solution of the problem is not this or that small reform but . . . complete independence and sovereignty. . . .[11]

Shortly after the general strike, Singh was placed under detention. He was not released until eleven years later. Kubai was re-arrested on an unsuccessful charge of attempting to kill an African Councilman who had co-operated with the Nairobi authorities during the Charter celebrations.[12]

A Reappraisal of Policy

The EATUC mobilised workers at the grass roots to wield their labour power to further a subjectively political aim. If such political action has not been forthcoming from Kenya's second generation of trade unions, the answer is unlikely to rest with the greater reprisals it risks or the fewer civil guarantees it enjoys.[13] For as the political action of a few trade unions escalated after World War II, so did the government's actions to contain political trade unionism.

To begin with, several of the most outspoken labour leaders happened to experience detention or arrest. It has also been asserted by the old-timers that police permission was not always forthcoming for African mass meetings and that District Commissioners ignored requests by union organisers for permits to travel and recruit. Eventually, the government reviewed its Essential Services (Arbitration) Ordinance which made strikes illegal and arbitration compulsory in scheduled industries. According to the Labour Department, 'The schedule had to be extended as the result of the politically inspired general strike in Nairobi during 1950 . . .' and then came to cover '. . . a wide range of undertakings'.[14]

In 1952, the government passed a new Trade Union Ordinance. It served to strengthen several provisions of a 1948 Amendment Bill which were designed to frustrate political action. First, moved by many sad stories of labour leaders misappropriating hard-earned dues, the government imposed more stringent controls over union finances. The legality of making contributions to a political party was hedged in doubt (although most unions were hardly in a position to pay their own officers). Second, the '52 Ordinance stipulated that all labour executives had to be employed in the industry represented by their union. This provision was designed to prevent a politician from capturing a union for his own use. Third, the '52 Ordinance enabled the government to register trade unions on a probationary basis (all unions in Kenya and other British colonies were required to meet statutory registration requirements). If the character of a union was deemed questionable, full registration privileges could be withheld. Fourth, it became difficult for a general union to win registration. Such a model was viewed by the Labour Department as a camouflage for political activity. Fifth, a trade union could be de-registered if its actions violated its constitution. A catch-all provision similar to this one (under the Societies Ordinance) was invoked against the Kenya Federation of Labour. During the early years of the Emergency, African political parties were outlawed. Tom Mboya writes in his autobiography:

after the banning of KAU, the work of the KFL (and mine as its Secretary-General) became as much political as trade unionist. For the KFL became the voice of the African people, in the absence of any other African organisation to speak for them.[15]

In 1956, the KFL was called upon 'to show why its registration should not be cancelled on the grounds that its general political activities were beyond the scope of its constitutional objects as declared at the time of its registration'.[16] Sir Vincent Tewson, General Secretary of the British TUC, flew to Nairobi to defend the KFL. The defence performed a successful operation but the patient died. Registration was still to be the KFL's but only after a promise had been extracted to the effect that its political ventures would be restricted to matters of industrial relations.

Finally, in the shadow of the East African Trade Unions Congress, the government temporarily adopted an entirely new approach to industrial relations. It endeavoured to encourage the growth of staff associations and works councils. It hoped that joint consultation in industry would pave the way towards the development of a more responsible trade union movement and collective bargaining.

In the words of the Labour Department:

> Much more harm would be done to the movement by permitting the registration of a large number of illiterate, ill-disciplined groups of persons mainly actuated by a political and not an economic bias than by restricting such registration. It has become clear that the proper approach to industrial organisation lies through the development of staff associations, Whitley councils and the like as a means of giving practice to both sides in industry in the art of consultation.[17]

Recently, echoes of a similar approach have been heard throughout Africa. A case in point is Mr Guy Hunter's indictment against the trade union policy of the British Administration:

> The idea of necessary conflict in working relationships, which take up so much of life and matter so desperately to economic advance, is perhaps the most defeatist and destructive which the West exported to the developing world.
> There is still time and opportunity for African nations to avoid the unhappy precedent of European industrial relations . . . and to invent institutions based on more co-operative attitudes.[18]

What Mr Hunter suggests is the need for vision and experimentation: with variants of worker participation, building on 'a long African tradition of communal co-operation'.[19]

Before continuing on an historical examination of trade unions in Kenya, these and other suggestions for experimentation will be discussed in some detail. Feasible or otherwise, they have recently aroused enthusiasm. With incidents such as the Nairobi general strike fresh in mind, proposals for experimentation which hinge on an alleged African tradition of co-operation are best assessed. The British

Government's trade union strategy also comes into perspective. For if such a strategy was ultimately designed to prevent radical political change, the very same change may be a pre-condition for meaningful worker participation.

The Alternatives

The theoretical concept of worker participation is as vague as it is broad. The spectrum it spans may be delimited at one end by the idea of workers' self-management, where, as practised in Yugoslavia, workers are empowered to decide what is produced, and how. Bounding the other limit may be the idea of joint consultation, where, as conceived at least in the literature, worker representatives and management meet regularly to *consult* on matters of interest to both (or either) of them. Associated with worker participation is a range of opinion complementary in breadth and diversity. Some observers have regarded it as little more than a pernicious form of employer control. Others have viewed it as a step towards the achievement of industrial democracy. This latter concept, however, also defies easy definition. It is perhaps best conveyed as a moving target. The strains united under the rubric of industrial democracy all signify a movement away from the abject state wherein workers have no personal control over their work situation: the organisation of production and its management.

The policy of joint consultation adopted by the Kenya Government in the early 'fifties was already something of a museum piece elsewhere. Its origins in Britain date back to the two World Wars when the airing of problems common to management and labour was hailed as a deterrent to the interruption of wartime production. It has come to be recognised, however, that works councils largely devoted to joint consultation will be eclipsed by trade unions as vehicles for meaningful industrial relations.[20] Bread and butter issues are claimed by trade unions to be within their jurisdiction, subject to collective bargaining and the strike weapon, if need be. Non-concrete issues, conceded to be suitable for consultation, are, at best, neglected.

Measures to boost productivity habitually fall within the latter category and so it is not too surprising that employers are generally the most enthusiastic champions of joint consultation. This was certainly the case in Kenya. But 'consultation' is about as far as employers there have appeared willing to go. Another mechanism often acclaimed for boosting productivity is profit-sharing; a device which has won support from government officials in Kenya since Independence. Profit-sharing is traditionally endorsed as a form of worker

D

participation (in profits) more far-reaching than joint consultation. But it is a poor man's industrial democracy, for it affords labour little chance to decide how their productive efforts are to be organised. Even so, the Federation of Kenya Employers has been lukewarm to the idea—an inkling of the reception management in Kenya is likely to give to some of Mr. Hunter's alternatives to trade unions; particularly those which feature greater self-determination for workers.

Whatever its advantages as a channel of communication, joint consultation has rarely been viewed (not even by the Kenya Government) as an alternative to trade unions and collective bargaining. For to view it as such is to deny that disagreements between managements and labour may ultimately terminate in conflict. To uphold joint consultation as more than a marginal institution of industrial relations is, in effect, to place reliance on the good behaviour of management in seeing to it that workers get the benefits to which they are 'justly' entitled. Yet, it is precisely this which Mr. Hunter seems to do. He states that instead of European institutions, 'the highest standards of modern personnel management could work in Africa'.[21] Why in Africa? (and why, given the FKE's coolness to a form of worker participation as mild as profit-sharing, should it be expected that the highest standards of personnel management will even be introduced in Africa?). Because, writes Mr. Hunter, in Africa, there is not yet the hundred year old Western tradition of enmity between the two sides of industry, and the chance remains to build on co-operative attitudes. Hence, joint consultation alone may afford adequate protection to labour against exploitation. The West, as mentioned earlier, is indicted by Mr. Hunter for having infected the developing world with the idea of necessary conflict in working relationships.

It is highly questionable, however, whether Western agents (such as government or employers) exported industrial conflict to Africa, clad in the garb of trade unions, or whether such conflict was inevitable with the coming of industrialisation and a sophisticated form of capitalism (which employers did export). Evidence has been mustered on the natural inclinations and unspoiled tastes of African workers before trade unions were furthered from above. Did such tastes incline towards historical norms of behaviour or towards the Western class struggle? The few cases available are contradictory but a moot point is in dispute. It is inconsequential whether traditional co-operation prevailed at the beginning of industrialisation in Africa: and should an up-to-date attitudinal survey of African workers now more accustomed to factory life disclose a pugnacious mood, the result could be ascribed to the active presence of trade unions. Nevertheless, the evidence is interesting. On the one hand, African workers on the Copperbelt more than 25 years ago rejected the exercise of industrial relations through the medium of tribal elders. They eventually formed trade unions.[22] Mossi villagers in an industrial environment (the Niger Project) also appear to have given their traditional chiefs little support.[23] On the other hand, Africans in the Cameroons Development Corporation *initially* chose their local union leaders from amongst senior, presumably European, administrators.[24] In Nigeria after World War II, '. . . in some instances the employer himself became President of the Union!'[25] In Kenya, the services of two African chiefs were prevailed upon by the government during disturbances at the docks in 1945.[26] When a strike erupted on the waterfront ten years later, the services of Mr. Mboya were prevailed upon by the workers.

It is noteworthy that disturbances at the docks in 1945 provide only one example of unrest in Kenya before the advent of trade unions. Early labour history throughout East Africa is dotted with countless other spontaneous strikes. The naïve pre-trade union era of paternalism is hardly a paragon of industrial harmony. Indeed, the Nairobi general strike may be seen as part of this tradition. 'Necessary conflict' was manifested by the EATUC long before the Colonial Office's model of trade unions had taken effect.

The mystique of an idyllic socialist past has assumed critical importance since the changeover to independent rule. Its implications for labour policy and for experimentation with proxies to Western institutions have transcended the realm of theoretical possibilities. For whereas Mr. Hunter and others have been careful to question as myth the glorification of an innate socialism, both past and present, numerous African governments have been too quick, perhaps, to accept it as reality.

From Sekou Toure to Tom Mboya, the theory has been advanced that African society before contact with imperialism was unstratified.[27] Class antagonisms are a European import. Before Independence, it was appropriate to fight imperialism on its own terms, i.e. to mobilise sectional pressure groups such as trade unions to drain the ruling class of its power and privilege. Since Independence, the class struggle rages between rich and poor countries. It is not an internal phenomenon. Nor are divisive pressure groups such as trade unions warranted any longer under a régime of African Socialism.

Guided by this rationale, or rationalisation, one government has rapidly followed another in bringing trade unions under tighter control. In Ghana and Guinea, for example, mammoth trade union machines have been created, to function as industrial wings of the ruling political party. Autonomous trade unions have been disbanded.

It is superfluous to question the justification for such a move in societies where classlessness and the socialist persuasions of political parties are highly suspect. More germane is to question the payoff within the context of worker participation which the confection of state-run unions affords to underdeveloped countries: even those countries which have evinced a genuine interest in avoiding the hardening of class divisions by trade unions representative of an already elitist segment of the population. It is difficult to see how a centralised state-run union encourages worker participation, industrial democracy, or any other form of democracy for that matter. Where works councils function within the legal framework, they typically fall closer to the 'consultative' rather than 'workers' self-management' end of the spectrum.

Between the two lies the political transformation of the fundamental social and economic order.[28] So to talk of essays at workers' self-management in anglophone Africa, Tanzania apart, is to talk mainly in theory. To appreciate the divide, it is useful to explore briefly the philosophy of participation which has of late engaged the attention of sociologists in the West.[29] It features an attack on the unimaginative use to which the factory system has been put. It features the variable of active and creative participation by workers to escape the strait-jacket of human organisation of the productive process narrowly conceived of today. Mr. Guy Hunter refers to an early manifesto:

> Simone Weil, asked to prepare for General de Gaulle a Paper on the regeneration of France after the last war, replied in *The Need for Roots* with a direct and fundamental attack on the whole social system incorporated in and radiating from the factory, and on the whole set of motives upon which both employers and Trade Unions relied. This is not, as Mlle. Weil pointed out, a question of private ownership versus State Control.[30]

It may not be a question of private ownership versus state control in so far as state control does not guarantee meaningful worker participation. This holds for Tanzania, where an attempt at works councils strayed but little from the Western 'consultative' pattern.[31] But what is the outlook for worker participation under private ownership?

Paul Blumberg writes in his recent study on industrial democracy:

> Despite the almost unanimous evidence on the favourable effects of participation . . . in industrial settings—almost no one has raised the question: to what extent does private ownership and control of modern industry place sharp limits upon the amount of participation that is structurally possible? . . . Is it true, as T. B. Bottomore has said, that the

full development of workers' participation is possible only on the basis
of social ownership?[32]

Mr. Hunter stresses the need for vision, and with little strain on the
imagination, African workers and the management of an international
firm in Kenya can be pictured co-operating on novel team-work output
systems and group incentive bonuses. But what standards of industrial
democracy are to be invoked when management is unwilling to pay
the amount of bonus thought equitable by labour?

Certainly a radical and hard-won change in the basis of ownership
and control was a necessary pre-requisite in Yugoslavia for the
evolution of its controversial practice of workers' self-management.
Only a revolution in thought about power relationships and industrial
democracy could have allowed a system of decision-making by workers'
representatives, in conjunction with a manager elected by those whom
he manages, on almost every aspect of the firm: how much is to be
produced, at what price, how much workers are to be paid, for how
much output, etc. Such decision-making proceeds within legally
circumscribed limits and often under the Party's shadow. Surely it is
an adherence to Western property relationships and their intrinsic
ideologies of consent which precludes experimentation in Africa with
workers' self-management on the Yugoslav model, or even a variant
of it. Indeed, it is tempting to note in passing that, on the practical
level, the Yugoslav model may not be altogether as alien to African
soil as is readily assumed. As in most of Africa:

> Workers in Yuogslavia are even now for the most part first generation;
> many still work part time on the land. To master technical skills is a
> tremendous problem. . . . [The] education level is still low—30 per cent
> of Commune deputies still had less than four years schooling in 1963.
> [Yugoslavia is] a semi-developed, culturally disparate society with a large
> peasant minority . . . it is hardly possible to maintain a family without
> alternative work at the lower income levels.[33]

Finally if 'social ownership' (the term is Bottomore's) does not
prevail, there is the danger that worker participation may assume a
perverted form. According to Mr. Blumberg:

> . . . participation has lately become quite fashionable in management
> and business school thinking in the United States, having replaced the
> human relations approach which was considered too manipulative and
> thus self-defeating, and the new fad has given rise to concepts and
> approaches such as bottom up (!) authority styles, theory 'Y', T-Groups
> and an assorted alphabet soup of participative and pseudo-participative
> techniques.[34]

In the last analysis, there is much to suggest that if a search is to be made in Africa for new models of industrial relations to replace those exported by the West, a prior search may be necessary for new models of ownership and control. Those extant may not only inhibit the adoption of more co-operative and participatory methods in the factory. Private enterprise and the authority it bequeathes to the entrepreneur may make trade unions and conflict, however institutionalised, unavoidable, in Africa or anywhere else. The practical question at issue then becomes the nature of trade unions: was it unavoidable in Kenya that they came to concern themselves largely with bread and butter matters rather than political change which might have altered the economic and social setting in which they operated? To answer this question, discussion of employer associations and early labour history in Kenya is resumed.

From Works Councils to Trade Unions

The Kenya Government's short-term policy of works councils and joint consultation in the early '50's—superimposed on its long-term policy of trade unions and collective bargaining—was hardly a spectacular success. Indeed, the one might have counteracted the other. Mistrust of works councils hardened amongst Africans interested in labour organisation when it became obvious that several employers (including local government authorities) were using them as sops to more militant unions.[35] The most vocal organisers, such as Singh and Kubai, rejected consultation from the start. In the extreme, the two leaders may be regarded as trouble-makers, unrepresentative of the labour force at large. Still, it does not appear that most workers welcomed the opportunity for consultation in works councils, although a number of firms reported some progress. Nor does it appear that most workers actively resisted their presence, although a number of them did. It is significant, however, that when disturbances over bread and butter issues erupted, works councils were frequently by-passed.[36] The experiment on the whole seems to have floundered amidst apathy, but on the eve of 'Mau Mau', a co-operative mood could hardly have been at its peak.

More soul-searching has been expended on the fundamental question of why business unions also evoked faint enthusiasm. Although dues-paying trade union members on the eve of 'Mau Mau' numbered some 30,000 out of a work force nearly twenty times greater, there was almost nothing in the way of routine collective bargaining for better terms of service.[37] Business unions seemed to figure more in the thoughts of the Labour Department than in the lives of most workers.

That some employers played works councils off against fully-fledged trade unions provides an unsatisfactory explanation, if only because works councils operated on a limited scale. Several more plausible explanations have been posed by the East African Royal Commission.[38] First, the interests and concerns of many African workers after the war were deeply rooted in agriculture. Trade unions were as fly-by-night as the African work force was transient. Second, the educational backwardness of most workers and the inexperience of most union leaders made communication between the two difficult. Shortages of ready cash also barred the efforts of organisers to travel throughout the countryside, recruiting new members and keeping established branches in contact with one another. The services of less than competent administrators were often the only resort of meagre budgets and there was always the possibility of a raid on the union coffer to finance a night out on the town. Awakening interest in trade unions amongst a labour force on the thin edge of subsistence then became doubly difficult. Third, the Royal Commission suggested that the paternalism of the government and many employers pre-empted the benefits normally fought for by a union. To this list might be added not just paternalism but the downright hostility of some employers to trade unions.

An additional handicap in the immediate post-war years may have been the reluctance of Africans to participate actively in multi-tribal organisations. Voluntary associations other than trade unions flourished at the time but in many cases, though by no means all, these organisations were formed along tribal lines.[39] The Luo Union is perhaps the best example.[40] It provided its members throughout the urban areas of Kenya with a number of friendly benefits, the principal one being insurance for funeral and burial costs. It also protected the morals and reputation of the tribe. Luo women of questionable character were shipped back to the reserve at the Union's expense. Besides having a tangible basis for unity (namely, the tribe), voluntary tribal associations were easier to administer than trade unions, not being restricted in their choice of administrators by a work requirement. The services they offered were also tangible, unlike the pay-offs a trade union could only promise. Indeed, the provision of friendly benefits by tribal associations effectively robbed the unions of a potential attraction for members.

The position of the skilled worker created further difficulties. In most Western countries, skilled workers pioneered union organisation. Although artisan guilds were known to exist in the Kikuyu Reserve, they evolved into employer associations rather than worker associations in the money economy.[41] The ranks of artisans in Kenya were filled by Asians who made few moves to form trade unions after the war. They may have been wary of identifying themselves with a labour movement increasingly associated with African struggles for political and economic redress. Their craftsmanship was also at a premium. If trade unions did materialise, moreover, they were often segregated by race and occupation. In the railways, for example, African, Asian, and European unions largely represented manual, skilled, and white collar workers respectively. When a strike by the former erupted in 1947, the latter were conspicuous in their efforts to keep services running. In this instance, a co-operative spirit in industry was not only absent vertically, between management and labour, but also horizontally, within the labour force itself.

If the government were to stand trial for the sluggish pace of union growth after the war, it could be charged on a number of counts. To some extent, the measures invoked to curtail political trade unionism inadvertently overflowed to cramp bread and butter unionism. The Essential Services Act blunted the thrust of trade unions by outlawing strikes in key industries. Several illegal strikes were, however, waged. The stipulation of the '52 Trade Union Ordinance requiring all officers, barring the Secretary, to be employed in the industry represented by their union meant a dearth of officers who had both the requisite work background and a sufficient level of literacy and sophistication. The 'Secretary', however, soon came to designate a union's top executive, rather than clerical administrator, thus widening the field of choice. Another stipulation of the '52 Ordinance, which took an unkindly view of general unions, threatened to fragment what limited skills and resources were available. Faced, however, with an absence of unions altogether, the demarcation of 'industry' under the jurisdiction of one union eventually came to be given a more liberal interpretation.

Finally, the measures invoked to curtail political trade unionism may have directly checked the labour movement's momentum. By legislating the formal structure out of political life, the government reduced it to sterility, at a time when the country was on the brink of profound political change and vital issues of politics, rather than 'small reforms', were monopolising the attention of many workers. Even major terms of employment were thrashed out in other theatres: minimum wages and equal pay for equal work were under the jurisdiction of bureaucrats and committees. As one union leader recently reminisced, the question is not why few trade unions existed after the war but how a few managed to exist at all.[42]

The tide began to turn gradually with the coming of 'Mau Mau'. Bread and butter trade unionism showed signs of life in spite of the fact that efforts to organise were severely hampered by extraordinary

Emergency measures. A greater interest in 'small reforms' seemed to show itself as Independence became less of a remote possibility. Why demands for fundamental political change went no further than demands for Independence; why African 'moneylords' in Nairobi, Black or White, were no longer a target for strikes, open to question the imminent efforts of employers to build business unions. Two events in 1955 suggest the impending change and set the stage for the future.

On the third of March, 6,000 dockers in Mombasa went on strike. Soon the walk-out spread to other undertakings on Mombasa Island and 14,000 workers became involved. 'Mau Mau' was then at its height but the demands of the strikers appear to have been limited to better working conditions. The initial contacts and subsequent negotiations between the strikers, the employers, and the government were handled by Tom Mboya. He registers the importance of the walkout as follows:

> The whole dispute was one of our biggest tests. . . . It was . . . the first time a trade union leader had personally represented the workers in the settlement of a strike. The employers began to realise that they were dealing with a new type of trade union.[43]

In the same year, members of the Kenya Local Government Workers' Union (KLGWU) confined a dispute with the Nairobi City Council to the issue of recognition. The findings of a Board of Inquiry appointed to investigate the matter were two-fold.[44] First, it was advised that the Nairobi City Council should recognise the KLGWU and permit it to nominate representatives to the Council's staff association. This had the effect of discouraging employers from patronising consultative bodies instead of supporting fully constituted trade unions. Second, it was recommended that a trade union be accorded recognition even if it was not as yet fully representative of the workers for whom it purported to speak. This broke a vicious circle, for workers would only join a trade union after it had demonstrated its worth and a trade union could only demonstrate its worth by winning wage improvements. These, in turn, depended on the willingness of an employer to bargain, which presupposed recognition. By recommending that employers grant a trade union recognition before it became representative, the door was opened to future organisation.

Conclusion

Even in 1955, the field was virtually wide open. Few trade unions could boast a coherent following or a customary say in working conditions. Uncertainty surrounded the direction which trade unionism would take in the light of 'Mau Mau'. The political militancy exhibited by the East African Trade Unions Congress may have remained fresh in the memories of African workers. The Mombasa strike and the KLGWU decision were evidence of the labour movement's future rather than actual position. The chief importance of these developments lay in the spectre of union power they were able to evoke. This spectre made a profound impression on private employers whose ensuing activity served to further unionisation. Most important, as bread and butter trade unionism gained momentum, political trade unionism abated. It is to the activity of private employers that attention is now turned.

REFERENCES

1 George Bennett, *Kenya: A Political History; The Colonial Period* (London: Oxford University Press, 1963), p. 95.
2 *East African Standard*, January 14, 1949.
3 Colony and Protectorate of Kenya (hereinafter referred to as Kenya), *Labour Department Annual Report, 1947* (hereinafter referred to as *LDAR*), p. 13.
4 Makham Singh, *History of Kenya's Trade Union Movement to 1952* (Nairobi: East African Publishing House, 1969), p. 170.
5 *East African Standard*, January 21, 1947.
6 Singh, *History of Kenya's Trade Union Movement to 1952*, p. 177.
7 Kenya, *LDAR*, 1950, p. 12.
8 Bennett, *Kenya: A Political History: The Colonial Period*, pp. 125–26.
9 Singh, *History of Kenya's Trade Union Movement to 1952*, p. 254.
10 *Ibid.*, p. 256.
11 *Ibid.*, p. 261.
12 Great Britain, Colonial Office, *Historical Survey of the Origins and Growth of Mau Mau*. Cmnd. 1030, 1960, p. 89.
13 It is reported in a recent interview with Fred Kubai that Kenyatta himself opposed the 1950 general strike as inconsistent with the objectives of KAU. It was feared that such extremism would alienate workers of tribes other than the Kikuyu and educated Africans. KAU's policy was then reappraised and it was decided to use the trade unions for industrial issues only. (Carl G. Rosberg Jr., and John Nottingham, *The Myth of 'Mau Mau': Nationalism in Kenya* [New York: Frederick A. Praeger for the Hoover Institution on War, Revolution, and Peace, Stanford University, Stanford, California, 1966], pp. 267–69.) While such a reappraisal sheds light on the character of Kenya's nationalist movement, it is doubtful whether the political character of Kenya's trade union movement in subsequent years can be traced back closely to this tenuous policy decision.
14 Kenya, *LDAR*, 1952, p. 12.
15 Tom Mboya, *Freedom and After* (London: André Deutsch, 1963), p. 35.
16 Kenya, *LDAR*, 1956, p. 14.
17 *Ibid.*, 1949, p. 23.
18 Guy Hunter, *The Best of Both Worlds? A Challenge on Development Policies in Africa* (London: Oxford University Press for the Institute of Race Relations, London, 1967), p. 90.
19 Guy Hunter, *The New Societies of Tropical Africa* (London: Oxford University Press for the Institute of Race Relations, London, 1962), p. 223.

20 Hugh Clegg, *A New Approach to Industrial Democracy* (Oxford: Basil Blackwell, 1960).

21 Hunter, *The Best of Both Worlds?*, p. 90.

22 Roberts, *Labour in the Tropical Territories of the Commonwealth*, pp. 51–61.

23 Peter B. Hammond, 'Management in Transition', in *Labor Commitment and Social Change in Developing Areas*, ed. by Wilbert E. Moore and Arnold S. Feldman (New York: Social Science Research Council, 1960), p. 116.

24 W. A. Warmington, *A West African Trade Union: A Case Study of the Cameroons Development Corporation Workers' Union and its Relations With the Employers* (London: Oxford University Press for the Nigerian Institute for Social and Economic Research, 1960), p. 27.

25 T. M. Yesufu, *An Introduction to Industrial Relations in Nigeria* (London: Oxford University Press for the Nigerian Institute of Social and Economic Research, 1962), p. 84.

26 Kenya, *LDAR*, 1945, p. 13.

27 See, for example, William H. Friedland and Carl G. Rosberg, Jr., 'Introduction', in *African Socialism*, ed. by the same authors (Stanford, California: Stanford University Press, 1964), pp. 1–11.

28 Ken Coates, 'Democracy and Workers' Control', in *Towards Socialism*, ed. by Perry Anderson and Robin Blackburn (The Fontana Library/New Left Review, 1965), p. 293.

29 The institutional constraints on this philosophy as well as the main body of thought are discussed by Maurice Payet, *L'integraction du travailleur à l'enterprise* (Paris: Payot, 1961).

30 Hunter, *The New Societies of Tropical Africa*, p. 221.

31 William Tordoff, 'Trade Unionism in Tanzania', *Journal of Development Studies*, Vol. 2, No. 4 (July 1966), p. 420.

32 Paul Blumberg, *Industrial Democracy: The Sociology of Participation* (London: Constable, 1968), p. 129.

33 David Riddell, 'Social Self-Government: Theory and Practice in Yugoslavia', *Anarchy*, No. 95 (January 1969). Riddell makes mention of the fact that it was only in 1960 that the Yugoslav peasantry became a minority of the population.

34 Blumberg, *Industrial Democracy: The Sociology of Participation*, pp. 123 and 129.

35 See, for example, Tom Mboya, 'Trade Unionism in Kenya', *Africa South*, Vol. 1, No. 22 (1957); Kenya, *Report of a Board of Inquiry into a Trade Dispute at the Athi River Premises of the Kenya Meat Commission* (Nairobi, 1960).

36 Kenya, *LDAR*, 1952, p. 14.

37 Mention has been made of the existence of underground trade unions at the time, but these were clearly not of the 'bread and butter' variety. Mary Parker, *Political and Social Aspects of the Development of Municipal Government in Kenya with Special Reference to Nairobi* (London: Colonial Office [1949]), p. 43. (Mimeographed.)

38 Great Britain, *The East Africa Royal Commission Report, 1953–55*, Cmd. 9475, p. 161.

39 Parker, *Political and Social Aspects of the Development of Municipal Government in Kenya with Special Reference to Nairobi*, pp. 38–46.

40 Gordon Wilson, 'Mombasa: A Modern Colonial Municipality', in *Social Change in Modern Africa*, ed. by Aiden Southall (London: Oxford University Press, 1961), p. 111.

41 L. S. B. Leakey, 'The Economics of Kikuyu Tribal Life', in *East African Economic Review*, Vol. 3, No. 1 (July 1956).
42 Interview, Duncan Mugo, General-Secretary of the Hotel Workers' Union, Nairobi, 1966.
43 Mboya, *Freedom and After*, pp. 40–41.
44 Report and Recommendations of the Board of Inquiry Appointed by the Minister for Labour on 4th April 1955, under Section 13 to Inquire into a trade dispute between the Kenya Local Government Workers' Union and the Nairobi City Council, Nairobi, April 1955. (Mimeographed.)

CHAPTER FOUR

THE NEW LOOK OF EMPLOYERS

The shattering experience of 'Mau Mau' led private industry to reassemble its forces and re-cast its policies. In April 1956, the Association of Commercial and Industrial Employers (ACIE) was formed, later rechristened the Federation of Kenya Employment. In the following pages, the birth of the ACIE will serve to symbolise the demise of paternalism in strength throughout most of the colonial period and the dawn of a new philosophy. The mother of change was the modern corporation, as distinct from the small entrepreneur of the earlier phase, and the new tradition was part of the new capitalism which was coming of age in many underdeveloped countries.

Private Industry's Political Power
Under Colonialism

In the years before 'Mau Mau', the behaviour of employers in Kenya largely accorded with the caricature of a European class of entrepreneurs in a colonial setting. It is worth examining the old stereotype if only to contrast it with the new image of private industry after 'Mau Mau'.

The wherewithal of private industry to shape government policy under Colonial rule was extensive in spite of what may appear to have been a handicap: urban interests were under-represented on the Legislative Council in comparison with rural interests, and after the war industry was increasingly centred in townships.[1] Settlers and European businessmen, however, tended to share common aims in the Legislative Council. The settlers had long stressed the need for solidarity amongst the white community to present a united front against Indians, Africans, and even official government representatives. Many of the rural delegates to the Council also combined business pursuits with those of farming.

By way of illustration, the leader of the Europeans and member for Nairobi (South) in 1947 was Mr. (later Sir) A. Vincent, a prominent businessman in East Africa. Vincent owned Motor Mart and Exchange, Ltd., and the settlers provided the leading outlet for his cars and lorries.[2] Mr. W. G. Nicol, the member for Mombasa, was a partner in and managing director of East Africa for Smith Mackenzie and Co. He was also a director of the African Wharfage Co., and the Kenya Landing and Shipping Co. He served as the liaison between elected members and the Associated Chambers of Commerce and Industry of East Africa. Mr. F. J. Couldrey, member for Nakuru, was owner of the *Kenya Weekly News*, President of the Nakuru Chamber of Commerce, and a member of the Pyrethrum and Wheat Boards. Major Joyce (Ukamba) was Chairman of the Kenya Dairy Association and on the Board of the Kenya Stockowners Association. Mr. Trench (Rift Valley) was a farmer and member of the Pyrethrum Board.[3]

Besides being influential on the Legislative Council, private industry directly exerted its will on the government in other important ways.

In 1944, Kenya's Governor had called for the establishment of a Labour Advisory Board with the following terms of reference:

. . . to advise the Government upon all matters of high general policy relating to labour and labour conditions in the Colony.

To consider and report upon any existing or proposed legislation.

In 1947, the Chairman of the Labour Advisory Board was Mr. S. W. P. Foster-Sutton, an old settler and the Colony's Attorney-General. Other members included: the General Manager of the Kenya and Uganda Railways and Harbour Administration, the official Chief Native Commissioner, the General Manager of the European-owned African Highlands Produce, Ltd., the Director of Companies, the General Manager of the Magadi Soda Company (a Subsidiary of Imperial Chemical Industries), an official of Shell Co., a sisal farmer, a mixed farmer, the Leader of the Indian Elected Members on the Legislative Council, the representative of Indian employees, and the government-appointed Representative of African interests.[4] A trade union was not directly represented on the Labour Advisory Board until a year after the Emergency had begun. Before this, private industry and the settlers were well placed to advise the government on the framing of all major labour ordinances and directives.

Private employers pressed their advantage after the war through the machinery of the Central Minimum Wages Advisory Board. Its make-up was not unlike the Labour Advisory Board before 1953, for it was only after 'Mau Mau' that African trade unionists were given a voice in the fixing of statutory rates.

The Joint East and Central African Board (largely composed of British expatriate businessmen) gave a new coating to its African wage policy in 1947. It informed the Secretary of State for the Colonies that it fully recognised the necessity for stabilised labour, decently housed:

The important objective at the moment is to decrease the number of workers who have one foot in the reserve and the other in employment.[5]

Principle and practice, however, parted ways. As noted by Mr. E. M. Hyde-Clarke, Labour Commissioner in Kenya after the war: 'everyone was in favour of a stabilised African work force but no one wanted to pay for it'.[6] Private employers played a strategic part before the Emergency in securing statutory minima which were geared to the essential needs of a bachelor rather than to the requirements of a married man.

Of equal importance were the innumerable extra-constitutional channels through which private industry could make its weight felt. European employers in Kenya were organised into exclusively white Chambers of Commerce. (Indian and African businessmen ran their own separate Chambers.) European Chambers formed a network across the colony which united in the Associated Chambers of Commerce and Industry of East Africa, with headquarters in Nairobi. Influence was wielded in Kenya through a liaison in the Legislative Council and during the post-war boom in investment, the Associated Chambers did not suffer from a lack of government assistance.[7] Their affiliation to the Joint East and Central African Board, with head-quarters in London, gave them easy access to the Colonial Office and Parliament, both through private and official contacts.[8]

Finally, communication between European employers and the official side of the government was effected through casual social links. Hyde-Clarke has indicated that much of the Labour Department's day-to-day business was handled informally. Employers telephoned him when problems arose and the 'old-boy' network served as the principal means of contact.

Against this background, the impact of 'Mau Mau' on private industry becomes more meaningful. The Emergency discredited businessmen almost as much as the settler community, for both were of the ruling class. The government was at pains to make reparations to African workers at management's expense so that reliance could no longer be placed on the political largesse of colonial administrators. To survive, employers were faced with the challenge of devising new policies and opening new avenues of influence.

The ways in which they did so manifested important structural changes undergone by private industry after World War II. The new corporate entity which emerged behaved unlike the stereotyped white entrepreneur of the haut colonial epoch. The fundamental philosophy of this new business circle was responsible for the adjustment of private industry to the changes ushered in by 'Mau Mau'.

Structural Changes in Industry

Kenya's economy after the war sported features which had long been operative as well as new traits which completely altered the face of economic organisation.

On the one hand, Kenya remained an overwhelmingly agricultural country. A great percentage of total exports was accounted for by cash crops. Roughly 40 per cent of the labour force was employed in commercial agriculture. The public services remained the second major source of employment, leaving only 30 per cent of the total in private industry.[9] This category comprised mining and quarrying (never very significant in Kenya), building and construction, transport and communications, manufacturing, and especially commerce. Thus, to talk about Kenya's economy in terms of industry after the war belies the true weight of industry in the economic picture. On the other hand, whilst private industry continued to account for only a third of recorded employment even as recorded employment grew, the increase in the net product of private industry was phenomenal. New industries bloomed overnight and old firms raised their output. The annual report of the colony for 1948 stated: '. . . the arrival of so many enterprises profoundly changed the colony's economic potential'. By 1950 it was noted: '. . . the value of local manufacturers now plays an important part in the economic stability of the country'.[10]

The building industry in particular experienced a boom. Between 1948 and 1952 its net product almost trebled.[11] Simultaneously, industries connected with the building trades began to grow: light engineering, plastics, and chemicals. Plans were drafted for the erection of two cement factories and by 1953 one near Mombasa began operating. An oil refinery was projected for the Coast.

Other secondary industries flourished as well and sold their goods in a market which differed from that of the pre-war period. Before 1940, most secondary industries had been geared to the demands of the settlers. After the war secondary industries increasingly catered for (or whetted the appetites of) African consumers. The wares made available included soft drinks, canned goods, beer, cigarettes, knit-wear, woollens, pottery, machine-made shoes, vegetable oils, baked goods, packaged biscuits, and furniture.[12] Between 1948 and 1952, the net output of firms in commerce, finance, and insurance increased by seventy per cent.

Besides catering for an African market, three other new character-istics distinguished post-war industry from the pre-war variety. The consequences for labour affairs were often of major importance.

First, a great number of firms which registered in Kenya after 1945 were expatriate and a preponderance of these were British. Writing about industry in Kenya in 1962, H. W. Ord notes:

> On the whole, American business enterprise in Kenya took on a restricted form, being limited to oil companies and services such as cinemas. Continental interests were important in coffee and trading, notably French and Dutch respectively. Other sterling area interests were mainly Indian and South African insurance companies. The dominant position of the United Kingdom among overseas owners is evident.[13]

The arrival of international firms based in London (later in other capitals) saw the ownership and control of production slip out of local hands—although local enterprise continued to be of importance.[14] A preponderance of British investment meant that management imported into Kenya its convictions of British industrial relations.

Second, the new industries which mushroomed tended to be comprised of a number of fairly large-sized firms. This is not to say that Kenya ceased to be a country of predominantly small-to-medium sized industrial units. As late as in 1967, there were more firms employing less than 50 workers than firms employing more than 50 workers.[15] Nevertheless, the large enterprise tipped the scales, for a majority of the labour force found employment in factories over the 50 worker mark: approximately 75 per cent in 1957.[16] Paternalism could not always thrive under these circumstances. The concentration of employment in large industrial units lent itself to the organisation of trade unions.

The third important characteristic was that many of the new secondary industries began settling in Nairobi and Mombasa.[17] This differed somewhat from pre-war practice where much industry (which processed agricultural products) was located in rural areas. The growth of secondary industry in urban vicinities had the effect of increasing population congestion, taxing already overworked social services, and aggravating the severe post-war African housing shortage. The location of industries in municipal areas also harboured the growth of a more coherent urban African proletariat, much different in outlook and temperament from its more docile rural counterpart. The employer community also became more cohesive.

In short, whilst large enterprises continued to co-exist with the predominant small family business, like skyscrapers in a metropolis they came to dominate the horizon of industry. Thus is came to be the international firm with the 'new' look that pioneered developments in industrial relations after 1945 through the medium of an employer federation.

The 'new' look has also been popularised under the title of mono-

E

poly capitalism, neo-capitalism, and the new industrial state. Differences in terminology reflect differences in politics but there are some linking threads. At issue is the growth of giant corporations which have come to replace the self-made entrepreneur, the development of a professional class of managers—the organisation men— which has come to displace the tycoon, and a diffusion of share-holding, although concentration of ownership in the hands of selected families obtains even in the United States to no small degree.[18] According to Baran and Sweezy, two inter-related factors distinguish the old and new models: the corporation has a longer time horizon than the individual capitalist and is a more rational calculator.[19] Perforce, the volume of investment and intricacy of technology require a long time horizon and the vastness of operations and specialisation of production require a rationalisation of the managerial function. As far as trade unions are concerned:

> The interests of managers have turned them to a 'rational' study of industrial relations. Anxious to maintain continuity of production, they have realised the necessity for securing good labour relations as a pre-requisite of smooth administration.[20]

One commentator on the American scene, Galbraith, goes even further:

> . . . the industrial system has how largely encompassed the labour movement. It has dissolved some of its most important functions, it has greatly narrowed its area of action, and it has bent its residual operations to its own needs. Since World War II, the acceptance of the union by the industrial firm and the emergence thereafter of an era of comparatively peaceful industrial relations have been hailed as the final triumph of trade unionism. On closer examination it is seen to reveal many of the features of Jonah's triumph over the whale.[21]

It is questionable whether the distinguishing features of the new corporation in a Western setting hold fully in an underdeveloped one. Big business may have a shorter time horizon for its investments abroad, where political uncertainty conditions capital outlay decisions.[22] Firms may seek the pay-offs they can get as quickly as they can get them, without bothering to launch a public relations campaign to win loyalty and affection. Much would depend on the nature of the investment and the time span in which capital gains could be realised. Much would also depend on the nature of the expatriate business community as a whole, which might put pressure on the hit-and-run establishment to behave with decorum. On the other hand, to survive at all in an underdeveloped climate may demand of the expatriate establishment even sharper and more rational calculations: both internally and externally with respect to political rapport. Certainly the new political strategy of the international firm is more subtle than of old.

Politics and the New Corporation

Whilst traditional and less traditional employers alike manoeuvred politically to further their aims in Kenya after the war, the political involvement of both strains differed. The great majority of employers in agriculture and small-scale industry embroiled themselves in the growing racial struggle. Most professional managers of the larger corporations maintained a studied measure of aloofness. Margery Perham wrote in 1955:

> I find it frequently necessary to remind myself that if Europeans are a minority in Kenya, the settlers . . . are a minority amongst Europeans. There are many thousands of white men, officials; missionaries, employees of large firms, such as banks, merchant houses, tea-planting companies, and professional men of all categories and grades, who are not settlers and who do not share the settler viewpoint. Many of them have little or no dealing with politics. . . . It has been a great loss to Kenya that this element has never made itself felt in political life.[23]

The dispassion displayed by international firms towards politics allowed a more rational approach towards trade unions. The Labour Department noted in 1949:

> Newcomers to the secondary industries of the Colony . . . bring with them a background of United Kingdom industrial relationship and are ready to discuss terms and conditions of service with their employees or their representatives, which augers well for the future—a very different attitude to that adopted by some of Kenya's 'old-timer' employers.[24]

Three years later 'Mau Mau' erupted. Newcomers to the secondary industries then brought with them from the United Kingdom a feeling expressed in private business circles that it was time the messy business of 'Mau Mau' was cleaned up.

The London-based Overseas Employers' Federation (later the Organisation of Employers' Federations and Employers in Developing Countries) was instrumental in putting across this view. The OEF aimed to modernise personnel management in the colonies. As a first step, employers were encouraged to organise locally. Considerable success was met with in Africa, the Caribbean, and the Far East. Organisation by employers at the national level is by no means limited to the case under study. As a second step, employers were encouraged to collaborate internationally. Today, OEF members number some fifty confederations, the smallest being that of Fiji, with 100 affiliated companies, the largest being possibly that of Kenya. A letter dated September 1954 from the OEF to a British TUC international organiser reads as follows:

> The purpose of the Federation is primarily to represent the interests of overseas employers at international conferences, particularly where those conferences have a strong left-wing bias and are likely to impose conditions on employers that are not in the best interests of the economies of the territories concerned.

In the same year, the Secretary of the OEF, one time Labour Commissioner in Kenya, made an exploratory visit to Nairobi. Two years later the Association of Commercial and Industrial Employers was founded.

Sir Philip Rogers, first President of the ACIE and former director of the British and American Tobacco Corporation in East Africa, lends a perspective to the rationalism of his organisation in its early days.[25] Sir Philip suggests that it was necessary to form a federation during the Emergency to correct the hostile image created by some of Kenya's 'old-timer' employers. It was necessary to create an agency through which employers might determinedly co-operate with the labour movement, for to do otherwise would have been political suicide. To do otherwise would also have been to invite the possibility of extremist opposition or the foregone opportunity to create a labour movement in the image of the new industrial state. At a time when African nationalism was in its ascendency, it was necessary to organise a cohesive pressure group to exert influence on the government, for the chances were growing remote for Europeans to exert their will through the constitutional process. Finally, Sir Philip stresses that it was necessary to launch a concerted campaign against the racial bitterness then at its most virulent. Before the Emergency, management and labour were divided on racial lines. A white and black face rarely came into contact. The ACIE viewed collective bargaining as a medium for co-existence. The two sides of industry would confront one another in their conventional roles as management and labour, not as white man and black man.

In later years, the policies of Kenya's expatriate business community were dominated by the same concern. The Federation of Kenya Employers has repeatedly lent its support to the political safety-valve of Africanisation. The pay-off was appreciated by the Managing Director of Esso Standard (East Africa):

> The climate vis-à-vis the government brightens, pressures for nationalisation reduce, and a feeling of empathy develops for the enterprise as a good corporate citizen. All such results enhance profitability.[26]

Economic Exigencies

The transition from rubber baron to technocrat has occasioned debate about economic goals. Do corporations seek to maximise profits? Mr. Galbraith thinks not; at least not entirely. Satisfactory profits are sufficient. Baran and Sweezy disagree. They refer to James S. Earley's theory of the 'excellently managed' company:

> Like Samuel Gompers' ideal union leader, the exemplary man of management seems to have 'more!' for at least one of his mottoes. . . . My behavioural postulate could best be briefly described as 'a systematic temporal search for higher practical profits'.[27]

Certainly the expatriate corporation which set up operations in Kenya after the war displayed less of the ruthless avarice at the margin usually associated with the self-made industrialist. But in the long run, a picture of bountiful indulgence hardly describes the international firm either. When one American oil syndicate gave signs of exceeding the bounds of benevolence, the other new companies were active in seeking to bring the profligate back to the existing norm of generosity. The ACIE seems to have reasoned that whilst trade unions were unavoidable, employers could ensure that they upset the wage cart as little as possible.

Two of the more specific circumstances which gave rise to the ACIE's 'rational' policies may be noted. Traditions of British industrial relations show themselves in the ACIE's behaviour.

Throughout most of the colonial period, the government maintained a stewardship over African wages in two respects. Even when some of the corporations offered higher than average pay, the norm was that of the public sector. In any case, current rates for unskilled operatives were pegged to statutory minima. The detailed standards for rations, housing, and medical services laid down in an Employment Ordinance also served as the private sector's standard.

Before 1947, few employers voiced complaints against government paternalism. Statutory terms of service were sufficiently austere to be tolerated. It was only in 1947 and later in 1955 that the advantages of the government's protectorate began to be seriously questioned. In these years, two arbitration awards appreciably pushed up the labour costs of a large number of firms. Employers then asked if it would not be more in their interest to institute voluntary collective bargaining and dispute settlement machinery. In the absence of such machinery, arbitration was more or less inevitable.

The Mombasa Tribunal was set up in 1947 to investigate a strike at the Coast in which 15,000 Africans participated.[28] Although the Tribunal's award applied to only 50 per cent of the Mombasa labour force, employers elsewhere were pressured to fall in line. The Tribunal's award called not only for cost of living allowances above statutory minima but also for overtime pay for overtime work, higher wages for employees with five years' seniority, wage advances, the provision of uniforms, paid annual leave, and better medical care.

Significantly, several Mombasa employers reacted to the award by associating. They constituted themselves into the Mombasa and Coast Province Employers' Association and the Port Employers' Association. Their activities, however, were limited to representing management on the numerous regional consultative committees which proliferated after the strike. In the absence of coherent trade union activity, little effort was made to institute independent machinery and the threat of another Mombasa Tribunal persisted.

The award handed down by an arbitrator in the wake of a strike on the waterfront in 1955 made a much more dramatic impact. The ACIE was formed a year later. The award was considered highly favourable to the strikers, the dockers improving their terms of service by 33 per cent.[29] Like the Mombasa Tribunal eight years earlier, the '55 award rippled through industries other than long-shoring.

The growing antipathy of employers to arbitration crystallised. It was objected that arbitrators sued for peace at any price, were unaware of the peculiar problems of each industry, and tended to make awards over too wide a range of issues.[30] By contrast, voluntary collective bargaining held greater benefits. At least through collective bargaining employers would have some say as to when and by how much their labour costs rose; and if wages did rise, part of the credit would redound on them.

The government's wage leadership prompted employers to launch a system of collective bargaining for another reason. Whenever the conditions of civil servants were improved, a general fever for wage reform was kindled.[31] International firms with branches in West Africa had long experienced this. The Nigerian Labour Department's annual report for 1955–56 reads as follows:

> It is unfortunate that many workers are still under the impression that any wage adjustments in respect of Government servants should also be applicable throughout private industry . . . the refusal of managements to be bound by the elaborate scales . . . of Governmental employment . . . leads to much friction.[32]

If wages in private industry were reviewed in annual collective bargaining rounds, the agitation following public pay improvements would be minimised. Nor would private industry be forced to swallow conditions in the public services whole.

'Corespectivism'

It only remained for signs of trade union activity to give the final fillip to employer combination. Leading employers had met as early as in 1945 to explore the possibility of combining. The forum for discussions was the Associated Chambers of Commerce and Industry of East Africa and it was under the auspices of this body that the ACIE was eventually created.[33]

The urgency to combine was squared, taken to the second power, when African nationalism intensified, and with it, the trade union potential. A Federation was wanted to hold the line against inroads made by the unions' divide and conquer tactic known as whipsawing. A federation was also wanted to resist outroads made by nervous directors (the oilmen were conspicuous) anxious to buy security with higher wages. The ACIE was viewed as the agency to take the sting out of competition over labour costs. Schumpeter terms such behaviour in product markets 'corespective' but the label is also apposite in labour markets. Large concerns 'refrain from certain aggressive devices', political or otherwise, and 'play for points at the frontiers'.[34] The success met with by the ACIE's organising drive in later years may be loosely credited to the principle of reciprocity convenient to big business.

Conclusion

'Mau Mau' was a watershed in Kenya's history and perhaps the most profound lesson it taught was that if a class of people is kept oppressed, violence may prove its only alternative. In the last analysis, this *caveat* was central to the behaviour of leading firms after 'Mau Mau'. Forewarned, the ACIE encouraged the growth of business unions just capable of winning sufficient bread and butter benefits. Under these conditions, political unrest would be less likely. With a change of government on the horizon, employers endeavoured to ensure that a change in the ownership and control of industry would not accompany it. What remains to be seen is whether the self-protective measures adopted by the ACIE have achieved peace and stability in the long run; and at what price to political and economic development.

REFERENCES

1 According to George Bennett, '. . . the South African principle of weightage in favour of the rural areas was taken to a more extreme conclusion . . .' in Kenya. (*Kenya: A Political History: The Colonial Period* [London: Oxford University Press, 1963], pp. 39–40.)

2 Negley Farson, *Last Chance in Africa* (London: Victor Gollancz, 1949), pp. 44–45.

3 S. Aaronovitch and K. Aaronovitch, *Crisis in Kenya* (London: Lawrence and Wishart, 1947), pp. 32–33.

4 Colony and Protectorate of Kenya (hereinafter referred to as Kenya), *Labour Department Annual Report* (hereinafter referred to as *LDAR*), (Nairobi, 1947), p. 14.

5 P. G. Powesland, *Economic Policy and Labour: A Study in Uganda's Economic History*, East African Studies No. 10, ed. by Walter Elkan (Kampala: The East African Institute of Social Research, 1957), p. 77.

6 Interview, Mr. E. M. Hyde-Clarke, London, 1966.

7 See Great Britain, Colonial Office, *Annual Report on the Colony and Protectorate of Kenya* (London: HMSO, 1948 and 1949), p. 62; p. 6.

8 Interview, Mr. A. J. Don Small, then President of the Associated Chambers of Commerce and Industry of East Africa, Edinburgh, 1967.

9 Kenya, *Reported Employment and Wages in Kenya, 1948–60* (Nairobi: East African Statistical Department, Kenya Unit, 1961), p. 4.

10 Great Britain, Colonial Office, *Annual Report on the Colony and Protectorate of Kenya*, 1948, p. 2; 1951, p. 1. See also William A. Hance, *The Geography of Modern Africa* (New York: Columbia University Press, 1964), p. 423.

11 East Africa High Commission, *Quarterly Economic and Statistical Bulletin*, No. 19 (March 1954).

12 See A. M. O'Connor, *An Economic Geography of East Africa* (London: G. Bell & Sons for the London School of Economics and Political Science, 1966), pp. 155–74.

13 H. W. Ord, 'Private Ownership of Physical Assets in Kenya', *South African Journal of Economics*, Vol. 30, No. 4 (December 1962), p. 329.

14 For an up-to-date account, see *Who Controls Industry in Kenya?*, Report of a Working Party [National Christian Council of Kenya] (Nairobi: East Africa Publishing House, 1968).

15 Republic of Kenya, *Statistical Abstract* (Nairobi, 1967), Table 65(a), p. 68.

16 International Bank for Reconstruction and Development, *Economic Development of Kenya* (Baltimore: John Hopkins Press, 1963), p. 152.

17 Kenya, *Reported Employment and Wages in Kenya, 1948–60*, pp. 10–11.

18 G. William Domhoff, *Who Rules America?* (Englewood Cliffs, New Jersey: Prentice-Hall, 1967).

19 Paul A. Baran and Paul M. Sweezy, *Monopoly Capital: An Essay on the American Economic and Social Order* (Penguin Books, 1966), p. 58.

20 Asa Briggs, 'Social Background', in *The System of Industrial Relations in Great Britain*, ed. by Allan Flanders and H. A. Clegg (Oxford: Basil Blackwell, 1964), p. 35.

21 John Kenneth Galbraith, *The New Industrial State* (London: Hamish Hamilton, 1967), p. 281.

22 The political factor was found to be of great importance in a survey of investors in East Africa, albeit the survey was conducted at the time of

Kenya's Independence when the political climate was particularly uncertain. D. J. Morgan, *British Private Investment in East Africa* (London: Overseas Development Institute, 1965).

23 Elspeth Huxley and Margery Perham, *Race and Politics in Kenya: A Correspondence between Elspeth Huxley and Margery Perham* (Rev. ed.: London: Faber and Faber, Ltd., 1956), p. 281.

24 Kenya, *LDAR*, 1949, p. 8.

25 Interview, Sir Philip Rogers, London 1968.

26 R. J. Belknap, 'The Role of Private Enterprise in a Developing Nation', *East African Management Journal*, Vol. I, No. 1 (October 1966).

27 Baran and Sweezy, *Monopoly Capital*, pp. 36–37.

28 Kenya, *Report on the Economic and Social Background of the Mombasa Labour Dispute*, by H. S. Booker and N. M. Deverall (Nairobi, 1947). (Mimeographed.)

29 Tom Mboya, *Freedom and After* (London: André Deutsch, 1963), p. 41.

30 Association of Commercial and Industrial Employers, 'Memorandum on the Essential Services (Arbitration) Ordinance From the Employers' Point of View', Nairobi, 1958. (Mimeographed.)

31 Kenya, *LDAR*, 1948, p. 15.

32 T. M. Yesufu, *An Introduction to Industrial Relations in Nigeria* (London: Oxford University Press for the Nigerian Institute of Social and Economic Research, 1962), pp. 60–61. Reference is made by Yesufu to the Nigerian Labour Department's annual report.

33 Overseas Employers' Federation, 'Industrial Organisation: Kenya', London, [1956]. (Mimeographed.) The Sisal Control Board had formed an employer association for its industry in 1952 in the hopes that this would eventually lead to the formation of a colony-wide federation. (*East African Standard*, April 22, 1952.)

34 Joseph A. Schumpeter, *Capitalism, Socialism and Democracy* (London: George Allen and Unwin, 1943), p. 90n.

SECTION II

THE INTERMEDIATE YEARS: 1956-63

CHAPTER FIVE

BLUEPRINT FOR MODERNITY

From the ACIE's appearance in 1956 to the celebration of Kenya's Independence in 1963, trade union organisation, collective bargaining, and an assortment of paraphernalia for dispute settlement proliferated dramatically. No less striking was the degree to which the ACIE shaped the course of labour history and the degree to which Independence left the course uninterrupted.

The ACIE held its Second General Meeting on February 11, 1957, attended by thirty-seven members. The minutes of the meeting read as follows:

> As has been made clear on a number of occasions, we have a wonderful opportunity in this country to build up good and lasting relations between employers and employees, for the field of organised labour is virtually empty.
>
> Let us remember that we are organising for a situation which does not yet exist, but almost certainly will exist in the future. The important thing is that I think we are organising in time.[1]

The Development of Policy and Procedure

In the autumn of 1957, the ACIE initiated, in its own words, 'the project of setting up a system of voluntary negotiations in Kenya, which it was envisioned would be supplementary to and would gradually supersede the paternal industrial regulations set up by the government'. As a first stage, a *Joint Consultation Report* was prepared by a select committee of the Association and approved at a general meeting.[2]

One measure in the Joint Consultation Report recalls an early policy of the Colonial Government. The familiar figure is works councils:

> All employers should encourage the growth of Works Councils within their own organisations. In the early stages where no responsible Trade Unions exist these Works Councils should have a dual function. They should operate as Consultative Committees. . . . Their second function should be to act as negotiating bodies. . . .

The possibility that trade unions might develop autonomously, however, free from the ACIE's 'guiding hand', caused the Association to pay considerable attention to union growth:

How rapidly the stage is reached that the negotiating trade union becomes entirely distinct from the Works Council must depend upon the speed with which the trade union element develops those characteristics of responsibility which must be regarded as a pre-requisite of their recognition.

The ACIE recommended that employers observe the following criteria for granting a union recognition:

1. The Union's paid-up membership over a substantial period must be such that it can reasonably claim to speak for not less than 40 per cent of the employees involved.
2. Its scope should not overlap that of any other recognised union.
3. It must be organised on an industrial basis.
4. It must not attempt to operate the 'closed shop' policy.

The little hope which employers had for using works councils as substitutes for trade unions or, alternatively, as embryos for company unions is manifest when the ACIE's next major policy is considered. Instead of opting for company unions, the *Joint Consultation Report* emphasises:

Encouragement should be given by employers to the development of unions of an industrial basis. . . .

By accepting this principle, the ACIE also acceded to collective bargaining on an industry-wide basis and the formation of employer associations along the same lines:

As a development of the system [of industrial trade unions] indicated above and in order that matters affecting an industry as a whole might be discussed on an industry-wide basis, there should be created in due course Joint Industrial Councils at which employees would usually be represented through their unions and employers either individually or by their Employers' Associations, which would be an association of employers in that particular industry.

In connection with collective bargaining, the ACIE also enumerated the fundamental rules which it hoped would apply when arbitration was agreed to by both parties in a dispute.

The ACIE demanded the enumeration and limitation of arbitrable issues, financial punishment for bringing 'frivolous' claims before arbitrators, and a clear definition of the points in dispute in each arbitration case. In line with this, the *Joint Consultation Report* touched on the controversial Essential Services Ordinance.[3] The *Report* comes out strongly in favour of voluntarism:

. . . the Essential Services (Arbitration) Ordinance has been applied to such a wide field that it constitutes an unreasonable fetter. . . . It is recommended that the number of trades and industries to which the Ordinance is to apply should be reviewed and reduced to those which are truly 'essential'. It would then be more politically possible to enforce the penalties provided by the Ordinance in a genuine emergency.

The policy statement in the *Joint Consultation Report* which encountered the most disagreement amongst ACIE members con-cerned the 'check-off':

> . . . the system by which the employer makes himself responsible for deducting dues on behalf of the union, known as the 'Check-off', should not be adopted in this Colony.

Apparently, against the belief of a minority of employers that the check-off would promote the financial stability of the unions and make them more 'responsible', the majority of firms recoiled at the prospect of substantial funds at the disposal of 'inexperienced' union leaders.

Finally, the *Report* concludes:

> the plan of gradual development of negotiating machinery outlined above should not be put forward in the form of something to be imposed by employers on their employees, but rather, as an agreed programme. To this end, it is recommended that the employers' proposed policy should be put before the Labour Department . . . and the KFL [Kenya Federation of Labour], in the hope that it can be agreed and that co-operation can be achieved.

Towards this end, the ACIE drew up eleven broad principles based on the *Joint Consultation Report* and invited the KFL to meet and discuss them. According to the ACIE, the KFL 'responded with enthusiasm' and on the 22nd November 1957, chaired by the Minister of Labour, a conference between representatives of the two bodies took place 'which was something of a historic occasion in the develop-ment of industrial relations in Kenya'.[4] The ACIE judged the meeting 'a success' although there was 'considerable debate and some amend-ment of the propositions put forward. . . .' A *Joint Statement* was issued to the Press which records the changes to which the ACIE's original ideas were subject.[5] Behind the amendments lay the labour movement's assertiveness and the government's persuasiveness (not altogether anticipated by employers from an invited guest).

Apparently, the KFL was untroubled by the ACIE's preoccupation with works councils. Once it was solemnly agreed between the parties that works councils would not be substituted for recognised trade unions they faded from the picture. The KFL invested much of its bargaining power in insuring that trade unions won recognition easily, and with high returns. In the *Joint Consultation Report*, the ACIE stipulated that a union should be recognised only when its paid-up membership reflected 40 per cent representation of the employees concerned over a lengthy time period. In the *Joint Statement*, this rigorous criterion was ditched:

> . . . To be recognised . . . a union . . . must be able to show that it can insure that agreements reached will be observed by the workers in the industry.

Mr. Mboya argued his case before the ACIE along the same lines on which he presented his brief for the recognition of the Kenya Local Government Workers' Union before a Board of Inquiry in 1955: it was impossible, so the argument ran, for a union to become representative until after it had obtained recognition. With the Minister of Labour's support, Mboya forced the ACIE to retreat—and to retreat substantially. For the ambiguity of recognition requirements in the *Joint Statement* eventually came to mean no requirements at all. Presently the ACIE urged its members to recognise the appropriate industrial union as soon as such a body was formed and registered by the government, the degree of representativeness notwithstanding.

Apart from the check-off, which remained unimplemented in spite of the KFL, other principles proposed by the ACIE met little opposition. The KFL gladly accepted that the Essential Services Ordinance be limited to 'truly essential services', that joint industrial councils be created and, less enthusiastically, that trade unions be organised on an industry-wide basis.

Trade Union Structure

The structure assumed by the trade union movement excited the passion of the corporations unlike any other issue. A memorandum was prepared on the subject by the ACIE which drove home the case for and against various prototypes.

The ACIE stressed that if industrial relations were to progress or if 'relations' were to obtain at all, it was incumbent on employers to cease pressuring for company unions. The memorandum put it rather mildly:

> Company unions on the American pattern, although they have much to recommend them, would probably prove unacceptable to employees on the grounds that their officers, being of necessity members of the Company, were susceptible to undue pressure from the Company management.[6]

Having surrendered this type of structure, the ACIE proceeded to note the chaos in British labour relations caused by the compounded existence of craft, general and industrial unions. For this reason, the ACIE maintained that in Kenya,

> where unionism is a new and, to a considerable extent, a synthetic product, it is possible to learn from the mistakes of others and in many cases to make a deliberate choice between the three types of union.

The merits and demerits of each structure were then enumerated.

The development of craft unions was more or less dismissed out of hand. Such organisations were considered inappropriate in an under-developed country 'where craft standards have not been highly developed'. It was also argued that this type of union 'tends to create a stoppage of work by key men in a large number of industries over a dispute concerning a few men in one industry only'.

Next, the ACIE treated academically the possibility of forming general unions. The drawbacks to this structure for employers were stressed: general unions enmesh themselves in politics, suffer from indiscipline, and promote the worst form of 'whipsawing'. The following remarks are indicative of the ACIE's attitude:

> The basic disadvantage of this type of union is that it tends to become too big. This may be acceptable under a Bevin or a Citrine but under the usual type of leader thrown up it leads to dissatisfaction amongst members and insubordination.
>
> [Moreover, the general union] . . . is prone to the general strike technique . . . and is likely to become converted into a revolutionary political body.

Thus, if only by default, it remained most appropriate for the ACIE to promote the growth of unions organised on industry-wide lines. It was argued:

1. 'The most obvious advantage of this type of union is that its negotiators will be well-informed as to the workings of the industry, its difficulties, and capacity to pay.'
2. 'Whipsawing' will be minimised.
3. Most employers will be forced to deal with only one union.
4. Wage rates negotiated by an industrial union will produce a rational wage structure within one industry.
5. Industry-wide unions will be sufficiently strong to be responsible.

With these thoughts in mind, the ACIE met with the KFL in the winter of '58 'to thrash out the thorny problem of the demarcation of the spheres of operation of the various unions [which either existed or might usefully be formed]'.[7]

If the KFL paid lip service to the creation of industrial unions in the *Joint Statement* issued to the Press in 1957, it was hardly amenable to this type of structure when it actually came down to deciding which unions were to be built and what their jurisdictions were to be. For the KFL was inclined to favour the development of general unions with mass striking power. Certainly in 1958, the major unions already in existence (such as the Kenya Distributive and Commercial Workers' Union and the Transport and Allied Workers' Union) tended to be organised loosely on multi-industry lines.[8]

From winter to spring, prolonged debate skirted the politics governing the preferences of each side. The KFL adopted the attitude that it was unable to organise a pantheon of industrial unions because of a critical shortage of qualified union leaders, Section 29 of the Trades Union Ordinance (1952) being held culpable. Undeterred, the ACIE gratuitously offered to petition for the revocation of Section 29 so that no longer would all union officers be required to gain employment in the industry to which their union was attached, one officer could administer more than one union, etc.

The ACIE carried the day and, with it, many of Kenya's labour institutions in days to come. A *Demarcation Agreement* was drafted on May 8th, 1958. The ACIE commented to its members:

> [Although] this agreement did not go the whole way towards setting up separate unions for separate industries. . . . This was a necessary concession made by the ACIE representatives in recognition of the fact that . . . the KFL had moved a very considerable way from their original plans as to demarcation in order to meet the views of the employers[9]

Thus, apart from minor exceptions, the May 8th *Demarcation Agreement* embodied the principle of industry-wide unions. It set precise limitations on the scope of the unions already in existence and, more important, called for the creation of other unions with carefully delimited spheres of influence. As a result, the following major trade unions amongst a host of others eventually came into being:

1. Kenya Electrical Trades Workers' Union
2. Kenya Petroleum and Oil Workers' Union
3. Kenya Chemical Workers' Union
4. Tobacco, Brewing and Bottling Workers' Union
5. Kenya Dyers, Cleaners and Laundries Workers' Union
6. Kenya Timber and Furniture Workers' Union
7. Kenya Engineering Workers' Union
8. Kenya Motor Engineering and Allied Workers' Union
9. Kenya Shoe and Leather Workers' Union
10. Kenya Quarry and Mine Workers' Union

Mr. Sammy Muhanji, the General-Secretary of the Kenya Distributive and Commercial Workers' Union and a veteran of the labour movement, has emphasised the fillip which the *Demarcation Agreement* gave to union growth.[10] Mr. Muhanji began his career as a clerk in a law firm. He soon sought to recruit white collar workers in other companies for membership in what he termed a craft union. In the Kenya context, Mr. Muhanji's organisation was eclectic. It called itself the Nightwatchmen, Clerks and Shop Workers' Union and sought to organise workers in all these sectors. In 1953, however, labour leaders gave second thoughts to union structure. In that year, Tom Mboya entered the union movement and he and other officials decided to organise unions on an industry-wide basis. Apparently, Mr. Mboya and his colleagues were influenced in their decision by Mr. Jim Bury, a Canadian representative of the International Confederation of Free Trade Unions stationed in Nairobi. Mr. Bury stressed the advantages of industrial unions as he knew them in Canada.[11]

In Kenya, however, it was by no means clear what an industry-wide union constituted. According to Mr. Muhanji it was most important that an employer or industry was not forced to deal with more than one union. But a union was perfectly free to organise beyond the confines of one industry. By 1954, Mr. Muhanji's union had been renamed the Distributive and Commercial Workers' Union, and sought to organise workers in a wide range of undertakings. It met head-on opposition from the government who refused to grant registration on the grounds that the Distributive Union failed to protect the sectional interests of its affiliates (the clause of the '52 Trade Union Ordinance designed to impede the growth of general unions). For the next few years, the recruitment of the bulk of workers as yet unorganised made little headway. 'Mau Mau' security restrictions hampered organising activity. Mr. Muhanji was busy battling with the Trade Union Registrar. Other officials were occupied in the time-consuming jurisdictional disputes between the Dockworkers' Union and the Transport and Allied Workers' Union in Mombasa. Thus, as Mr. Muhanji maintains, despite the sound and fury in the labour movement beginning around 1950, little was done on the decision to form industrial unions until employer associations took the lead in 1958.

Much has been written about the influence of the ICFTU on trade union affairs in Kenya.[12] Mention of the Canadian representative stationed in Nairobi only scratches the surface. Much has also been written about the influence of the American CIA on the ICFTU.[13] It is suggested that the pragmatic and conservative character of the unions (as well as the pro-Western and politically conservative nature of the government) reflects the CIA/ICFTU presence. Certainly before Independence the ICFTU exercised sway with the youthful labour movement by means of the money it proffered (discussed in Chapter

Seven), the advisers it made available, and the pseudo-professional training it afforded labour leaders. To give these externalities undue emphasis, however, is to overlook the internal dynamics of the situation. Kenya's expatriate employer movement (as briefly sketched above and as described more fully below) provided an able and omnipresent guardian in rearing the unions along the right lines. The activities of the ICFTU appear in the long run as little more than frosting on the cake.

Agricultural Labourers

The ACIE refrained from broaching the subject of trade unions for rural workers in negotiations preliminary to the May *Demarcation Agreement*, lest it spark off such a development. When, however, an organiser from the Plantation Workers' International Federation (PWIF; an ICFTU Trade Secretariat) arrived in Kenya late in 1958 after a successful membership drive on the sisal plantations in Tanganyika, the ACIE turned its attention to agricultural trade unions, lest they develop autonomously. The PWIF's representative, Mr. Bavin, was invited to address the ACIE and his first bid for employer co-operation proved most effective.

Mr. Bavin warned that the Communist menace was making headway in the African trade union movement. If employers did not permit the PWIF to organise, the World Federation of Trade Unions would capitalise on this. The second of Mr. Bavin's suggestions met with a much different reception. Bavin maintained that his Federation proposed to help the KFL organise one union for all agricultural workers. He argued that an omnibus union functioned well in Malaya and that conditions in Kenya were also suitable for this structure. To put it mildly, the ACIE disagreed. It emphasised that it could only accept the creation of industrial unions in agriculture just as in industry. That is, recognition would be forthcoming only if a separate trade union were created for mixed farming, another for coffee; another for tea; sisal; and sugar.[14]

Diverse and sundry arguments were summoned by the ACIE in support of its case but the real fear was that an omnibus agricultural union would play one sector of employers off against the other. The peculiar characteristics of each crop permitted this. For example, coffee growers are in a vulnerable position since coffee must be picked as soon as it ripens or a whole harvest is lost. Sisal growers, on the other hand, are not subject to such pressure since sisal leaves do not ripen all at once. Employers reasoned that if one union represented all rural workers, a strike could be threatened just when the coffee crop was ready to be picked. Coffee employers would be forced to meet union demands to prevent the wastage of a whole year's take. Other industries within the coffee growers' bargaining unit would then be forced to meet the same exacting conditions. To prevent this and other permutations, the ACIE demanded seperate unions for each sector and hoped that sympathetic strikes would prove unfeasible.

After prolonged wrangling, the KFL acquiesced to the ACIE's demands but its decision to do so was more in the nature of a tactical retreat than a total surrender. In a letter to the KFL by an officer of the PWIF it is suggested that the KFL humour the ACIE. The letter notes that once sectoral unions are organised, they will prove easy enough to amalgamate.[15]

The Organisation of Employers

Meanwhile, not to be outdone, steps were being taken by the ACIE to organise employers into industry-wide associations: the basic purpose being 'to present a united front of the employers in an industry to the united front which the corresponding trade union presents in negotiations over wages and terms of service'.[16] In 1956, the Group Organisers' Committee was formed. The urgency of the Committee's activities was noted at a meeting of the ACIE's general council, 17 March, 1958. The minutes of the meeting read:

We are engaged in a race to complete our development and get ourselves firmly established before we are swept away in the current of events which is moving so swiftly around us in the field of industrial relations.

As a first step, the Group Organisers' Committee sub-divided private industry into some thirty categories—each of which qualified for the formation of an employer association. Next, leading firms were urged to pioneer associations within their own jurisdiction. They were then prevailed upon to organise the smaller companies. It was recognised that as an interim measure it might be necessary to permit companies to join the ACIE directly. They would then be encouraged to affiliate themselves to their appropriate industry-wide body and their direct membership in the ACIE would lapse.

In addition to this organisation drive, the ACIE was also engaged in negotiations over the formation of a colony-wide federation with the Mombasa and Coast Province Employers' Association.[17] The major points at issue between the two groups were administrative. A formula had to be devised for representing both sets of officers on the governing board of the new body. This body was named the Federation of Kenya Employers. It was formally registered under the Society Ordinance on the First of January, 1959. Henceforth, the ACIE will no longer be mentioned and reference will only be made to the Federation of Kenya Employers (FKE).

Collective Bargaining

The creation of a colony-wide federation considerably strengthened the efficiency and scope of the employer movement. In a more united spirit, the FKE turned its attention to establishing ground rules for collective bargaining.

FKE members had already agreed that voluntary collective bargaining was preferable to a system leaning heavily on compulsory arbitration. Their reasons for doing so are worth repeating. They provide an interesting contrast to the FKE's attitudes after Independence. In a memorandum on the drawbacks to the Essential Service Ordinance prepared in 1957, the FKE listed the following general shortcomings of compulsory arbitration:

1. An employer is compelled to leave conditions in a particular industry to the judgment of an outsider who may have little expert knowledge of that industry's particular problems.
2. An employer may be compelled to accept the verdict of an arbitrator appointed by the government although he may consider the arbitrator unsuitable.
3. Arbitrators tend to have the preservation of industrial peace as their first objective. Their inclination to play for safety at the expense of the employer's pocketbook is intolerable.[18]

For these reasons, the FKE embodied the voluntary principle in the models it prepared as guides for employers on negotiating and dispute settlement procedures. These models were designed to systematise collective bargaining. One model applied to employers bargaining on an industry-wide (or sub industry-wide) basis under the auspices of an employer association. Another was directed to employers bargaining on a company-wide basis. All the parties had to do was fill in the numbers and sign on the dotted line.

The steps for collective bargaining and dispute settlement enumerated in both company and industry-wide models were similar.

First, two stages were envisaged for bargaining. Negotiations would commence on a plant-wide or regional basis. (In fact, very little negotiation ever occurs here.) Then discussion would continue on a company-wide basis or at the national level of each industry (depending on the model of negotiation). If no agreement was reached at these summits:

1. Either party could refer the dispute to conciliation.
2. If conciliation failed, and after due warning, a strike or lockout could commence twenty-one days later.
3. Compulsory arbitration could be invoked after unsuccessful conciliation only if both parties agreed to this step.

Second, distinctions were drawn in the FKE's models between general grievances (or matters of interest) and individual grievances (or matters of right). General grievances concerned such topics as wages and hours of work. Individual grievances centred primarily on questions of promotion and discipline. In the models prepared by the FKE, certain general grievances were 'bargainable'. That is, strikes or lock-outs could be held over them. Individual claims, on the other hand, or questions of right, were not 'bargainable', nor theoretically could strikes or lockouts be used in their defence.

Third, the FKE distinguished between issues which were bargainable and those which were only appropriate for consultation. Bargainable issues (which gave rise to general grievances) were fair game for strikes and lockouts. Consultative issues were not. In the early stages of drafting negotiating machinery, the FKE outlined a very limited number of bargainable issues. Under pressure from the KFL, however, the FKE was forced to extend this list substantially.

One of the FKE's most basic objectives was to centralise as much control as possible over the terms of service offered by each of its members. It followed from this that the FKE strongly favoured multi-employer bargaining. It encouraged employer associations to bargain over the greatest number of issues leaving only minor matters to the discretion of individual firms. Towards this end, the FKE prepared additional model collective bargaining agreements. The general rule embodied in these models was that a subject was suitable for bargaining at the national level if it had a bearing on all companies—regardless of size or location—within one industry. Only a few issues which the unions eventually forced to the bargaining table were left for determination at the level of the firm.

The FKE also made headway with the second stage of its plan. This was to promulgate colony-wide norms of employment which would serve as bench-marks for all bargaining units in an effort to hold the line. A 'Report on Terms of Service' prepared in 1959 reads as follows:

We suggest that the FKE is the organisation best suited to ascertain the facts and figures necessary to establish the rate for the job and that this could best be approached by deciding on 'key' jobs appropriate to each grade and using these as a yardstick for purposes of comparison. These facts and figures would then be passed to the individual industries concerned as a guide to determining their own wage structure.

Although this programme was never implemented, the feeling being that most employers would resent such undisguised interference, the FKE continued to preach basic policy for private industry to follow from the pulpit of Management Board meetings and from bibles of recommended terms of service.

Thus, when the jousts of collective bargaining were about to begin in the late 'fifties, the structural characteristics of the players had been determined and the rules governing the behaviour of each team established. By the end of 1963, roughly 150 collective agreements were being drafted each year, many of which embraced a large number of firms. Approximately 60 per cent of all employees within the private industrial sector (or 100,000 workers) were covered by collective bargaining arrangements.[19] Negotiations were also under way in the plantations. The unions demarcated in 1958 materialised quickly and were poised for the fight. Whilst 9 predominantly African unions existed in 1956, approximately 30 unions were operative by 1962. Whilst union membership totalled 17,000 in 1956, it reached 100,000 by 1963.[20] These figures are probably overstated but typically understate the true strength of the union movement—as employers were soon to discover. On that note, attention will now be focused on the fate of the FKE/KFL machinery in operation.

Rules and Realities

In 1962 alone, the number of man-days lost from strikes was greater than the cumulative record for 1948–59.[21] Figures for other years privy to the opening scenes of collective bargaining tell the same dramatic story. Management was 'authoritarian', labour was 'irresponsible'. The unions were unable to control junior officers, the FKE could not control some small (and not so small) employers. The political scene kindled a militancy in labour leaders and the rank and file, employers refused to meet 'exorbitant' wage demands or to discuss encroachments on their managerial 'prerogatives'. The screaming headlines of the Press added fuel to the flames.

Emphasis on the sensational aspect of strikes after the commencement of collective bargaining, however, distorts the picture. The leaks which the young system sprung and the box of tools used to repair them exhibited a striking resemblance to the labour experiences of Great Britain and other Western countries. The 'new look' internal to the modern corporation was spreading externally to the labour affairs of an underdeveloped country.

By far the greatest number of work stoppages and man-days lost occurred in agriculture. The years 1960 and 1962 were particularly marked by unrest.[22]

In 1960, employers were apprised that an absence of trade unions did not necessarily mean utopia, whilst their presence might have its advantages. Agricultural labourers rose up against their supervisors and participated in go-slows in the virtual absence of trade union organisation (except in the tea industry). The Labour Department ascribed the outbursts to '. . . the relaxation of Emergency restrictions' and '. . . the political fever sweeping the country . . . which served to give rise to a new spirit of militancy among the workers'. It was also recognised that '. . . on a number of occasions, union officials were able and willing to secure a return to work by the strikers'.[23] In the coffee industry, labour disturbances ended when an agreement on picking rates was reached between the Kenya Coffee Growers' Association and the nascent Coffee Plantation Workers' Union. The greatest number of man-days lost in agriculture in 1960, however, was accounted for by a strike in the tea industry. The Tea Plantation Workers' Union demanded higher wages than the Kenya Tea Growers' Association was willing to offer. After lengthy protests from the employers, the strike was finally sent to arbitration.

The circumstances which gave rise to unrest in agriculture in 1962 differed from those which prevailed in 1960. In 1962, labour leaders made the first move to amalgamate the five trade unions in the plantations and mixed farming. The precarious agreement reached between the KFL and FKE in 1959 was ignored. Amidst much confusion, the Sisal and Coffee Plantation Workers' Union was constituted. It asked the Kenya Coffee Growers' Association (KCGA) for recognition but this request was rejected outright. Nor were the remonstrations to the KCGA by the Labour Department of any avail and so a strike began in the coffee industry on June 19th, 1962. The circumstances surrounding the strike could not have been more dramatic. For one thing, the KFL threatened to call a general strike (which it did not) if the KCGA failed to relent.[24] Moreover, a bumper coffee harvest was forecast and there was a good chance that Kenya's major export industry would be ruined if the strikers held out. After four days, an interim compromise was reached (which the KFL did call for) and a Board of Inquiry was appointed. Nevertheless, the excitement surrounding the coffee walkout and the call for a general strike prompted a host of other stoppages. For the next few weeks, June strike-fever swept Kenya: both in the private sector and in public employment (where there was no collective bargaining).

The Board of Inquiry appointed by the government lost no time in coming to the heart of the coffee dispute and counselled that since the new union had agreed to negotiate separately for each industry, the KCGA should overcome its fears of whipsawing and should grant the merger recognition.[25] When the KCGA complied shortly thereafter, the way was open to further amalgamations. Today, the Kenya Plantation and Agricultural Workers' Union (registered in 1963) represents workers in tea, coffee, sisal and mixed farming. Only the Sugar Workers' Union remains distinct. The executive officers of the leading agricultural employer associations have since asserted that amalgamation proved a desirable step: there are fewer spokesmen with whom to deal or to make a muddle of things.

The June '62 strike wave hit the oil, transportation, banking, printing, motor engineering, chemical, hotel and food processing industries, to mention only a few. At a meeting of the FKE convened to analyse the wave, it was contended that behind it lay a lack of discipline in the union movement. The minutes of the meeting could equally well be those of a contemporary employer association in Britain:

> The biggest trouble . . . appears to be the taking of strike action by Branch Secretaries or other junior officials of the Unions without the consent of the General Secretary . . . in a few cases the endeavours to insure good industrial relations have been destroyed by the action of Shop Stewards. . . .[26]

According to the FKE, unofficial disturbances had two causes. Junior trade union officers envied the publicity and power accorded national figures. They hoped either to engineer a coup by their unofficial action or to bring themselves into the public eye. Shop stewards or branch secretaries were also ill-paid or unpaid and open to factional power squabbles amongst themselves. The FKE claimed that by calling a strike, local representatives created an opportunity to make a collection and retain part of the booty for themselves.

The check-off appeared a palatable remedy and the FKE finally sung its virtues to employers in a policy statement issued soon after June 1962. For with more money flowing to central union headquarters, national executives would have the means not only to pay themselves, which might stem the tide of official strikes, but also to pay off branch delegates and shop stewards, which might bring such junior officers under tighter control from the top—if not from the top of the employer movement. It does not appear, however, that management used the check-off as ransom to make the unions toe the line. Nor does it appear that the check-off succeeded in stamping out wildcat strikes.[27]

The issues over which wildcats were waged are worth closer

examination. Some figures prepared by the Labour Department in 1962 are revealing.[28]

TRADE DISPUTES 1962

Subject of Strike	Percentage of Total
1. Protest against disciplinary action taken by management (generally dismissal)	41
2. Demands for removal of supervisors	11
3. Demands for improved terms of service	15
4. Protest against excessive tasks (mainly in agriculture)	10
5. Alleged victimisation, recognition, implementation of agreement, etc.	24

N.B. Whereas dismissals account for a large number of strikes, other figures indicate that a large proportion of man-days lost is accounted for by strikes over better terms and conditions of service.

From these figures it is apparent that approximately 50 per cent of all strikes in 1962 concerned subjects which FKE members considered 'non-bargainable' and it was over subjects such as these that wildcats in particular were waged.

Demands for the removal of supervisors (11 per cent of total) are not difficult to explain. There were innumerable instances of headmen mistreating labourers.[29] A new dimension to the problem appeared as Independence approached and many of the corporations began appointing African foremen. They were often found more objectionable by operatives than Europeans or Asians. They were accused of 'brotherisation' (job patronage by tribe) or of meting out harsher treatment than that formerly dispensed by non-Africans.

Strikes over dismissal (41 per cent of total in 1962) are less easily explained: except insofar as management refused to open its disciplinary measures to discussion. But not only do other African countries report a comparably high figure: data for Great Britain (1962) also show that over 50 per cent of all strikes were fought on issues other than wages and hours, with discipline and dismissal coming high up on the list.[30] Trade union leaders in Kenya proposed one set of explanations. Many suggested that a dismissal provided the occasion to demonstrate over other grievances. Some mentioned that if working class solidarity was not at play, racial identity was. Still others claimed that the fear of unemployment, already chronic by 1960, motivated Africans to come to the defence of a dismissed co-worker in the hope that, if threatened with the same fate, similar support would be mobilised. Employers offered a different set of reasons. The FKE maintained that if a dismissed worker was a union member, trade union leaders felt obliged to prove their worth by pleading the member's case. If a dismissed worker was not a trade union member but approached a trade union for assistance under duress, the union agreed to demonstrate its strength by championing the worker's cause—on the condition that the worker joined the union and paid a little extra fee for the union's trouble.

Today, most firms continue to regard dismissal as a sacrosanct managerial prerogative but allow prolonged negotiation over 'difficult' cases. If palaver fails, the government importunes both parties to settle up in a civil court: an unlikely proposition for the poor and un-educated trade unionist.

If the union movement suffered from indiscipline, the FKE was occasionally no more successful in controlling the behaviour of employers. Industrial conflict between 1960 and 1963 raged in firms which had failed to don the FKE's 'new look' or which had failed to associate with the FKE altogether. One of the causes of a very bitter strike at the Macalder-Nyanza Mines is illustrative.

In a report on the strike by a Board of Inquiry, Macalder was described as 'a tough mining community, with all their pent-up problems'.[31] It was noted that one key executive's treatment of African workers bordered on the sadistic, racial hatred underlay much of the conflict, and, complicating matters, the Kenya Quarry and Mine Workers' Union suffered from inefficiency and factional rivalry. The union approached Macalder with a view towards negotiating a Recognition Agreement in the autumn of 1961. Little progress was made, however, since deadlock was reached over the proper role of a works council. Finally, after a strike threat, the Executive Officer of the FKE flew to Macalder, a Recognition Agreement was signed, and a Negotiating Committee set up. The Board of Inquiry, however, emphasised that whereas the Management of Macalder agreed to collective bargaining in principle, its willingness to bargain in practice was questionable. Thus, the strike at Macalder erupted in part because the Company Director served as Chairman on the Negotiating Com-mittee at all its meetings, established the Committee's agenda, and steered its discussions—until the inexperienced union officials on the Committee rebelled.

Employers twisted the 'spirit' of the FKE's policies in other ways. The FKE warned its members that their position on hiring and firing would be undermined if this management 'right' was abused. Yet, some firms obviously victimised trade union officials to the tune of much adverse publicity. The FKE also stressed the importance of not squandering the value of a works council. It cautioned employers against finagling for consultation over legitimate bargainable issues.

It further cautioned that all workers were eligible for election to works councils and that if active trade unionists were popularly chosen, employers should accept this. Several did not.

The Peacemaking

On the occasions when the smoke on the industrial battlefield cleared between 1960 and 1963, various parties could be seen making vigorous efforts to end skirmishes or to prevent others from erupting. The government was a principal peacemaker, from its Labour Officers in the field, to its conciliation services made available at the Ministry of Labour, to its ministerial influence exerted to check strikes threatening to paralyse the country. It is significant, however, that only limited use was made of arbitration during these years. The Labour Department stated in 1962: 'The Unions appeared to prefer trials of strength with the employers'.[32]

Leading officers of the FKE and KFL also acted as trouble shooters. Representatives of both organisations would jointly visit a scene of unrest, soften up their respective members for a settlement, and then put pressure on both parties to accept a compromise.

Nevertheless, in 1961 the FKE felt it necessary to establish more formal machinery. In conjunction with the KFL, a National Joint Consultative Council was created, under whose umbrella functioned Joint Demarcation Committees and Joint Dispute Commissions. Demarcation Committees were charged with sorting out inter-union jurisdictional claims and judging which categories of workers were elegible for unionisation. Dispute Commissions were to serve as alternatives to statutory conciliation or arbitration. It is noteworthy that the FKE was inspired in 1961 to set up 'independent machinery which would operate without the patronage of the Labour Department'.[33] It was believed that in its efforts to right the favouritism shown to employers before 'Mau Mau', the government had gone too far and was now partial to labour. The FKE objected that the government was not consulting it on proposed legislation; that the police were too permissive over strikes; and that nothing official was done about the 'professional agitators' hired by some unions.

But these moves were not enough. More was needed to restore peace, particularly by a Coalition Government (in which Tom Mboya served as Minister of Labour). Its two month old regime was weakened by the wave of strikes in June 1962. The prospect of African self-government had caused capital formation to all but cease and unemployment to sky-rocket. Even Mboya, however, could push the unions only so far. The KFL's leadership had passed to Peter Kibisu and hardly remained a mirror of Mboya's desires. With these thoughts in mind, a series of conferences was convened between the KFL and the FKE under Mboya's chairmanship. What resulted was the Industrial Relations Charter, born on October 15, 1962.[34]

Although much has been made of the Charter, it was essentially a statement of faith by the government and the two sides of industry to relieve tensions and to rebuild the country's economy. No forms of coercion were adopted. Indeed, the Charter had little novel in it, for nearly all its provisions incorporated policies embodied in the FKE's blueprint.

What could be described as remarkable about the Charter was its efficacy in bringing about a ceasefire and the fact that it *did* vindicate the FKE/KFL blueprint, despite the intensity of labour troubles during the preceding months. Whilst the colonial mentality of management was routinely attacked by some trade union leaders; whilst the international firms in the FKE were evidently influential, they were not to be subjected to greater checks and balances as Independence approached. Nor just yet were the trade unions. The British Government was still lodged in State House. Anti-strike proposals in neighbouring Tanganyika had raised such an uproar in KFL headquarters that Mboya was forced to make reassurances on the right to strike.[35] The General-Secretary of the KFL described Nyerere's proposals as 'the first step towards the denial of the rights of ownership and property. . . . We look upon this legislation . . . as a limit on trade union freedom . . . for which the people of Tanganyika and all of East Africa have fought'.[36] The Liberal doctrines of industrial relations set in motion by the corporations had taken root. This would have to be taken into account in years to come by activists of all political persuasions in disagreement with Liberal ideology.

Thus, as KANU swept into office and led Kenya to Independence in December 1963, it brought the Industrial Relations Charter with it. It also appropriated a sizeable labour movement adept at industrial warfare with a mentality aimed at winning some fairly high rewards. It is somewhat ironic that this should be a stark reflection of the planning and activities of a predominantly expatriate employer federation.

REFERENCES

1 On January 1, 1959, the ACIE merged with the Mombasa and Coast Province Employers' Association to form the Federation of Kenya Employers. To simplify matters, all documents prepared by the ACIE will be credited to the Federation of Kenya Employers (hereinafter referred to as the FKE). FKE, Minutes of Second General Meeting, February 11, 1957). (Typewritten.)

2 FKE, 'Joint Consultation Report', August 22, 1957. (Mimeographed.)
3 See above, Chapter Three, p. 33.
4 FKE, 'Notes on the first ACIE/KFL Meeting', 1957. (Mimeographed.)
5 *East African Standard*, November 26, 1957.
6 FKE, 'Memorandum on Industrial (Vertical), Craft (Horizontal) and General (Horizontal) Unions', [1958]. (Mimeographed.)
7 FKE, 'Notes on the Demarcation Agreement', 1958. (Mimeographed.)
8 This may appear surprising given that the Trade Union Ordinance of 1952 viewed such unions unfavourably. (See Chapter Three, p. 33.) By 1958, however, the 'industry' under a union's jurisdiction was given a more liberal interpretation. The Transport and Allied Workers' Union, for example, not only represented workers in trucking companies but also workers in firms which assembled transportation equipment. The ACIE adopted a stricter interpretation of 'industrial' union.
9 FKE, 'Notes on the Demarcation Agreement'.
10 Interview, Mr. Sammy Muhanji, Nairobi, summer 1966.
11 The influence of Jim Bury on Kenya's union movement is noted by Tom Mboya in his autobiography, *Freedom and After* (London: André Deutsch, 1963), p. 42.
12 D. Schecter, M. Ansara & D. Kolodney, 'The CIA is an Equal Opportunity Employer', *Ramparts* (July 1969).
13 George Morris, *CIA and American Labor: The Subversion of the AFL–CIO's Foreign Policy* (New York: International Publishers, 1967). Morris gets a fair amount of his information from the *New York Times*.
14 The attitude of the ACIE on the demarcation of agricultural trade unions is expressed in the minutes of various meetings held in 1958 and 1959. Mr. Bavin's visit is recorded at an earlier date. (FKE, Minutes of informal meeting of Central Council, December 3, 1957.) (Typewritten.)
15 Letter contained in files of International Federation of Plantation and Agricultural Workers' Union, Headquarters, 17, Rue Necker, Geneva. I am indebted to Mr. Tom Bavin for permitting me to examine these records.
16 FKE, 'Memorandum on the Organisation of Employers for Industrial Negotiations (The Two-Tier Structure)', 1959. (Mimeographed.)
17 For information on this Association, see Chapter Four, p. 56.
18 FKE, 'Memorandum on the Essential Services (Arbitration) Ordinance from the Employers' Point of View', 1958. (Mimeographed.)
19 For a break-down of these figures, see Chapter Nine, pp. 143–4.
20 Colony and Protectorate of Kenya (hereinafter referred to as Kenya), *Labour Department Annual Report* (hereinafter referred to as *LDAR*) (Nairobi, 1956–62). Also, Republic of Kenya, *Ministry of Labour and Social Services Annual Report 1963* (Nairobi, 1965), Table 9, pp. 38–41.
21 Republic of Kenya, *Statistical Abstract* (Nairobi, 1966), Table 154, p. 127.
22 In 1960, out of a total of 756,806 man-days lost in the private sector, 637,933 were accounted for by agriculture. (Republic of Kenya, *Statistical Abstract*, 1966, Table 154, p. 127.)
23 Kenya, *LDAR*, 1960, p. 15.
24 *Daily Nation*, June 16, 1962.
25 [Colony and Protectorate of Kenya], *Report of the Board of Inquiry Appointed to Inquire into the Question of the Sisal and Coffee Plantation Workers' Union being afforded by the Kenya Coffee Growers' Association Recognition for the purposes of voluntary Collective Bargaining on Terms and Conditions of Employment in the Coffee Industry and the Right of Access*

to its *Members and Potential Members Residing on Coffee Plantations* (Nairobi, 1962), p. 14.

26 FKE, Minutes of 39th Management Board Meeting, 29 June, 1962.

27 Peter Dodds, 'Current Problems in Industrial Relations', *East African Management Journal*, Vol. 2, No. 4 (September 1968).

28 Kenya, *LDAR*, 1962, p. 11.

29 See, for example, Kenya, *Report of a Board of Inquiry Appointed to Inquire into a Trade Dispute at the Athi River Premises of the Kenya Meat Commission* (Nairobi, 1960).

30 Great Britain, *Ministry of Labour Gazette*, April 1963, p. 146.

31 [Government of Kenya], *Report of a Board of Inquiry Appointed to Inquire into Labour Unrest at the Macalder-Nyanza Mines and into the Machinery for Negotiating with the Kenya Quarry and Mine Workers' Union* (Nairobi, 1963), p. 14.

32 Kenya, *LDAR*, 1962, p. 12.

33 FKE, 'Newsletter', No. 27, 28th September, 1961. (Mimeographed.)

34 Part of the Charter is reproduced in Mboya's autobiography, *Freedom and After*.

35 *Daily Nation*, June 14, 1963.

36 *Daily Nation*, June 13, 1963.

SECTION III
THE YEARS OF INDEPENDENCE

The effect of Independence on Kenya's house of labour may be likened to a tightening of some nuts and bolts which bear the stress, a renovation of the roof, and a paint job. The Kenyatta Administration's vigilance has seen to it (through legislation and police power) that trade unions continue to keep out of politics and that strikes become a more remote possibility. The top of the union pyramid has undergone an important restyling. The KFL no longer exists although the industry-wide unions have survived the transfer of government in strength. The Western framework of labour relations sprung from the FKE/KFL blueprint persists today. More profoundly, the exercise of Africanisation has left the basic colonial economy unchanged, save for a new coating. On May Day, 1968, President Kenyatta's speech to a workers' rally read as follows:

> Let me emphasise that employers who co-operate fully with the Government and establish training programmes aimed at placing Kenyans in positions of growing responsibility will find no difficulty in pursuing their commercial policies and objectives.*

Thus, a more thorough analysis of the employer side of the equation will follow as an overture to the *Uhuru* era. The influence of the FKE does not appear to have abated under African rule.

* *East African Standard*, May 2, 1968.

G

CHAPTER SIX

THE EMPLOYER MOVEMENT

In 1967, the President of the Federation of Kenya Employers stated in his annual address:

> We cannot conduct our traditional industrial relations activities in a vacuum and have constantly to take cognisance of the political and social trends around us when we make decisions on points of principle.[1]

A pragmatic approach is the key to the FKE's success. Kenya's post-Independence conventions of behaviour have been dutifully adopted, short of the rhetoric of African Socialism. Apart from this, the FKE's position rides on three other factors: government co-operation; the internal locus of authority prevailing within the employer movement; and trade union power. The reciprocal strength which the employer and labour movements derive from each other is a basic theme in Kenya's industrial relations. The interplay of these variables helps explain how the FKE has managed to forge a coherent empire of impressive proportions in a relatively small underdeveloped country.

Organisation

Membership in the FKE (initially the Association of Commercial and Industrial Employers) advanced in a series of waves. In the first year of its existence, the number of ACIE affiliates totalled little more than thirty of the largest firms in Kenya.[2] Within the next two years, these firms were joined by associations representing the five sectors of agriculture. This followed the trade union organisation drive launched by the Plantation Workers' International Federation and, later, the agreement on agricultural trade unions reached between the ACIE and KFL. Another major deluge arrived soon after the government acted on a joint KFL/ACIE request to limit the number of industries classified as essential services. De-classified industries (oil, food processing, hospitals, and road transportation) flocked to the ACIE once they were no longer invulnerable to legal strikes. The Port Employers Association became federated when the ACIE merged with the Mombasa Coast Province Employers Association on January 1,

1959. The next deluge materialised around 1960, when trade unions arising out of the 1958 *Demarcation Agreement* began to consolidate their strength. Industries touched by union activity which sought representation in the FKE included: brewing and bottling; baking; chemicals; engineering; motor engineering; mining and quarrying; airways; timber and furniture; shoes and leather; textiles and spinning; retail and wholesale; banks; insurance and real estate; hotels.

Then came the public services, specifically the railways and the Nairobi City Council, whose ample dues swelled the ACIE's finances and enabled the hiring of a full-time staff and the provision of services which in turn attracted additional members. Other local government authorities and quasi-public corporations soon threw their lot in with the rest, confronted with trade union pressures and the Labour Department's policy in favour of association amongst employers. Indeed, the Department aided the ACIE's growth by way of deliberately neglecting the problems of non-federated firms.[3]

Finally, a manifold increase in size coincided with the Industrial Relations Charter, signalling as it did the coming of Independence. Over 300 firms not wishing to appear reactionary sought a more enlightened image under the FKE's colours.

By the end of 1967, total membership in the FKE stood approximately as follows:[4]

Industrial Sector: 1,200 companies (including those in industry-wide associations);
Agricultural Sector: 700 undertakings (most of which are associated).

In the industrial sector the FKE's representation is extensive. The 1,200 or so member firms employ, at a very conservative estimate, at least 100,000 workers (excluding those in the hotel industry and a number of major groups). In 1966, all of private industry (excluding domestic help) employed 194,283 workers.[5] Of this total, however, approximately 25,000 workers found employment in firms with fewer than 10 workers each. Making allowance for this, the FKE's Industrial Sector comprises around 60 per cent of employees in firms with at least ten workers each and in 1966, approximately 65 per cent of all employees in private industry were engaged by companies over the 50 worker mark. Numerically, a large bulk of the FKE's following falls under this rubric but at least 400 federated companies are small. FKE support is by no means confined to the cadre of the expatriate business community.

As far as the Agricultural Sector is concerned, performance is more modest. A fair number of the larger mixed farms are not FKE members, either directly or indirectly. Nor are a great percentage of small farms, although the cash revenue accruing to small producers accounts for a large fraction of total agricultural revenue. Nevertheless, the employer associations covering the plantation industries together account for a sufficient percentage of total output and engage a large enough bloc of rural workers to be well set to influence employment standards.

The rub is one which transcends aggregates, for after membership margins are seen to be more than comfortable, it remains a harsh fact in the FKE's political life that support is not being mobilised as rapidly as African enterprise is growing. There are signs of impending change although most African concerns are today relatively small, often paternalistic, and frequently exempt from union pressures. Whatever their hue, they would be difficult to organise but because they are African they perhaps feel little need to acquit themselves of the colonial stigma by joining the FKE. The small African farmer keeps aloof, although the Kenya African Farmers' Union has recently disbanded, to merge with the Kenya National Farmers' Union, an arch-institution of the colonial era and the parent of an employer association in mixed farming. The small African businessman also keeps aloof, although the FKE has added a few of the more prosperous African companies to its membership roster. Whilst a considerable number of small Asian outfits are associated, their support is no longer passable for multi-racialism, and the FKE is at all times constrained to tread lightly in the affairs of an increasingly and determinedly African society.

Breakdown in Membership

There have also been disappointments, albeit minor ones, about the internal array of firms within the FKE's orbit. The number of industry-wide associations and the coverage of each have fallen short of the ACIE's original plan, which provided that firms join the ACIE directly only under exceptional circumstances. To meet this situation, the FKE now welcomes as members both individual firms and industry-wide associations (or associations representing a sub-part of an industry). The latter total 17 in the FKE's Industrial Sector and speak for approximately 600 firms. The number of independants affiliated to the FKE is of the same order.

The existence of an industry-wide association generally means that collective bargaining approaches the industry-wide scope but the fact that some industries do not sport associations does not necessarily imply that collective bargaining is otherwise. The FKE classifies its direct members into 'groups', many of which have been prevailed upon to bargain on a multi-employer basis. This mode of negotiation appears to be the most popular in Kenya today.

It is difficult to assess the coverage of each industry-wide (or sub industry-wide) association because it is difficult to reconcile the government's official employment figures for an 'industry' with the spheres covered by various associations. Therefore, in the following sketch of selected industries, estimates of coverage are only approximate and are supplied by the FKE.

Agriculture

Kenya's five agricultural employer associations were formed as off-shoots by long-standing trade associations. Gentlemanly pressure (and not so gentlemanly pressure) was exerted on estates to band together as employers under trade union fire. Unity has also been re-inforced by a fear of political censure should employer associations cease to exist and work with the unions. The level of union membership on individual estates throught the countryside is admittedly low. Only one-third of all sisal workers (20,000 in number) are organised. It is estimated that the Kenya Plantation and Agricultural Workers' Union (KPAWU) can at the most claim 15 per cent union affiliation on each coffee estate. Some estates claim to have no unionised members at all. This has meant that the dues flowing to union headquarters are negligible and that the quality of administration is low. If union officials were forced to seek out geographically isolated estates in the absence of associations to bargain with them, the extent of bargaining would undoubtedly diminish. In this respect, employer organisation has certainly proved a boon to the union movement, but it soon becomes evident that the planters have organised to suit their own best interests.

The Sisal Industry

The Sisal Employers Association (SEA) covers 40 sisal estates out of 50 or 95 per cent of output and employment in the industry. The Secretary of the SEA, an old Kenya planter, claims that the SEA is uninterested in recruiting the 10 pariah firms all of which are small (non-African) and all of which, he alleges, bribe union officials to pay less than SEA rates.[6] The cohesiveness of the SEA appears to rest on the fact that most sisal estates (which are primarily syndicates and not family-owned establishments) prefer to hand their labour problems over to a specialised agency to save time and trouble. Sisal prices have also dropped sharply in the international market since

1964 and the SEA stands in readiness to hold the line against the KPAWU's wage demands, so far, with apparently considerable success.

The Coffee Industry

The Kenya Coffee Growers Association (KCGA) represents coffee farmers who together account for no more than 22½ per cent of total coffee acreage. Most of the growers who have joined the KCGA are the largest in the principal coffee growing area which is east of the Rift Valley. The remainder of coffee is grown by small African cultivators and by European mixed farmers west of the Rift Valley. The KPAWU has been unable to organise African cultivators and consequently, so has the KCGA. The union was more successful in bothering the wealthier European growers, now KCGA supporters. The Secretary of the KCGA claims that the union began playing one coffee 'ridge' off against another in the early 'sixties.[7]

The Tea Industry

Like the others, the Kenya Tea Growers Association (KTGA) was formed as a result of trade union pressures. Because most tea estates are large and hence, relatively easy targets for union activity, the KTGA represents estates producing roughly 90 per cent of Kenya's tea output. The industry, however, is rapidly changing in consequence of the government's crash programme to encourage the cultivation of tea on small African holdings. At present, the Association keeps together to prevent the labour upheavals which it is predicted would result if standardised wage rates were not maintained throughout the industry. This very important factor is operative in other sectors as well.

Mixed Farming

The Agricultural Employers Association (AEA) can speak for only a minority of mixed farmers. This reflects the fact that the KPAWU has been unable to unionise many mixed estates, a large proportion of which are small, European or African owned. Consequently, there is little collective bargaining in this sector. AEA rates duplicate the bare minima laid down by law, the lowest in the country.

Industry and Commerce

To pass from agriculture into industry and commerce is to pass from a land of erratic labour strength into more militant trade union territory. Even so, whilst a number of employer associations in industry and commerce evolved under the assumption that trade union whipsawing would otherwise be rampant, the consensus amongst employers today is that the ability of the unions to whipsaw is exaggerated. The present policy of the FKE, therefore, is to obtain the best terms for each of its members within every industry rather than uniform terms across the board, as the ACIE originally proposed. This has made for some interesting patterns of employer organisation as well as collective bargaining.

The Engineering Industry

Employers in the engineering industry are affiliated to the FKE in four capacities: 22 companies have constituted themselves into the Engineering and Allied Industries Employers Association; 36 companies are direct FKE members and are informally classified as the Minor Engineering Employers Group—they bargain on a multi-employer basis; 20 Kisumu firms have also banned together for collective bargaining; 8 companies, all FKE members, negotiate on an individual basis. All these firms allegedly comprise about 90 per cent of the 'reputable' engineering industry. On October 7th, 1959, the Kenya Engineering Workers' Union was registered.[8] On its heels came the Engineering and Allied Industries Employers Association, reflecting the wish of many employers to put a floor under price competition by enforcing a common rate of pay. The EAIEA represents the largest (generally expatriate) engineering firms and pays the highest wages in the industry. The Minor Engineering Employers Group and the Kisumu organisation comprise small, predominantly Asian firms which claim to be unable to pay EAIEA rates, and do not do so. Both the unions and the larger engineering firms abide by this arrangement. The unions, of course, may have little choice in the matter but appear wary of pressuring the smaller establishments under the threat of redundancy. The larger companies, it is claimed, are unperturbed by the competitive edge which lower wages afford the smaller engineering outfits. The two groups are in a different class and operate on a different plane. This point was generally conceded at a Management Board meeting of the FKE in 1959.[9] Instead, leading firms expressed concern that notably bad conditions should not be allowed to prevail in small companies lest the image of private enterprise in Kenya become tarnished.

The Motor Trades

The Motor Trades and Allied Industries Employers Association (MTAIEA) was formed in 1962 amidst trade union activity which forced each of the large motor companies to hire additional personnel staff. To minimise costs, the companies decided to form the MTAIEA, with a paid executive to handle the labour relations of the whole industry.[10] The MTAIEA is comprised of 27 companies employing about 4,500 workers. All the major companies are affiliated with the exception of one Asian firm which is not unionised. The lower wages it pays are used as a bargaining strong-point by the Association with the Motor Engineering and Allied Workers' Union. Four small firms in Kisumu have constituted themselves into the Motor Engineering Employers Group for purposes of collective bargaining. They, too, pay lower rates than the MTAIEA. Together, these two bodies cover only half of all establishments within the industry. The remaining enterprises are dubbed 'bamboo garages' and are small, fly-by-night, and non-unionised. To ensure that the wages in these garages do not get too far out of line with FKE member rates, and to protect the workers in these establishments, the government constituted a wage council in the motor industry in 1963.

The establishment of wage councils was at one time encouraged by the FKE to protect its small-sized members against competition in industries characterised by a multitude of small non-unionised firms. Such a step was opposed by the labour movement, which expressed a preference to fight it out, since a strike could not be used to ensure a favourable wage council order.[11] Nevertheless, the minima established by wage councils today are determined largely as a result of negotiations between FKE members and industry-wide unions. Not infrequently, collective agreements are negotiated above these rates.

The Building Industry

In the building trades, a wage council was the precondition for association laid down by 122 contractors. They wanted a floor imposed on terms of service before they united and exposed their broadside to the unions for collective bargaining, since together they represented only 60 per cent of the industry. When a council was convened in 1965, the Kenya Association of Building and Civil Engineering Contractors was constituted within the FKE. Eleven additional construction firms remain independent of the Association. Some of the eleven are expatriate and like to be known as high payers, a phenomenon common in a number of sectors.

The Banks

The Bank Employers Association (BEA) was formed in 1962 after a strike in one of Kenya's nine banks. Conscious of publicity and fearful of unrest, the BEA evolved 'to deal with the unions'.[12] The full-time Secretary of the BEA claims that all the banks pride themselves on being good employers and want to keep their employment conditions in line with those in the oil, brewing, and tobacco industries. The BEA prevents all the banks from needlessly scoring political points on each other. It speaks for all the major banks in Kenya (and in Uganda) with one exception (a consortium of American, Dutch, and South African interests) which pays rates similar to those of the BEA.

The Oil Industry

The nine firms comprising Kenya's oil industry began bargaining on an industry-wide basis in 1962. This followed one of the few instances in Kenya where a trade union (the Petroleum and Oil Workers' Union) was sufficiently well organised and aggressive to play one firm off against the other with finesse. The wage increases which followed became a source of anxiety in employer circles and pressure was exerted on the oil men to combine. Although the industry negotiates one collective agreement, an association has not been formally constituted, for the American syndicates are wary of anti-trust suits.[13] The oil industry is represented as a 'group' within the FKE and barely manages to hold together.

The Distributive (Wholesale) Industry

The Distributive and Allied Trades Employers' Association (DATA) was formed in 1960 and covers 33 large firms in the wholesale distributive industry. There is much talk, however, that DATA will break up in the near future since there is little geographical or occupational similarity amongst the firms.[14] Forty distributors in Kisumu also have an association which pays lower wages than DATA.

Miscellaneous Industries: Multi-firm Bargaining

Employers in a large number of industries bargain on a multi-firm basis principally as a result of FKE pressure and the advantages of putting a floor under competition. In some cases, employers negotiating on this basis have formed associations. In other cases, to avoid the expense and bother of associating, they have remained classified as 'groups'. Some of the former type include: Nairobi and District Retail Dairymen's Association; Nairobi Petrol Stations' Association; Timber Industries Employers' Association (Rural, Urban, and Nyanza divisions). Some of the latter type include: Nairobi Coach Builders'

Group; Nairobi Spray Painters' Group; Laundries, Dyers, and Dry Cleaners; Fort Hall, Kitui, and Thika Merchants' Groups; Kisumu and Mombasa Service Stations' Groups; Charitable and Religious Organisations; Education Group.

The Longshoring Industry

The East Africa Cargo Handling Services, Ltd., is a consortium of private firms operating at the docks. It bargains with the Dockworkers' Union over employment standards for approximately 8,500 longshoremen.

Local Government

A major association in the FKE comprises some 30 local government authorities embracing roughly 22,000 workers. Within certain limits, each authority is responsible for its own employment conditions and hence negotiates on an individual basis with the Kenya Local Government Workers' Union. The Association within the FKE exists to co-ordinate the policies of all local councils, which have experienced persistent labour troubles. The emergence of the Association attests the co-operation of the FKE and the government in its role as employer. The FKE is also afforded the chance to keep terms of service in local councils in line with those in private industry.

The Chemical Industry

Kenya's chemical companies constitute a major industry which neither sports an employer association nor bargains on an industry-wide basis. The major factor precluding the formation of an association in the ACIE's heyday was disparities in size and product. Since that time, the chemical companies (numbering 26) have altered their approach and have expressed their preference for industry-wide negotiations. The efficient Chemical Workers' Union, however, with whom all the companies negotiate separately, has successfully opposed this move, a rare case in Kenya where a union has unilaterally determined bargaining structure.

Miscellaneous Industries: Company-wide Bargaining

Disparities in size and ability to pay, the diversity of product or occupational and geographical incompatibility have worked against the association of FKE firms in the following industries: airways, co-operatives, agriculture marketing, mining, food manufacturing and distribution, shoe and leather working, and textiles. Companies within these industries bargain on an individual basis, including an appreciable number of international firms, which may wish to deal with the unions on a separate footing.

Thus, the FKE's membership breaks down into diverse patterns. Employer associations (or equivalent groups) flourish in a great many sectors although large firms remain independent in considerable numbers. Whatever the option followed, chiefly at work is the unfailing and almost uncanny ability of Kenya's labour movement to threaten management's peace and prosperity—despite considerable handicaps. Of complementary importance are the peculiar politics of labour relations in an underdeveloped country such as Kenya—which constrain management to modify its behaviour in a manner unaccountable in purely economic terms. This is one factor making for differences between the FKE and a Western employer movement. Another is the extremely small size of each industry by European standards, which may mean an insufficient number of firms within one industry to warrant combination, or a sufficiently limited number of firms in contact to cement unity. The prevalence of higher concentration ratios in Kenya's manufacturing and service sectors also makes for 'corespectivism' and joint bargaining amongst oligopolists. Clearly monopolists will bargain alone as will monopsonists in rural areas. Nevertheless, despite these and other distortions of often considerable consequence, the same assortment of variables governing patterns of organisation in the Metropolitan countries may be said to operate within the FKE. Indeed, traditions of association in Britain may condition association overseas.

As for inter-African comparisons, quite briefly, whilst employer federations at the national level are active almost everywhere, employer associations at the industry-wide level are not. This is suggested by information available from the ILO and from the Organisation of Employers' Federations and Employers in Developing Countries. Constellations of industry-wide associations have not for the most part materialised in strength in Africa: Kenya being an exception. Some of the discrepancy may reflect uneven paths of industrialisation. Employers are necessary for an employer association and there may be more of them in Kenya than elsewhere. More of the discrepancy, however, may reflect past history: the timely and energetic empire building of the ACIE. Significant problems confront association at the industry-wide level, no less in Kenya than in other countries south of the Sahara. Hence the need to marshal a centralised supra-federation to initiate association at the grass roots and to mop up

independent firms not readily fileable into a sub-national compart-
ment, and otherwise lost to unity. The important implication is that
today, a viable network of employer associations at the industry-wide
level plus a large number of federated independents allow the FKE
to act with authority. Neither did the ACIE's energetic empire building
imply a diffusion of authority. Power flows to the top in Kenya's
employer movement, which redoubles the FKE's ability to manoeuvre
as a compact and formidable force on the industrial scene.

Locus of Authority

If the locus of authority in Kenya's employer movement is firmly
rooted at the top, such authority has largely been garnered indirectly.
An exploratory debate on whether or not the ACIE should serve as
an agency for collective bargaining as well as merely a forum for
consultation approached the limit to which most firms would entertain
outside interference in their affairs. In a Code of Conduct adopted on
the eve of Kenya's Independence, formal discipline is lax, for FKE
members undertake no more than:

(a) To seek the advice of the FKE on the handling of trade union demands
and, '. . . bearing in mind the possible effects on other employers, its
suggestions as to an acceptable area of settlement'.

(b) 'To take note of such advice and, unless impracticable, not to act
contrary to it without further consultation with the Federation,
further, in this event, immediately to advise the Federation'.[15]

Nevertheless, the FKE's wherewithal to operate effectively has suffered
but little from a withholding of legal sanctions. The 'advice' which
employers must seek from the Federation has taken on a stronger
meaning than the term would imply. According to the Federation's
Executive Officer:

No member . . . is allowed to negotiate without first obtaining advice
and guidance from the Federation. A mandate is given to individual
companies, or groups of companies, who are parties to negotiations . . .
which defines the limits within which they can seek agreement.[16]

Compensatory power has also been garnered from other sources: the
kind of dues formula adopted; the quality of professional staff
employed; the extent of services made available; and the mechanics
of government prevailing internally.

Dues Formula

The ACIE realised early in its career that if it was to expand without
an undue fragmentation of control, sufficient funds were required to

hire a full-time staff adept at offering attractive services. The FKE has not lost sight of this objective and levies fairly high dues on its affiliates. The exception is the small firm, whose loyalty is coveted, and subscriptions for companies with fewer than 50 workers are nominal. Such a formula places the burden of expense on large enterprises, allowing them, obliquely, to hold the whip over Federation affairs.

Professional Staff

With ample dues, a secretarial staff has been recruited of sufficient scope to make FKE headquarters a clearing-house of information which few firms are in a position to forfeit. Every controversy in employment, every piece of impending legislation, occasions an FKE memorandum on advised policy, dispatched to all members. A newspaper is published once a month. Affiliates are sampled on practices such as the payment of provident funds and the employment conditions of African college graduates. The FKE remains informed and incursive of developments in the field by providing secretarial services for a substantial number of industry-wide associations and groups: their negotiating proposals, correspondence and minutes of meetings are processed.

Ample finances have also allowed the FKE to pick and choose a full-time executive staff of high calibre which in no small part is responsible for the FKE's position in the industrial arena. The executive corps is comprised of five officers who in Kenya's small industrial community exert a personal influence in handling the unions. The five are familiar with the terms of service prevailing in almost all bargaining units and have learned the tolerance levels of almost all union leaders. Many firms, particularly small ones operating without the aid of a personnel department, have joined the FKE to take advantage of this pool of experience and expertise. Two of the executive officers are European; their assistants, African. This breakdown is somewhat difficult to explain, considering the FKE's policy in support of Africanisation. Nevertheless, the services of the chief executive officer, David Richmond, may be too valuable to forgo since Richmond is particularly able and is, in any case, said to be free of a 'colonial hangover' in his personality. The choice of African assistants reflects more closely the new look cultivated by the big business sector. The senior African executive, for example, Mr. Adam Kutahi, was once a leading trade union figure. Rumour has it that Tom Mboya feared Kutahi's popularity and squeezed him out of the union movement allegedly because Kutahi held pro-Communist sympathies and had a prison record as a result of some hard-fought strikes.

Services

By taking advantage of the manifold services made available by the FKE, a firm opens itself to interference from the top, and centralisation within the employer movement began evolving in this way from the start. When trade unionism showed signs of spreading on a significant scale in the late 'fifties, a parade of employers arrived at the ACIE's doorstep seeking aid. Already a going concern, the ACIE synthesised industry-wide associations and provided them with a cookbook of recommended procedures and practices. Most important, an executive officer of the ACIE frequently became secretary to an industry-wide association. This was more than an administrative procedure. Often, the executive would speak for the association with one or two other representatives at the bargaining table, thus affording the FKE considerable say over employment standards.

The FKE has also managed to exercise suzerainty over some of its groups and smaller direct affiliates by two procedures. First, groups like associations may be administered by an FKE executive. Second, it is accepted practice for individual companies and groups bargaining on a multi-firm basis to establish Joint Negotiating Councils. Not infrequently, FKE executives serve as independent chairmen on these bodies!

Most of the highest-paying associations within the FKE employ their own executive staff. A sizeable number of international firms bargain independently. Nevertheless, the independents are by no means entirely without the FKE's shadow. Their bargaining sessions may be attended by an FKE executive in an advisory capacity. Their personnel directors will meet with an FKE executive bi-monthly and will be informed of recent agreements concluded in the country. In short, the pressure exerted on wage leaders may frequently meet with success: the zone defined by the FKE within which the leaders are free to play may be quite fine.

It is not at all unlikely that as African firms expand into more than family-run establishments, they too will come under the FKE's shadow. There is some slight indication that this has already begun to happen. The upwardly mobile African entrepreneur stands to benefit; and not just from the specialised services the FKE makes available at nominal cost. In a recent study on the African businessman in Kenya, it is argued that neither a shortage of capital nor managerial skill constitute the primary obstacles to enterprise.[17] Rather, the African is handicapped because he is socially isolated from the business community. This makes it difficult for him to appraise his market and the scope of his competition. Membership of the FKE may ease these difficulties. Through contacts with other employers in all parts of the country, labour problems and other facets of business are likely to grow more familiar. In this respect, the FKE may serve as a high priest in initiating the African novice into the ways of modern capitalism.

Decision Making

The procedures by which the FKE governs itself have been a principal factor contributing to centralisation.

A General Meeting of the FKE is held annually. Each member is entitled to one vote per 200sh. paid in dues, which are assessed according to numbers employed. Apart from elections for seats on the Management Board, few votes are taken on substantive issues at General Meetings which are largely perfunctory affairs. The FKE's governing powers are effectively vested in its Management Board.

The FKE's Management Board bears responsibility for 'formulating and controlling' policy throughout the year.[18] It meets once a month and on special occasions when necessary. Its composition has been strategic in enhancing the FKE's stature. First, the Board is large: sufficiently large to mirror the diverse patterns of organisation prevailing at the industry-wide level and vouchsafe the implementation of policy down the line. Second, membership on the Management Board has by custom been restricted to large proprietors or leading executives. Company directors founded the ACIE and have been prevailed upon to continue running Federation affairs. It follows that decisions are made by men who have ultimate authority to make decisions within their own organisations. Such men are also the most likely to pull weight with the government.

Whilst the aim is to elect representatives of as many industries as possible, the complexion of the Management Board is decidedly that of big business. An association characterised by a large number of small firms and a small number of large ones may nominate the director of the largest in the hopes that his voice will speak the loudest. Several small firms or associations together covering more than one industry may effectively get one man on the Board to put forth the views of the 'small guy'—although a key industry with fewer votes at its command may get one man on the Board as well. Most company directors sitting on the Board (often of more than one company) hold British citizenship and reside in Kenya. Several 'Africanised' Africans are also members as are some prominent Asians.

The personal element is as important in the governing arm of the FKE as in the executive arm. Since 1962, Sir Colin Campbell has

presided over the Management Board in his capacity as FKE President.
He holds 19 directorships in East Africa, including one in Consolidated
Holdings, which owns a majority share in the *East African Standard*,
Kenya's leading newspaper. (Consolidated Holdings is in turn con-
trolled by Lonrho Ltd., a British company with subsidiaries in
Rhodesia, South Africa, Mozambique, and elsewhere.[19]) Famous for
his forceful personality, Sir Colin has weathered the Africanisation
storm so far.

The Management Board is empowered to delegate responsibility for
carrying out day to day decisions to an Executive Committee. The
Committee consists of the Federation's President, Vice-President, and
two Management Board representatives. In fact, the handling of
routine affairs devolves on Richmond and his assistants, with
occasional telephone calls to Sir Colin's offices. This makes the FKE
a wieldy and efficient body, free from bureaucratic encumbrances.

Efficiency has also been enhanced by the maintenance of regional
branches, although the FKE is centrally governed. The set-up in
Mombasa is a miniature of FKE headquarters, offering on-the-spot
advice to employers at the Coast. Branches in smaller townships,
however, are more modest in scope.

It is significant that a formal network of communication amongst
employers extends well beyond Kenya's borders. Representatives of
the FKE meet every two months with representatives of employer
confederations in Uganda, Tanzania, Malawi, Zambia, Ethiopia, and
the Sudan. Notes are exchanged on wage trends, government policy,
and the trade union situation. Since the politics and economics of
neighbouring states have repercussions in Kenya, the FKE seeks a
consensus amongst private firms on how far and in what directions
new developments on the labour front should be allowed to go.

The FKE and the Government

A telling indication of the changing times is Sir Colin Campbell's
statement to the effect that since Independence, the *modus vivendi*
between his organisation and the government has improved.[20] Whereas
the FKE once voiced complaints against the Colonial Administration's
failure to consult it on proposed legislation, the permissiveness of
police during strikes, and the laxity displayed in the discipline of
union 'thugs', such complaints are rarely heard today. The third
major factor contributing to the FKE's external and internal strength
is the co-operation it receives from the Kenyatta Administration.

There is little doubt that cordiality rests foremost on mutual
interest: keeping wages down (growth rates and profits up) without

H

disturbing political stability (loss of power and nationalisation). Partnership finds expression in innumerable ways. The government publicly acknowledges the status and legitimate problems of management, listens to the FKE, and helps it win new adherents. The FKE, in turn, is sensitive to the problems of the government: the colonial look has been discarded so that the presence of expatriate enterprise jars less awkwardly. The FKE also injects a professionalism into industrial relations on which the government has come to rely: empirically convincing arguments are produced; cooling-off meetings are arranged; orderly procedures for negotiation are established, and so forth.

The ways in which the government and the FKE collude to advance their common aims become apparent in the action taken by both parties over one of the most serious problems of recent times: unemployment. What happened in 1964 is a case in point. Whilst the FKE's actions nominally met the standards of political decorum and won the corporations warm praise, the cost sustained was more apparent than real.

Less than two months after Independence, political circumstance was such that it was crucial for the government to institute drastic short-term measures to reduce the pressure of unemployment. Even so, policy makers were sensitive to,

> the need for caution in the mounting of temporary . . . relief . . . which if too freely entered into might jeopardise the essential growth rate of the economy.[21]

A Tripartite Agreement on Unemployment was hit upon. It was allegedly voluntary but rumour had it that trade union leaders were threatened with detention if they refused to co-operate. The Tripartite Agreement was drafted in a matter of days.

The Agreement states:

> In acceptance of the fact that the unemployment problem has become so serious as to constitute a national emergency . . . sacrifices must be made if a potentially explosive situation is to be averted and the political stability of the State preserved. . . .[22]

The sacrifices called for in the agreement were as follows. Private employers pledged to increase their labour forces by 10 per cent. The trade unions agreed to a 12 month wage freeze after the expiration of existing negotiated agreements. No strikes or go-slows were permitted during the freeze. The government undertook to increase employment in the public services by 15 per cent. It proposed to establish an Industrial Court to settle disputes unresolved by voluntary negotiating machinery. The awards of the Court were to be final and binding for the duration of the Agreement. Price controls, of a sort, were also instituted. The government made it an offence to sell essential commodities (the staple foodstuffs bought by the poorest Africans) at a price higher than that ordinarily charged.[23] What 'ordinary' prices constituted and the machinery proposed to police this order were not clearly specified.[24]

Within a matter of months, approximately 28,000 workers received employment in the private sector. The government never came close to meeting its 15 per cent of the bargain.[25] Apparently it was financially unable to do so. The private sector, however, was taken off the hook by a loophole which the government was unprepared to close in the face of FKE resistance. Management was allowed to take on its 10 per cent quota without also filling vacancies created by annual attrition and turnover. Additions to total employment appear to have been no greater than what would normally have been experienced. Whereas 28,000 workers obtained employment soon after the Agreement was drafted, the Labour Department estimated in 1964 that annual attrition amounted to 20,000 in the wage-paying sector.[26] Whereas commercial agriculture was bound by the 10 per cent figure, annual labour turnover in most agricultural undertakings is easily 10 per cent. The FKE estimates in the roughest terms that turnover in industry is much lower; often less than one per cent for manual workers in the largest companies. The agreement, however, permitted employers to engage additional workers in any occupation. Many companies expanded their administrative staff but because of a shortage of middle-level manpower in the country, the FKE contends that turnover rates for this sector remain quite high. Not surprisingly, most firms announced in 1965 that they intended to retain the employees engaged under the terms of the Agreement. Whilst conditions of service other than wages were not frozen, the FKE reported only normal improvements in negotiated fringe benefits.

Conclusion

With ample dues to dispose of and manifold services to dispense, the FKE has recruited a large following and has manoeuvred as a tactical and united force on the industrial scene. With a centralised locus of authority, the FKE has exerted influence over bargaining behaviour and terms of service at the level of industry and the firm. From its observation tower at the top, well staffed and efficiently administered, the FKE has injected a certain professionalism into labour affairs. This has proved of use to the government and, in turn, the FKE has fared well under the Kenyatta Administration. Sir Colin Campbell

102   INTERNATIONAL FIRMS AND LABOUR IN KENYA

asserts that the incumbent government has given his organisation
confidence and the FKE has confidently gone about pursuing its own
interests.

What remains to be seen is how the trade union movement has
fared in light of the FKE's activities—or in spite of them. Just as big
business influenced trade unionism under colonial rule, so this
influence appears to have carried over to Independence. But neither
has reciprocal influence ceased. Trade unions remain a potent force,
suggesting that the FKE-government axis is better viewed as a triangle
with labour fighting well from its own corner.

REFERENCES

1 *East African Standard*, April 1, 1967.
2 FKE, Minutes of a Special Meeting, February 28th, 1956.
3 Interview, Mr. G. A. Lockhurst, Labour Officer, Nairobi, 1966. The Colonial
   Office also applied pressure on overseas Labour Departments to encourage
   the formation of employer associations. (Interview, Shiela Ogilvie, Assistant
   to the Labour Adviser to the Secretary of State for Commonwealth Affairs,
   London, 1966.)
4 FKE, 'Annual Report', 1966. (Mimeographed.) The employment figures which
   follow are also the FKE's.
5 Republic of Kenya, *Statistical Abstract* (Nairobi, 1967), Table 65(b), p. 69.
6 Interview, Mr. Daubenay, Secretary of the SEA, Nairobi, 1966.
7 Interview, Mr. Bown, Secretary of the KCGA, Nairobi, 1966.
8 Engineering and Allied Industries Employers' Association, 'Handbook for
   Employers', [1966], p. 1. (Mimeographed.)
9 FKE, Minutes of the Third Meeting of the Management Board, March 19,
   1959.
10 Interview, Mr. Field, Executive Officer of the Motor Trade and Allied
   Industries Employers' Association, Nairobi, 1966.
11 Colony and Protectorate of Kenya, *Labour Department Annual Report*
   (Nairobi, 1957), p. 7.
12 Interview, Mr. P. E. D. Wilson, Executive Officer of the BEA, Nairobi, 1966.
13 Interview, Mr. Dewar, Personnel Officer at Caltex, Nairobi, 1966.
14 FKE, Minutes of the Fifth Meeting of the Management Board, April 22nd,
   1966.
15 FKE, 'Constitution', 1965, p. 11.
16 Anthony D. Smith, ed., *Wage Policy Issues in Economic Development*
   (London: Macmillan, 1969), p. 128.
17 Peter Marris, 'The Social Barriers to African Entrepreneurship', Institute for
   Development Studies, Conference at Bellagio, Italy, Private Overseas Investment, October 1967. (Mimeographed.)
18 FKE, 'Annual Report', 1966, p. 1.
19 *Who Controls Industry in Kenya?*, Report of a Working Party [National
   Christian Council of Kenya] (Nairobi: East African Publishing House, 1968),
   pp. 145 and 158.

20 Interview, Sir Colin Campbell, Nairobi, 1966.
21 Republic of Kenya, Manpower Branch, Ministry of Labour and Social Services, 'A Note on Unemployment in Kenya', September 1964, p. 3. (Mimeographed.)
22 FKE, 'Copy of Agreement on Measures for the Immediate Relief of Unemployment, 10 February, 1964', 1964. (Mimeographed.)
23 *East African Standard*, February 3, 1964.
24 *East African Standard*, March 7, 1964.
25 The government engaged 5,950 workers by December 31, 1963. (Republic of Kenya, *Ministry of Labour and Social Services Annual Report 1964* [Nairobi, 1967], pp. 3 and 40.) Fifteen per cent of the labour force in the public services in 1964 should have amounted to an increase of at least 26,000.
26 Republic of Kenya, 'A Note on Unemployment in Kenya', p. 2.

CHAPTER SEVEN

TRADE UNIONS, POLITICS, AND AFRICAN GOVERNMENT

The trade union movement in Kenya since Independence conveys the impression of retaining more strength and autonomy than most trade union movements elsewhere in Africa. Certainly on the morrow of Independence it posed the same problems as the others: more political gumption and economic grasp than a frail African Government was willing or able to tolerate. Yet, the Kenyatta Administration has eschewed the approach adopted in several African countries, whereby existing trade unions are dissolved and a monolithic organisation fabricated, to function as the industrial wing of the ruling party. Instead, the Kenyatta Administration has re-organised only the top of the trade union structure, the confederation level, and has used police power and legislation to make doubly certain that politics are left 'strictly to the politicians'.[1]

The argument advanced here is that such an approach is in conformity with the fundamental nature of the labour movement which has evolved in Kenya since the 'fifties. The orientation of the industry-wide unions comprising the heart of the movement is decidedly economist. Action and ideology are geared towards winning higher wages and better working conditions—in Gomper's term, 'more'. Politically, it was thus unnecessary for Kenyatta to move against the centre. The argument also advanced and developed in earlier chapters is that the orientation of Kenya's labour movement is in large part attributable to employers. This not to belittle the complexity of the situation. There were other forces at play, namely the Colonial Administration, and notably its 1952 Trade Union Ordinance and sweeping Emergency measures; the International Confederation of Free Trade Unions; and British labour organisers. The FKE, however, produced something positive that worked: a model of unionism and a system of collective bargaining that offered gains and pre-empted potential radicalism.

Such radicalism, of course, might never have developed even in the absence of a deliberate employer offensive. Apart from the syndicalists, thinkers and activists alike have long been aware of an inherent conservatism in trade unions. By moving efficiently and in good time, the FKE might only have ensured that Kenya's trade unions strayed but little from the bread and butter path. It is the dynamics of the process that are interesting: the active role played by international firms. Many studies fail to note this dynamic process or the underlying nature of labour organisation because they dwell exclusively on the upper reaches of the union hierarchy.[2]

The Kenyatta Administration appears to derive positive advantage from its approach. The continued existence of a healthy number of industry-wide unions means the continued diffusion of power. To destroy the lower tier would have disturbed a system of collective bargaining that functioned smoothly. Leaving well enough alone, the unwelcome economic practices of the system could be doctored with a separate medicine. A dismantling of the established base would also have invited unrest amongst dis-employed union leaders and possibly their following. Indeed, the safety-in-numbers of the industry-wide base may go far in explaining its survival, just as the negligible organisation of some other African unions may explain their collapse under political duress.

To say that Kenya's labour movement pursues a pragmatic course is not to say that it is a-political. Such a term is almost meaningless in societies where the State plays a far more pervasive role than was the rule in 19th century Liberal European societies out of which evolved the classical conception of trade unions. Rather, industry-wide unions, including their regional branches and shop-floor cells, are pragmatic because they spend most of their time at the bargaining table and refrain from using labour power, particularly the strike weapon, to effect political change. The Nairobi general strike of 1950 is an exception. Significantly, it pre-dated the formation of an employer federation and mass unionisation. Since then, political action has for the most part been contained in the theatre of the 'TUC', the players being national union executives. The government's approach in remodelling only the TUC was aimed directly on target. Of course, the leadership of some industry-wide unions and that of the State-contrived Central Organisation of Trade Unions overlap. By a containment of political action at the top is meant that such action is not reinforced by an application of labour power from the bottom. Sometimes political action at the top exhibits an ideology. Sometimes it exhibits a struggle for power and money. Often it combines both.

Trade Unions and the Struggle for Independence

The polarisation of political and economic activity at the upper and lower strata of the trade union movement respectively began during the Emergency. Drawing inferences about the nature of the trade union movement, however, must date strictly from 1958, the onset of widespread organisation. Nevertheless, in the twilight period from 1952 until 1958, when 'Mau Mau' was intense and only a handful of trade unions was functioning, little supporting evidence appears for a popular myth in currency today. Politically inspired labour action designed to advance the Independence struggle was not apparent. The reputation of militance enjoyed by the EATUC seems to have spread groundlessly to its successors. The Nairobi Taxi Drivers' Union, dominated by Kikuyus, provides an exception, and others may have operated underground. But to all appearances, the two major industrial conflicts during 'Mau Mau' made few gestures of identification with nationalist politics. The unco-ordinated dock strike of 1955 was fought over the issue of better working conditions. The local government workers' dispute of the same year was waged over union recognition.

The Kenya Federation of Labour was involved in politics in 1956 insofar as it protested against some government measures unconnected with labour affairs: the Kikuyus' mass eviction from their farms and collective punishments. The KFL was also indirectly involved in politics through Tom Mboya, whose actions *qua* politician and *qua* KFL General-Secretary defy separation. What is significant is that some KFL affiliates seemed intent on their separation. Shortly after Mboya formed the Nairobi People's Convention Party (NPCP) in 1957, six officers of unions federated to the KFL issued the following statement against Mboya:

> The Federation is a workers' organisation for the benefit of the workers and not for scoring individual goals.[3]

In 1960, the NPCP called on all Africans to boycott public transport, cigarettes and beer to commemorate the day Jomo Kenyatta was detained. Trade union members (and there were many more of them by this time) gave the call a mixed reception. Although the boycott was almost 100 per cent successful in Kikuyu areas, it met with much less enthusiasm elsewhere.[4]

These isolated events shed some light on national politics and the early politics of trade unions in Kenya. Until recently, national politics were not for the most part oriented towards class. Both KANU and KADU appealed to the interests of workers, businessmen, and farmers. Trade union members responded to one or the other party as interested members of a tribe, region, and so forth. Alliance between party and trade union of divided political loyalties was thus difficult to cement.[5] Even after KADU disappeared from the scene, relations

between KANU and the KFL remained informal, perhaps because
closer ties would have worsened the split in KANU's ranks, mirrored
in those of the KFL. After supporters of Mr Oginga Odinga had been
hounded out of KANU and reassembled as the Kenya Peoples' Union,
the enlistment of the labour movement under the KANU banner in a
de facto two-party state was accomplished only by resort to coercion.

Mr. Mboya has some interesting things to say about the strategy
of those early years:

> The nationalist political parties must expect the unions to join with them
> at various points during the struggle, since the workers have as much
> interest in the struggle for independence as anyone else. Sometimes they
> expect the trade unions will call a strike as additional pressure. It is here,
> when strike actions may be used for general political purposes as against
> industrial purposes, that decisions have to be taken carefully. My own
> distinction has always been based on the view that the individual unions
> should act on an industrial basis, leaving the centre—the trade union
> federation—as the only body which should act politically.[6]

This was convenient gospel when Mboya ran the KFL; less so, for
him, when the KFL's leadership fell into other hands.

An incident in 1961 best sums up the deeds of the period. The
Kenya African National Union had been formed in 1960, with Mboya
serving as General-Secretary. In 1961, KANU planned a three day
general strike to press for the release of Jomo Kenyatta and other
political detainees. Kenyatta's release was the condition set by KANU
for its participation in a coalition government. Most surprising, the
strike had to be called off because the great number of trade unions
affiliated to the KFL refused to co-operate.[7] Nor does their attitude
reflect antagonism to KANU, which later swept the board in the
general election of 1963.

The Kenya Trade Union Congress

A split at the top of Kenya's trade union movement began in 1959
when the Kenya Trade Union Congress (KTUC) was formed. Arthur
Ochwada became General-Secretary but carried with him from the
KFL only the Building and Construction Workers' Union, of which he
was an officer. Job creation and a steadier income may have encouraged
Ochwada, for on his return to Nairobi from the Continent a few
months earlier, he found his old post in the KFL filled. His disenchant-
ment with Mboya at the time may explain his rebuff (and the KTUC's
challenge to the KFL). Ochwada was destined for Deputy General-
Secretary of KANU; a possible threat to Mboya.

On July 30, 1961, Ochwada declared a battle to free Kenya's trade union movement from neo-colonialism and the International Con-federation of Free Trade Unions.[8] (In 1957, Ochwada was a member of the ICFTU Executive Board. In 1958, he completed an advanced Management Course in Trade Unionism at Howard University, USA.[9]) Ochwada also announced the intention of the KTUC to join the All African Trade Union Federation, denounced by the ICFTU for its Communist bias. But Ochwada's career in the union movement was to end shortly. In October 1961, the Building Workers' Union gave him the sack and other officers of the KTUC did likewise. By October 1962, the KTUC was de-registered for lack of affiliates.

What did not end so shortly was the criticism directed against the unions for their adventures with international labour fronts. During a period of unprecedented strikes in 1962, Oginga Odinga said:

> I have never attacked the KFL but what I oppose is its financial aid which will make Kenya a slave to the West.[10]

Two months later, Kenyatta alleged at a rally that 'imperialist money' was corrupting the unions.[11] Money from either side could have riled him. The cold-war in Kenya was hotted up by internecine struggles to control funds from the same political source. Such struggles provide an ironic twist to the latest episode in the long history of the internationals (including the American AFL-CIO) in East Africa.

The 1963 General Election

Kenyatta's accusations of corruption were not allowed to drop and led to recriminations amongst top KFL officials. Amongst those to reappear in later events were: Dennis Akumu, head of the powerful Dockworkers' Union and the KFL's Mombasa Branch; O. O. Mak'Anyengo, head of the Oil and Petroleum Workers' Union and Assistant Secretary-General of the KFL; Patrick Ooko, Secretary-General of the KFL's Nyanza Branch; and Peter Kibisu, Mboya's successor as KFL chief. They talked much about forming a labour party to protect the unions from the under-handed politicians.[12]

Mboya quickly went into action. KANU was no doubt threatened at the prospect of a labour party only months before its showdown with KADU in the first of Kenya's general elections. Mboya stressed that trade union leaders should not use workers' organisations to further their own political ambitions. Whatever else was stressed privately, the KFL in Nairobi backed down. It also agreed to withdraw its call for a general strike planned to gain explicit protection for trade union freedoms in Kenya's new constitution. (Nyerere's anti-strike proposals in Tanganyika occasioned alarm over future trends.)

In turn, Mboya pledged to work for constitutional guarantees and also pointed out that any union leader was free to seek election as an independent candidate, or to run on the KANU or KADU ticket.[13]

The Coast Branch of the KFL was not so easily dissuaded. Hostile to Nairobi headquarters for weakening, it announced plans to sponsor the election of seven of its officers as independents. Some union leaders in Nairobi decided to stand without official backing; thus matters stood on the eve of the general election.

Trade unionists were heavily defeated at the polls.[14] Dennis Akumu, for example, lost his deposit. Mak'Anyengo received 351 votes out of 23,987 for Kericho East. Clement Lubembe, President of the Kenya Distributive and Commercial Workers' Union, was the exception to the rule. He became a Senator. He was also the only trade unionist to seek office as a KANU candidate. Workers clearly did not vote according to their trade union affiliation. Perhaps their grievances as workers were adequately ventilated at the bargaining table or occasionally on the picket line. The KANU-KADU campaigns, however, were overwhelming and the defeat of trade unionists at the polls can serve only as a poor proxy for the measurement of working class consciousness.

The Kenya African Workers' Congress

Dennis Akumu was a powerful man at the Coast but had received little KANU patronage. Neither had he been selected to run in the general election on the KANU ticket, nor had he apparently received unofficial backing in the KFL general election shortly thereafter. In the contest for Secretary-General of the KFL in August 1963 (Peter Kibisu had resigned to take up a post in private industry), Akumu was defeated by Clement Lubembe, Nairobi's Senator and Tom Mboya's political friend. There was little love lost between the men and, to a growing extent, few issues on which they saw eye to eye.

Akumu and Mak'Anyengo began their attack in March 1964. Lubembe's decision to boycott an AATUF Conference provided the occasion for charges of Western infiltration in the unions.[15] For this, Akumu and Mak'Anyengo were expelled from the KFL (Akumu had been elected second-in-command to Lubembe in August). A week or so later, they announced the formation of the Kenya Federation of Progressive Trade Unions. A year or so later, they were still unable to get the union registered by the Attorney-General. They finally met with short-lived success in September 1965 with a rechristened Kenya African Workers' Congress (KAWC).

Throughout their efforts to win legality for a KFL contender, Akumu and Mak'Anyengo reiterated their aim to free Kenya's unions from ICFTU domination. The issue may have been a wise choice politically but it was a poor one practically. In November 1964, the KFL broke with the ICFTU. Akumu and Mak'Anyengo made no move to rejoin the Federation but instead insisted that KFL men were still receiving ICFTU funds. No doubt they were, but no doubt, as Lubembe quickly rejoined, everyone was: indirectly through ICFTU International Trade Secretariats. The Colorado-based International Federation of Petroleum Workers had long maintained a representative in Nairobi. Mak'Anyengo had served as its Vice-President. (His contacts with the ICFTU stretched as far back as 1958 when he attended the Confederation's Labour College in Kampala. In 1959–61, he took a Labour Relations Course at the University of Chicago. Sometime later, he made a visit to the Socialist countries.)

Whilst counter-accusations of foreign domination were being exchanged with growing passion, the KAWC made known its intentions to create one large general union, similar to that in Tanzania. It argued that such a union would be more disciplined and in a better position to collaborate with the government and KANU.[16] Once again, the issue may have had more to recommend it ideologically than tactically. Soon the KFL announced a similar streamlining plan (which was subsequently rescinded).[17] More important, as one labour leader observed, to have one big union was foolish when the government advocated private enterprise.[18] In its awkward effort to raise party politics to trade union politics, the KAWC was severely hamstrung.

Unlike the KTUC which inflicted the loss of only one constituent union on the KFL, the KAWC created dissension and bitter power struggles all along the industry-wide front and down to the shop floor. Most interesting, despite the political intensity of the industrial conflict at the Coast, workers may well have entered the fight largely for the bread and butter spoils.

As an act of war against the KFL, Akumu began wooing workers of all trades stationed near the waterfront into his powerful Dockworkers' Union (and hence, indirectly, into the KAWC). In so doing, he poached the rank and file of unions affiliated to the KFL. Some branch secretaries, feeling the pinch of dwindling dues, put up a fight. Others retreated to the KAWC in the hope of better politics or better jobs. Violent jurisdictional battles ensued, for workers switched loyalties in considerable numbers. A union card from the Dockworkers', it should be noted, held out fair gain. The dockers earned the highest wages in the country and promises of similar terms to KFL defectors swelled Akumu's ranks. A Board of Inquiry reported on the feud:

> . . . when 2 elephants fight the grass suffers. Indeed, it would not be surprising [as testimony suggested] if the workers in whose name this split has appeared do not understand what it is all about.[19]

The FKE gave extensive evidence before the Board; and with much success. Documents were produced showing Akumu to be in violation of established trade-union demarcation rules in venturing to form one general union. It is hardly surprising that the FKE went to great lengths in the preparation of its testimony. The entire industry-wide model of unionism favoured by employers was in jeopardy and output erratic at the waterfront during the jurisdictional raids. It may, however, cause surprise that until provoked by production losses and the remote possibility of across-the-board wage increases on a par with longshoremen, the FKE had stayed aloof from trade union politics. Indeed, if impartiality was not maintained it was because the leadership qualities of Akumu were often remarked on. Nor did his politics appear to give much cause for alarm in employer circles. Events in 1969 showed the FKE to have judged the situation shrewdly.

The Central Organisation of Trade Unions

The tragic climax of the conflict at the waterfront came on August 30, 1965, when three workers were killed and over 100 injured at a Mombasa Branch meeting of the Kenya Distributive and Commercial Workers' Union.[20] The government quickly stepped in. Kenyatta appointed a Ministerial Committee and accepted its recommendations in September. Amongst other things, these called for:[21]

1. The de-registration of the KFL and the KAWC and the formation of the Central Organisation of Trade Unions (COTU) with exclusive rights to represent industry-wide unions.
2. The appointment of COTU's three leading executives by Kenya's President
   (a) from amongst nominees submitted to him by COTU's Governing Council;
   (b) the nominees (three per executive post) being popularly elected;
   (c) the officers of all constituent unions voting.
3. The dismissal of COTU's executives by the President at will.
4. The cancellation of all external trade union affiliations.
5. The reservation by the government to withhold check-off money
   (a) made payable (by law) to COTU by employers;
   (b) made payable by COTU to registered trade unions.

There was little segmentation in this chain of command. For example, the government firmly held power over the purse. COTU could not withhold check-off money, from constituent unions, their very lifeblood. It could only deny them voting privileges should they violate constitutional provisions, a marginal sanction. In a manner of speaking, if power flowed to the top in the employer movement, political power flowed out of the top in the union movement and into the government's hands. With the coming of Autumn 1965, labour saw the last of its freedoms to politicise, at least on paper. With the coming of autumn 1966, it saw more. For whilst the new legislation afforded the government by its ministerial committee was given limited application, mixing national politics and trade union affairs became a dangerous business in Kenya.

The Rift in COTU

The fusion of the KFL and the KAWC into COTU failed to mend the old schism. Indeed, history seemed to repeat itself. As in the KFL election of 1963, so in the COTU election of 1966, Clement Lubembe polled the highest number of votes with Dennis Akumu runner-up. Kenyatta ratified their appointments as General-Secretary and Deputy General-Secretary respectively. Soon, however, the COTU schism came to a head. A parallel split in national politics defined the underlying isssues and doubled the consequences.

In 1966, Odinga and his followers finally broke away from KANU and formed the Kenya Peoples' Union (KPU). Thirteen trade unionists did likewise including Akumu, Mak'Anyengo, Mr. Onudi (Sugar Workers'), Mr. Akama (Engineering Workers'), Mr. Awounda (Quarry and Mine Workers'), Mr. Wachira (Safari Workers'), Mr. Awich (Shoe and Leather Workers'), and Mr. Ooko (Common Services). Several of these unions are based in Mombasa, Akumu's old stronghold. Two have their headquarters in Luo territory. Most of the above union chiefs are Luo, which is Oginga Odinga's tribe. Only one is a Kikuyu. The following allegations were made against KANU in the Press: that employment was lower than under colonialism; that the government failed to produce a comprehensive wage policy; that no steps were being taken against rent increases; that the education system bred a privileged class; that co-operative state farming replace the government's 'yeoman' settlement scheme; that nationalisation of industry commence post-haste.

For this, the Executive Council of COTU suspended Akumu, Mak'Anyengo and Wachira from their posts. Its quasi-legal reasons for doing so were that since COTU had agreed to co-operate with the government, and since the government was run by KANU, and since the three had joined the KPU, they were acting contrary to COTU policy.[22]

These fractures seemed to leave the grass roots in the trade union movement unperturbed. The political loyalties of trade union leaders were apparently of little consequence to the rank and file. Nor is there evidence to suggest than the rank and file of *most* KPU-led unions was any less pro-KANU than the population at large. Akumu, Mak'Anyengo, Wachira, and Ooko retained their posts in their industry-wide bases. They continued their militance at the bargaining table. They persevered in embarrassing the government with demands for the pay-out of private provident funds. But all was to end shortly. After their suspension at the hands of the Executive Council, the four claimed that COTU was a puppet and KANU's industrial wing. Following this, the government passed the Preventive Detentions Act which allowed arrests in the interests of national security without public trial. A few weeks later, Akumu, Mak'Anyengo, Wachira, and Ooko were detained. More than three years later, Ooko was still in detention. Mak'Anyengo had been released after 23 months. Akumu and Wachira had served almost one year sentences.

Preliminaries to Change: 1967–69

Upon his release from detention on the 10th May, 1967, Akumu's fortunes began to improve whilst those of Lubembe began to worsen. The careers of both men are of interest in that they illuminate larger features of the trade union scene.

Dennis Akumu received his secondary education in Uganda. He then went on to medical training school in Nairobi at the outbreak of 'Mau Mau' and served as a laboratory technician with the East African Breweries until 1957. In the same year, he helped found the Nairobi Peoples' Convention Party with Mboya and worked as a Mombasa district organiser for the Kenya Local Government Workers' Union. Shortly after, he became General-Secretary of the Dockworkers' Union. He lost his post in 1966 over what appeared to be a tribal conflict.

Tribalism has infiltrated the trade union movement in Kenya if only because it has assumed an intensity in national politics. The crisis is one and the same. Political issues are clouded, if not eclipsed, by tribal ones. It is difficult to know when ideology is mere pretence and cover-up for tribalism and when it is genuine and discredited as tribal. Thus, officers of industry-wide unions may not necessarily support a faction in COTU on purely tribal grounds. Their support, however, may rest on the faction's association with a parallel coalition in national politics, which may speak for a peculiar tribal and political mixture.

Tribalism at the grass-roots in Kenya's trade union movement may be less intense. Certainly it has rarely broken the front presented by a union to an employer. Several union leaders themselves suggest that tribalism at the grass roots is latent until activated at the time of elections for industry-wide and branch officers. Candidates play on tribal loyalties as a ploy for securing votes.

This was the fate of Dennis Akumu in 1966. Akumu is a Luo whereas most dockworkers are from coastal tribes. Akumu's defeat as General-Secretary of the Dockworkers' Union came at the hands of Juma Boy, who is of the majority tribe at the waterfront. Apparently Akumu's affiliation to the KPU did not influence voting. Boy's victory and the dockers' socialism were hailed as triumphs for the KPU.[23]

Tribalism worked to Akumu's advantage after his release from detention. He was elected General-Secretary of the Sugar Workers' Union. Years earlier the sugar union had chosen to remain distinct from the general agricultural union. The former is largely a Luo affair. The latter draws much of its support from amongst Kikuyu workers in coffee, tea, and mixed farming. Two thousand sugar workers came out for higher pay in August 1968. Other workers in the industry followed. The Assistant Minister of Labour testified before a Commission of Inquiry that the strikes were politically instigated. A Commission member, however, said the Assistant Minister was alone amongst those from management, government, and the workers who had testified that the strike was due to 'political motives'.[24] Thus, after his detention, Akumu continued militating against the bosses; a militancy on which his reputation was built. He also continued to strike out at the old-guard COTU leadership: accusing it of softness, conservatism, and cold war prejudices. Indeed, despite a similar move which had ended in detention only months earlier, plans were announced for the formation of an action group with a view towards getting the COTU leadership changed. Somewhere along the line Akumu had dissociated himself from the KPU.

Clement Lubembe was educated at St. Mary's College and Commercial School. Employed by an advocate in 1950, he began organising clerks in 1951 as shop steward of the Kenya Distributive and Commercial Workers' Union. He became branch secretary in 1952 and president in 1955, an honorific post. Nevertheless, from his base in the KDCWU and later as ICFTU representative for East, Central and South Africa, Lubembe worked his way up through the KFL.

Using the KFL as a higher stepping stone and allying himself with
Mboya, he entered Parliament as a KANU Senator. In 1967, Lubembe
sat on the Board of Directors of the East African Cargo Handling
Services, Ltd., the consortium with which the Dockworkers' Union
negotiates.[25]

In May of the same year, the Minister of Labour remarked to the
Kenya Institute of Management that whilst financial support from
outside was prohibited for COTU unions,

> it is still not clear whether individual trade union leaders or individual
> trade union members may or may not accept such financial assistance.
> The Government will be providing clarification in the near future.[26]

It did so in January 1968. After a trip to Washington, Lubembe was
criticised in Parliament for making financial deals with the Ameri-
cans.[27] He subsequently denied them but admitted that some
American labour unions had proposed several projects to assist Kenya
workers. A statement was issued by the Vice-President, Daniel Moi,

> making it quite clear that the Government does not allow individuals or
> organisations to negotiate for aid or bring funds into the country without
> the Government's consent.[28]

Kenyatta had come a long way from merely delivering diatribes against
corruption at rallies in 1962.

If Lubembe was not a militant trade unionist he was an outspoken
watchdog on Africanisation. He spoke out against the views of the
East African Standard on the subject and was consequently faced with
a libel suit. The *Standard* was awarded £1,000 in July 1968. Lubembe
then seems to have turned to COTU for financial aid although
personally liable for payment. Naturally all this received much
publicity from the *Standard*. By February 1969, the Attorney General
was alleging in Parliament that COTU's funds were being misspent.
Large sums were earmarked for general purposes and travel.[29] If trade
union leaders wondered where the money came from after Lubembe's
trip to the US, they no doubt wondered where it was going. With
these thoughts in mind, COTU prepared for its second general
election on February 23, 1969.

The COTU General Election: February 1969

The Action Group of Akumu subsequently changed its name to the
Kenya Group. News broke on the eve of COTU's general election
that 76 union executives out of 100 eligible to vote had joined the
ad hoc body to depose Lubembe. The 76 were dissatisfied, according
to Akumu,

I

with the leader of what I will call the Moscow-Washington alliance in the trade union movement. By this I mean trade union leaders with foreign affiliations. . . .[30]

The Kenya Group drew up a 14 point programme and announced the candidates it would sponsor the following day. The Lubembe league selected its own slate of officers.

After the elections, placards were carried in Nairobi which read 'The Dollar has been devalued'.[31] The Kenya Group overwhelmingly defeated the incumbent COTU Administration. Akumu received 64 votes for General-Secretary compared with Lubembe's 37 and Mak'Anyengo's 41.

The Kenya Group was a cross-section of union leaders, both tribally and with respect to former KFL-KAWC loyalties. The decisive factors in voting seemed to be the obvious: Akumu's superiority as a bread-winner and his non-aligned policy. The East African Standard noted after the election that Kenyatta had the prerogative to appoint COTU's top officers from amongst three nominees submitted for each post. 'Applying the democratic principle, as he did for COTU's original officials, he will presumably ratify the appointment of those candidates polling the highest number of votes in each category.'[32] He did in fact do so. The Standard's editorial on the elections was glowing. Akumu was billed as 'well qualified by experience and character'. The Kenya Group's programme, according to the editorial, 'contains some hard-hitting points on which to rally the workers in their own interests'. Given that Akumu was once the trade union maverick and a thorn in the flesh of the establishment, the politics of COTU's second general election were far from obvious.

Some of the Kenya Group's 14 points were as follows:[33]

1. to defend the present trade union structure and to call for more autonomy for COTU affiliates;
2. to build strong trade unions to create security for trade union leaders;
3. to press for better living conditions for workers and increased pay;
4. to protect COTU funds;
5. to remain independent of any international labour organisation;
6. to press the government to Africanise the FKE;
7. to press for the recognition of trade union leaders as nation builders;
8. to work with KANU to ensure that trade union leaders were represented on local authorities and other bodies;
9. to support the government and KANU in their efforts to raise living standards.

Mr. Akumu clarified the political implications of the 14 points a few days later:

We shall support President Kenyatta, his Government and KANU. . .
[We shall] . . . pray for him for long life, as we all know that his wise
leadership and fatherly image have made the country stable.[34]

Akumu had learned his lesson well in detention. He may also have
learned the degree to which he depended on the votes of KANU trade
unionists in COTU polls.

The KPU's attack on the 'grandiose' 14 points rested chiefly on
what was interpreted as an implied COTU-KANU alliance.[35] This
interpretation was greeted by a defendant of the Kenya Group as
naïve. The alliance was explicit. The KPU, it was claimed. had put up
a candidate for COTU General-Secretary. He had met defeat after
joining forces with Lubembe.[36] (The candidate was Mr. Mak'Anyengo
and hence the reference to a Moscow-Washington alliance.) The
defendant argued that Mr. Akumu was a socialist. He differed from
the KPU only in that he was practical.

Mr. Mak'Anyengo clearly was not practical. When the government
outlawed the KPU in October 1969, he was once again detained.
Mr. Akumu's practicality and socialism, however, proved awkward to
reconcile. This is evident from his expanded version of the 14 points: [37]

> Employers can expect a new period of seasoned hard bargainers from us,
> but our approach will be an enlightened one in that we shall study the
> economy of an industry before submitting a demand.
>
> We believe that workers' right to strike should be retained but a strike
> is such a lethal weapon that it must be used very, very sparingly.
>
> We workers join hands with employers on issues such as increasing
> production, marketing, etc. What we will insist on is a fair share of the
> cake as its expands. . . .
>
> [Kenya is] one of the few countries where trade unions and employers
> [can] still bargain freely. COTU [hopes] to keep things that way and
> [looks] to the employers for co-operation in preventing a situation which
> could lead to Government intervention.

This expanded version of the 14 points does not entirely represent a
volte face. Past issues over which union leaders chose to express their
differences could hardly be described as radical. The rallying cry of
non-alignment appeared to serve as a watered-down proxy for
anti-capitalism.

Answering questions, Mr. Akumu said he was personally in favour of
nationalisation but COTU had many things to do and was not entering
into conflict with present government policy.[38] Thus, the Kenya Group
demanded no more than a 'fair share of the cake'. To do so would
have implied a recognition of exploitation and a manoeuvre to over-
throw capitalism. Nor did it settle for less than 'seasoned hard

bargaining'. To do so would have implied a recognition of labour's elitism compared with the mass of peasants and the unemployed. But given virtually the same political economy bequeathed at Independence, to demand less than 'seasoned hard bargaining' may have struck the Kenya Group as impractical. The question of why the same political economy obtained re-opens to question the role played by employers in the development of Kenya's industry-wide unions.

Conclusion

In summing up, it is clear that Kenya's trade union movement is no longer free to participate in opposition politics. With this avenue of activity blocked, COTU's new administration has taken the path of least resistance. It seemingly leads to the bread and butter pragmatism practised by the industry-wide unions. It is a pragmatism accommodating to the basic economic policies of KANU but not simply because the trade union movement has been enlisted under the KANU banner.

How many trade unionists would enlist voluntarily under the KANU banner is a difficult question to answer. How many trade unionists after 1950 wielded labour power to ensure freedom of choice is less difficult to answer: very few, both under British and African rule.

Fear of reprisal may not provide sufficient explanation. The East African Trade Unions Congress hardly had an easy time of it. Even in Spain, 4,000 workers went on strike in October 1969 to protest against the arrest of a Basque nationalist leader.[39] In the same month, the opposition party in Kenya was banned but no protest strikes were recorded. Perhaps the majority of workers in Kenya did not like the opposition party and the minority who did were reluctant to strike without cover from the rest. But neither was a strike registered when, two months earlier, M.P.s voted themselves handsome gratuities backdating to 1962.

The youth wings of political parties in Kenya play a conspicuous role in political demonstrations. Their members are often drawn from amongst the unemployed.[40] This, however, does not necessarily suggest that trade unionists refrain from political strikes for fear of losing their jobs. They are renowned for striking over dismissals, higher pay, overtime work, etc. It is arguable that the rewards from *these* strikes rather than fear of the sack make for business unionism.

Amongst the educated in Kenya, those who are socialists sometimes ascribe the political character of the labour movement to the character of its leadership. The argument (not a very Marxist one, however, for it takes little account of the underlying economic forces at play), holds that if only trade union leaders were of the right mind, the rank and file would think similarly. Certainly there may have been a correspondence between the militance of the EATUC and the politics of Makham Singh and Fred Kubai. (Today, however, Fred Kubai is hardly a radical Assistant Minister of Labour in the Kenyatta Adminstration.) The bourgeois character of Kenya's subsequent generation of union leaders (and union movement), the argument continues, is traceable to the intensified indoctrination of the ICFTU. Whilst theories of trade union leadership are diverse, one which continually reappears maintains that trade union leaders, whatever their education, will inevitably grow conservative and bureaucratic. Most of the new COTU Administration at one time passed through the hands of the ICFTU. Afterwards, however, it forgot the lessons taught and talked socialism. Now in power it has grown opportunistic. The inspiration for radical trade union politics may come from the intelligentsia externally or from the aggrieved and irrepressible workers internally. It is to the latter possibility that the international firms have applied their preventive medicine; and so far with marked success.

There are over 30 industry-wide unions in Kenya. Their dues receipts amount to more than £400,000 per annum. If their membership figures tend to be overstated, their influence tends to be understated by them. A union typically negotiates for more workers than dues payers. COTU has announced its intentions to employ an economist to arm negotiators with statistics and data. There is also talk of making COTU a clearing house for strikes. All point in the direction of sharper business practices and more bureaucracy. Of necessity, the union movement may increasingly adopt the FKE's characteristics. It is only in political matters that power flows over the top of the union movement and into the government's hands. In the realm of industrial relations, the unions are much less the government's handmaiden. A product of the new Liberal industrial state, they are viable and active, resorting to the ballot box to make frequent changes in officers. It is to how the Kenyatta Administration has coped with the economic demands of the unions that attention is now turned.

REFERENCES

1 *East African Standard*, May 2, 1968.
2 See, for example, Jean Meynaud and Anisse Salah Bey, *Trade Unionism in Africa: A Study of its Growth and Orientation*, trans. by Angela Brench (London: Methuen, 1967).

120   INTERNATIONAL FIRMS AND LABOUR IN KENYA

3   *East African Standard*, January 23, 1959.
4   *East African Standard*, October 20, 1960.
5   In 1960, the Colonial Government refused to register KANU if it enlisted the KFL as one of its constituent parts. Elliot J. Berg and Jeffrey Butler, 'Trade Unions', in *Political Parties and National Integration in Tropical Africa*, ed. by James S. Coleman and Carl G. Rosberg, Jr. (Berkeley: University of California Press, 1964), p. 343.
6   Tom Mboya, *Freedom and After* (London: André Deutsch, 1963), pp. 195–96.
7   George Bennett and Carl G. Rosberg, Jr., *The Kenyatta Election: Kenya; 1960–61* (London: Oxford University Press, 1961), p. 132.
8   *Daily Nation*, July 31, 1961.
9   *Who's Who in East Africa, 1965–66*, ed. by E. G. Wilson (2nd ed.; Nairobi: Marco Publishers [Africa], 1966).
10 *East African Standard*, June 25, 1962.
11 Ibid., August 16, 1962.
12 Some observers contend that the movement to form a Labour party was encouraged by the Odinga faction, to challenge Mboya.
13 *Daily Nation*, March 12, 1963.
14 Ibid., May 28, 1963.
15 *East African Standard*, March 21, 1964.
16 Ibid., October 28, 1964.
17 Ibid., January 9, 1965.
18 Ibid., December 30, 1964.
19 Republic of Kenya, Ministry of Labour and Social Services, *Report of a Board of Inquiry into (i) the claim by the Dockworkers' Union to represent certain categories of workers in Mombasa, and (ii) industrial unrest in Mombasa in the year 1964* (Nairobi, 1965), p. 25.
20 *East African Standard*, August 31, 1965.
21 Republic of Kenya, *The Policy of Trade Union Organisation in Kenya* (Nairobi, 1965).
22 This information was contained in the Minutes of Meetings of COTU's Executive Council.
23 *Daily Nation*, August 25, 1966. In fact, Boy only became General-Secretary after a brief power scuffle following Akumu's election defeat.
24 *East African Standard*, February 11, 1969.
25 *Who Controls Industry in Kenya?*, Report of a Working Party [National Christian Council of Kenya] (Nairobi: East Africa Publishing House, 1968), p. 90.
26 J. G. Kiano, 'Labour Relations in Kenya', *East African Management Journal*, Vol. 1, No. 4 (July 1967).
27 *East African Standard*, January 1, 1968.
28 Ibid., February 25, 1969.
29 Ibid., February 11, 1969.
30 Ibid., February 22, 1969.
31 Ibid., February 24, 1969.
32 Ibid., February 25, 1969.
33 Ibid., February 22, 1969.
34 Ibid., February 26, 1969.
35 The *Wananchi* Declaration of the KPU, which contains a short section on trade union policy, is reproduced, in part, in *Africa and the World*, May 1969 and June 1969.
36 *East African Standard*, March 10, 1969.

37 Ibid., February 26 and March 5, 1969.
38 Ibid., March 5, 1969.
39 *Le Monde*, October 3, 1969.
40 Peter C. M. Gutkind, 'The Energy of Despair: Social Organisation of the Unemployed in Two African Cities: Lagos and Nairobi', *Civilisations*, Vol. 17, Nos. 3 and 4 (1967), p. 395.

CHAPTER EIGHT

LEGISLATION AND THE STATUS QUO

On January 12, 1964, a successful revolution was staged on the small island of Zanzibar, which lies off the East African coast. On January 17, the workless demonstrated in Nairobi.[1] Three days later, disorders in Tanganyika's army and capital were put down by British soldiers at the request of President Nyerere. Then followed a mutiny of the Uganda Rifles, and British forces were invited to restore peace. On January 24th there was an uprising in a small division of Kenya's army and the government sent out a call for UK troops. *Uhuru* had come only 43 days earlier, the post-Emergency political situation not entirely settled.

The Kenya Government responded to the crisis with immediate relief for the jobless. The Tripartite Agreement on Unemployment commenced less than three weeks after the uprising ended. As indicated in Chapter Six, the Agreement lasted 14 months and called for a ten per cent increase in the labour force of private industry, a moratorium on strikes, a wage freeze, and the establishment of an Industrial Court with binding powers to resolve disputes for the duration of the Agreement. When the Agreement ended in April 1965, the government was loth to revert to the free-for-all of pre-Tripartite days. Although strikes were prohibited under the terms of the Agreement, many had occurred nonetheless. Fearing additional unrest with the lifting of its wage freeze, the government introduced a new Trade Disputes Act.

The new Trade Disputes Act viewed strikes as a concession, not a right. Apart from this, the Act was superimposed on existing labour practices. Trade unions substantially survived the experience. Collective bargaining persisted in a recognisable form. Even the ideology of industrial relations evolved under colonial rule was upheld in rhetoric. A tripartite model, rather than a state-administered one, was formalised.

The Trade Disputes Act

One of the principal parts of the 1965 Trade Disputes Act recalls an old colonial measure: strikes are prohibited in essential services and the industries scheduled as essential are relatively numerous.[2] If the Minister of Labour fails to take action on a dispute reported to him in an essential service after 21 days, he may refer such a dispute to the Industrial Court. In all cases, awards of the Court are binding. The penalties are relatively severe both for inciting an employee to break his contract of service in an essential industry and for wilfully breaking a contract of service.[3]

Section 21 of the Trade Disputes Act prohibits sympathetic strikes and lockouts. This conforms with the government's overall aim to prevent labour disputes from escalating and threatening the political *status quo*.

Strikes which are not of a sympathetic nature and which do not arise in essential services are subject to the following procedures.

The Minister of Labour may appoint a Board of Inquiry to investigate any dispute without the consent of the warring factions. But compliance with the recommendations of such boards is voluntary, at least on paper.

Any trade dispute, whether existing or apprehended, may be reported to the Minister by any party to the dispute. Before acting on a dispute, the Minister 'shall consult a Tripartite Committee. . . .' After such consultation, the Minister may take any of the following steps to promote a settlement:

(a) refer the matter back to the parties with proposals for a settlement;
(b) effect conciliation or investigation;
(c) appoint a Board of Inquiry;
(d) *recommend* to the parties that the dispute be referred to the Industrial Court.

In this Section, voluntarism is preserved. The Minister, however, is given greater powers elsewhere in the Act.

According to Section 20, where it appears to the Minister that there is an actual or a threatened strike or lock-out arising out of a trade dispute and the Minister believes

(a) that the matters to which that trade dispute relates have been settled by a collective bargaining agreement or an Industrial Court award,

the Minister may

(i) require the parties to that dispute to comply with that agreement and award, and
(ii) declare any strike or lock-out (whether actual or threatened) in that section of industry to be unlawful until the agreement or award ceases to have effect.

Section 19 contains the key provisions. It reads: 'where it appears to the Minister that there is an actual or a threatened strike or lockout arising out of a trade dispute in any section of industry, and the Minister believes

(a) that there is machinery of negotiation or arbitration for the voluntary settlement of disputes in that section of industry, and
(b) that all practical means of reaching a settlement of that dispute through that machinery have not been exhausted,

the Minister may

(i) require the parties to that dispute to make use of that machinery, and
(ii) declare any strike or lockout (whether actual or threatened) in that section of industry to be unlawful.'

The same penalties operative in essential services apply in all industries where breach of contract results in an unlawful strike.

Section 19 has given rise to prolonged debate and uncertainty as to whether or not strikes (other than those in essential services) are ever permissible in Kenya. The wording of Section 19 is partly responsible for this confusion.

It is stated in Section 19(a) that the machinery for the *voluntary* settlement of disputes must be implemented before a strike is lawful. But 'arbitration' is mentioned in conjunction with such machinery. This may only mean that if a collective bargaining agreement calls for arbitration as a final step in resolving a dispute, such arbitration must be invoked before a strike becomes permissible. Very few collective agreements in Kenya, however, do in fact make mention of arbitration so a strike may be lawful if conciliation fails to bring about compromise. On the other hand, reference in Section 19 to 'arbitration' may refer to the Industrial Court. If this is the case, no strike is ever allowable since Court awards are always binding. That is, Section 19 may amount to a 'Catch-22': a union may strike, but not before ordered to the Industrial Court, and after ordered to the Industrial Court, a union may not strike.

In 1966, the government insisted that '. . . the right of unions to call a strike has been preserved in Kenya'.[4] At the time, other African governments were insisting that strikes by the few lucky enough to labour hardly merited righteous defence. Kenyatta unfailingly congratulated the country on the liberalness of its industrial relations experiment. Yet, as it came to be interpreted, the Trade Disputes Act placed the strike weapon at the government's discretion. Whilst the government bothered to mouth the old colonial rhetoric, it referred disputes to the Industrial Court after ruling illegal strikes which had been waged prior to Court adjudication.

It may be said that the government has used its power calculatedly rather than arbitrarily. Strikes which threaten to paralyse production or political equanimity have been checked. Minor stoppages (over dismissal and redundancy) which relieve tensions rather than create them have been left alone. Even the inflammatory walk-outs, however, have been allowed to carry on a day or so. They give the appearance of old times: although it is by no means always the case that the disputant parties are eager for a showdown. They may welcome the immense pressure of the government to avert a stoppage and arbitrate differences. The face saving afforded by the Industrial Court as well as legal sanctions help explain why crippling strikes in Kenya are definitely on the wane.

Response to the Law

The response elicited by the 1965 Trade Disputes Act from employers and trade unions helps convey why the industrial scene has become more quiescent. It also sheds light on the relative strengths of employers and trade unions under African government.

The Federation of Kenya Employers estimates that most of its members are not at all unhappy with the new legislation. Indeed, there is evidence to suggest that the FKE prompted the government to introduce it. A letter from the Federation to the Minister of Labour on August 7th, 1964 reads as follows:

> We consider . . . it desirable that legislation should be enacted to render strikes or lock-out action only legal if the procedure in negotiated agreements and the Industrial Relations Charter are first complied with and the requisite notice given.[5]

The Trade Disputes Act takes these recommendations a step further. That the FKE has happily taken the step too represents a major policy tergiversation from pre-Independence days.

The Association of Commercial and Industrial Employers evolved partly to reduce the likelihood of disputes winding up before arbitration. Voluntarism was extolled at the time but then, trade union power was unimpressive. As the unions grew stronger, the employers had second thoughts. Former officers of the ACIE also indicate that their dislike of arbitration stemmed from misgivings that in the Emergency period, the situation was such that arbitrators would tend to be overly sympathetic to the demands of labour. That officers of the FKE express no such misgivings today is comment on the situation since Independence. Nor is Kenya alone reduced to such a situation. One writer generalises:

. . . employers in developing countries are typically much more amenable to governmental intervention than are their counterparts in more advanced societies.[6]

It is, however, noteworthy that whilst strong unions and unbiased arbitrators make employers in Kenya less shy of governmental intervention, the great majority of collective agreements get concluded at the bargaining table. The FKE very much prefers to settle out of Court. War-time Arbitration Order No. 1305 of Great Britain appears to have inspired Kenya's Trade Disputes Act and the outcome of both statutes is not dissimilar. Writing about British war-time experience, O. Kahn-Freund has noted:

> As a result of their operation, compulsory arbitration has not in this country killed voluntary bargaining. On the contrary, in some cases the action taken by the Minister under the Order may have stimulated voluntary negotiation.[7]

Since the same is true in Kenya, the Trade Disputes Act has been superimposed on existing practice.

The '65 legislation was initially accorded a hostile reception by the unions but this was short-lived. By 1966, the Central Organisation of Trades Unions announced:

> The trade unions support the existing legislation. . . . We believe that the operation of the Industrial Court has a wholesome effect upon labour relations.[8]

The unions appear to accept the Industrial Court's services when negotiations reach a stalemate because they are thereby spared the necessity of staging a strike.

The labour movement's finesse with the strike weapon has had a checkered history. Many unions, both in industry and in agriculture, have displayed great agility in staging full-scale strikes, and strikes, moreover, which are fought for better working conditions. Although spontaneous walkouts over dismissals and the personality of headmen have accounted for the great number of stoppages, strikes for higher wages have accounted for a fair proportion of man-days lost.[9]

The unions' behaviour in this respect appears to defy all economic laws. The pernicious extent of unemployment would seem to present a likely deterrent to strike action. Yet, many employers, wary of political censure, have shown reluctance to dismiss their entire work force in the aftermath of unrest. The unions' proficiency in staging strikes is also exceptional given the relatively small proportion of workers in Kenya who are actually dues-paying union affiliates.

The FKE has its own set of explanations. It reasons that the unions are able to strike because they are organised on industry-wide lines, and hence, bargain for the non-unionised, have sufficient if not abundant dues, good networks of communication, and paid administrators. Since employers were instrumental in persuading union leaders to organise along industry-wide lines, they were providing for their own opposition. The FKE also asserts that intimidation plays no small part in the obedience which union leaders command; but even the FKE does not place undue emphasis on this factor. A different set of explanations is offered by shop stewards and national officers. They suggest that most workers strike because they have nothing to lose, have something to gain, and generally feel aggrieved. They also suggest that some workers are not quite sure what a strike is all about and do what they are told.

It is interesting that whilst economic conditions provide a likely deterrent to strike action, living conditions may suffer it. Although workers in Kenya have access neither to strike funds nor to national assistance, they are able to live with friends temporarily and are in a position to send their families back to the reserve when out of work. Strike leaflets sometimes advise such arrangements. As industrialisation proceeds, however, the propensity to strike may lessen, as communal living arrangements become unacceptable and workers commit themselves to weekly hire purchase arrangements, etc.

The other side of the picture shows that whilst the strike technique has been learned, many unions have also learned to appreciate the difficulties of co-ordinating strikes in large numbers of firms for any length of time. Strikes have been less frequent in companies which bargain on a multi-employer basis than in companies which bargain independently. Thus, since 1965, many trade unions have gone to the Industrial Court quite willingly. There is, however, another factor at play. If the Court did not provide benefits on a par with those obtainable with the strike, the anti-strike legislation would undoubtedly be regarded with less than enthusiasm. Sensitive to this possibility, the President of the Industrial Court admits that arbitration and his job as arbitrator would have folded in a matter of months if respect had not been won from the unions.[10] Apparently, it has been won.

The interdependence of the FKE and the trade union movement has been a basic equation in Kenya's labour history. Each has provided for the other's growth and each has provided an adequate match for the other: given a peculiar mixture of political and economic realities. The Trade Disputes Act has been taken in stride by both parties and has merely changed the rules of the game. The power relations implicit in the game, however, are best seen within the context of Africanisation. Like the Trade Disputes Act, Africanisation has been superimposed on existing practices. Better stated, it has been superimposed almost single-mindedly by the Kenyatta Administration on the colonial political economy in which industrial relations proceeds. Because Africanisation figures so crucially in Kenya's political and economic ideology, and because it has largely been effected through legislation, it will be discussed now in some detail.

Africanisation

In preparation for Independence, the government realised the support to be won by job patronage especially among educated Blacks. In 1964, it was estimated that the proportion of jobs held by Africans in public employment totalled 92·6 per cent.[11] This figure is somewhat deceptive since much of it is accounted for by unskilled labourers, service workers, and teachers. Nevertheless, a year after Independence the proportion of Africans in the administrative, executive, and managerial category, and in the clerical and technical occupations in the public sector, was still impressive: 53·4; 70·6; and 40·6 per cent respectively.

The FKE took the cue and made assurances that it, too, was committed to greater African participation in the economy. As a demonstration of good faith, the convincing argument was posed that it was cheaper for employers to hire Africans than expatriaties. But it was not easier to do so and required time. The FKE's position was summed up at an international conference on localisation (i.e., Africanisation, Caribbeanisation), sponsored by the Organisation of Employers' Federations and Employers in Developing Countries (OEF). The Conference stressed the sensitive business

> . . . of integrating into an effective management team the products of two cultures whose origins, ethos and ways of thinking might be poles apart.[12]

The conference noted other serious problems as well.
First, target setting:

> If the business were a local one, the target could be 100 per cent localisation, despite the succession problems and lack of flexibility which this entailed. If the business were international . . . the target would be 100 — x, x being the residual percentage of expatriates needed to keep techniques up-to-date, to provide flexibility, and to enable local staff to be taken out for overseas training.

Second, there existed the problem of long-range planning:

> ... managers could not be trained overnight. ... Training methods must be adjusted to suit the material.

Employers were well advised to check all sources of recruitment:

> ... make personal contact with the schools and colleges most suited to the firm's purpose, show them what the work entailed, and interest them in recommending the right material. When a school or college was in its early days it was possible sometimes to gain its lasting goodwill by quite modest gifts of books, equipment or scholarships. ...

Third, there was the trade union problem:

> ... the reluctance of junior managers and supervisors who had come up through the ranks to relinquish their trade union membership; by the necessity senior staff sometimes felt to unionise in order to protect themselves against union pressures from below. ...

Finally, the OEF conference disclosed the variety in approach adopted by governments to localisation:

> In Malaysia companies had to appear before a board and justify their programme. ... In Kenya trade unions were also brought into discussion, but this was held to be acceptable [by the OEF] only where the trade unions had a record of responsibility.

Responsible or not, the unions in Kenya remained 'singularly unimpressed' with the pace of Africanisation in the private sector after Independence.[13] It lagged far behind the performance in public employment so the government began getting tough.

In April 1967, an Immigration Act was passed. It came four years after Independence, a delay which allowed the government to meet its own essential manpower requirements. As in other underdeveloped countries, there is an acute shortage of qualified Africans in Kenya for higher posts. The Act hit upon the localisation approach most displeasing to the OEF: 'an haphazard imposition of quotas and individual permits'. But the Act afforded the government the chance to Africanise at its own discretionary pace, minimising the possibility of a free-for-all Africanisation drive by the unions.

The Act purports to 'Kenyanise' rather than 'Africanise'. The government has committed itself to filling the jobs of expatriates with Kenya citizens, irrespective of colour. This, however, may merely be window-dressing. In its paper on Democratic African Socialism, the government has committed itself to improving the position of Africans in particular. There is little ground for optimism that Asians will be guaranteed fair chances of employment even if they become Kenya citizens (and roughly 70,000 have done so).[14]

The 1967 Immigration Act requires all non-citizens to apply for special entry permits if they wish to begin or continue working or engaging in their own business or profession in Kenya. The intention of the Act is to enable the government to grant permits to non-citizens only when qualified Kenyans are not available. At Kenyanisation of Personnel Bureau has been established to appraise the government of all local manpower and to survey the training facilities employers are expected to provide.

On November 30th 1967, the government made the first move towards implementing the Immigration Act. It called on non-citizens in the following categories to apply for permits: clerical, sales, skilled and semi-skilled wage or salary earners (other than technicians, works managers, shop foremen, and other supervisory tradesmen). Every company was required to submit the number of non-citizens it employed in these categories, enabling the government to keep an eye on the pace of Kenyanisation in each firm. The reverberations of the order echoed far outside Kenya. The number of Asians who declined to become Kenya citizens by December 1965 was in the vicinity of 100,000 and their jobs fell into jeopardy. Mr Guy Hunter writes:

> The other main grudge of Africans against Asians is that Asians, with a longer tradition of craft, commercial and clerical skills, have occupied just that middle level of technical, clerical and administrative posts to which tens of thousands of African school leavers now aspire. In a word, there is jealousy which can be focused on an 'other' group which is distinguishable by physique and culture, a culture not native to the African continent. This is plain, straightforward racialism, however it is disguised or rationalised.[15]

On January 13th, 1968, the Kenya Government passed a Trade Licensing Act which severely restricted the commercial activities of non-citizens. With trade and employment opportunities cut off, Asians holding British passports began to leave Kenya for the United Kingdom. Although many chose to go elsewhere, Britain panicked and passed legislation restricting the entry of UK citizens who could boast no substantial connection with Britain, either by birth or paternal parentage. The likelihood of such legislation had earlier provoked a panic amongst Asians intending to flee. For the British and Kenya Governments, the situation was clear-cut: black and white.

The November 30th order may have hit the hardest because it enumerated some job categories within reach reach of countless unemployed primary school leavers and Africans just short of school certificates. An address by the FKE's President indicates that follow-up Africanisation exercises are likely to be more drawn out in the short run.[16] About the long-run picture there is little uncertainty or room

for compromise. As more and more qualified African manpower becomes available, non citizens will be phased out post-haste.

The exercise of Africanisation exhausts the long-run picture envisaged by a lecturer at Makerere College, and the picture is a gloomy
one. In a reappraisal of the Kenya Government's paper on Democratic
African Socialism, Mr. Ahmed Mohiddin observes:

> No drastic changes in the economic system are proposed. . . . Africanisa-
> tion of the present capitalist system in Kenya is thus the answer. . . .
> Instead of having purely non-Africans forming the apex of the pyramid,
> as was the case before, now there is to be a predominance of Africans
> in the middle and upper middle classes . . . . it is very difficult to see how
> Africanisation of the incumbent elites could be equated with social
> justice.[17]

Mr. Mohiddin goes on to argue that Africanisation has been rationalised
by the government with a shift in emphasis 'from actual ownership
to effective control'. Mr. Mohiddin sees in this approach an acceptance
of basic capitalist assumptions: control by whom? Not, according to
to Mr. Mohiddin, the people. But for all that, neither is the approach
necessarily a guarantee of effective control by an *African* elite. The
OEF Conference indicated a willingness to entertain 100 per cent
localisation, which is not *ipso facto* synonymous with effective control. Much industry in Kenya rests in the hands of international firms
operating locally through private subsidiaries which neither offer shares
for sale nor publish financial accounts. Even if the boards of such subsidiaries as well as their managerial staffs are manned by Africans,
major decisions on reinvestment, sales and so on may still be taken
in London. In global terms, the polarisation of decision-making may
depend on the stature and assertiveness of the local elite, the relations
between its government and that of company headquarters, and the
overall mixture of foreign and indigenous enterprise in the local
economy.[18] Mr. Galbraith's cry of all power to the technocrats, however, may not be heard in every land.[19]

If Kenya's trade union movement has come to appreciate Mr. Mohiddin's class analysis, it has reduced pressures for Africanisation only
marginally. Less hotch-potch treatment for Asians is now favoured but
pressures spent on Africanisation have not been redirected to other
issues. For example, the new COTU Administration does not demand
even checks on the FKE's power, only Africanisation of the FKE's personnel. Like a bounty hunter, the old COTU guard boasted credit for
every Africanised expatriate. Victory, however, was hardly challenging
for employers scarcely resisted. Indeed, as the OEF conference recognised, employers were let off lightly by Africanisation 'when the ethos

K

and economics of independence impelled one developing country after another into a planned economy oriented towards socialism'.[20]

The implications of Africanisation may not have been clear immediately to the unions. Apart from his own finances, what exactly was the acclaimed leader of Kenya's workers thinking about when he spoke in Parliament against a proposal (later defeated) to lower M.P. salaries as a gesture of goodwill to the working class? Clement Lubembe, M.P. stated in 1968:

> . . . it was because members were not highly paid that some, like Mr. Omar, became directors of the East African Breweries, for example, and sat across the table from union negotiators during wage rise discussions.[21]

According to Mr. Mohiddin,

> . . . the implications of Africanising the existing economic and social institutions are precisely this. It is not socialists who are going to emerge from this exercise, but hard-headed capitalists.

The new COTU Administration appears not to have missed the point. In its 14 point programme, it joins hands with 'hard-headed capitalists', irrespective of colour, and the government, irrespective of choice, to enlarge the cake and to ensure a fair share of it for labour as it grows. A new frosting on the cake has not altered the basic recipe for containing class conflict in Kenya.

The Tripartite Approach

In his address on the Fourth Anniversary of Independence, the Minister of Labour joined hands with workers' and employers' organisations to minimise conflict through the tripartite machinery of the Trade Disputes Act.

The Industrial Court is officially tripartite in scope. The Chief Justice, however, may make provision for 'reference of matters in certain cases to be made by a single member of the Court'. Also, a government representative may cast the deciding vote in all proceedings. Nevertheless, in most hearings, particularly when a point of principle is at stake, COTU and FKE representatives deliberate. This, to some extent, affords them an opportunity to influence employment practices.

COTU and FKE representatives also sit on a Tripartite Committee provided by the terms of the Trade Disputes Act. The Minister of Labour, however, need only consult the Committee on the appropriate channel for the settlement of a particular dispute (the Committee has recourse to approximately six channels).[22] The power to declare a strike unlawful and to select one avenue for settlement ultimately rests with the government. Trade unions and the FKE, however, are afforded ample opportunity to participate in dispute settlement procedures and the procedures so arrived at are typically rubber-stamped by the Minister. The important implication is this: the tripartite committee is highly efficient and professional. It is likely to become even more so if COTU succeeds in consolidating authority over strikes called by industry-wide unions and industry-wide unions succeed in checking wild-cats called by branch officers and shop stewards. The bread and butter model of industrial relations in Kenya today, largely evolved under colonial rule, may in the future entrench itself through the very legal process which it viewed as a threat on the eve of Independence.

Conclusion

Neither the exercise of Africanisation nor the labour legislation of the Kenyatta Administration represents a radical departure from past tradition. Indeed, the one may reinforce the other. Strikes of any magnitude appear less and less likely as a result of the 1965 Trade Disputes Act although the dynamics of threatened walkouts figure behind the scenes. The power of the union movement prevails although greater checks and balances have been imposed on it. The Industrial Court attempts to put a ceiling on standards of employment yet much collective bargaining continues outside the scope of the Court. Whether these controls have rendered collective bargaining better suited to the needs of an underdeveloped country is the next chapter's concern. Since collective bargaining has become part of the fundamental political economy, which Africanisation has left unchanged, an assessment of it raises larger issues.

REFERENCES

1 *East African Standard*, January 18, 1964.
2 See Chapter Three, p. 33.
3 They amount to a fine not exceeding £250 and/or a maximum of 12 months' imprisonment in the first case and a fine not exceeding £25 and/or a maximum of 3 months' imprisonment in the second.
4 *East African Standard*, June 6, 1966.
5 FKE, Minutes of Special Meeting, August 7, 1964.
6 Arthur M. Ross, 'Introduction', in *Industrial Relations and Economic Development*, ed. by the same author (London: Macmillan for the International Institute for Labour Studies, 1966), p. xv.
7 O. Kahn-Freund, 'Legal Framework', in *The System of Industrial Relations in Great Britain*, ed. by Allan Flanders and H. A. Clegg (Oxford: Basil Blackwell, 1964), p. 96.

8   Central Organisation of Trade Unions, 'Forward With the Workers! A Statement of Policy', [August 1966], p. 3. (Mimeographed.)
9   This information was acquired from the strike records of the Ministry of Labour, Nairobi, 1966.
10 Interview, Mr. Saeed Cockar, President of the Industrial Court, Nairobi, 1966.
11 *Reporter*, April 27, 1967.
12 OEF, 'Localisation in Developing Countries: International Conference; November 1967', London, 1968.
13 Republic of Kenya, *Ministry of Labour and Social Services Annual Report 1964* (Nairobi, 1967), p. 8.
14 One writer notes: 'It would appear that currently only in Tanzania are "citizen Asians" being actively recruited into government service.' Emil Rado, 'Manpower Planning in East Africa', *East African Economic Review*, Vol. 3 (NS), No. 1 (June 1967).
15 Guy Hunter, *Education for a Developing Region: A Study of East Africa* (London: George Allen and Unwin, 1963), p. xvi.
16 *East African Standard*, March 28, 1968.
17 Ahmed Mohiddin, 'Sessional Paper No. 10 Revisited', *East African Journal*, Vol. 6, No. 3 (March 1969).
18 Some of these factors are suggested by Raymond Vernon, 'The Multinational Enterprise and National Sovereignty', *Harvard Business Review*, March/April, 1967.
19 John Kenneth Galbraith, *The New Industrial State* (London: Hamish Hamilton, 1967).
20 OEF, 'Localisation in Developing Countries: International Conference; November 1967', p. 16.
21 *East African Standard*, March 27, 1968.
22 The six channels include: boards of inquiry, Joint Dispute Commissions, Joint Demarcation Committees, investigation, conciliation, and the Industrial Court. Court proceedings will generally be invoked if a strike has erupted and is declared illegal.

CHAPTER NINE

COLLECTIVE BARGAINING

From 1956 onwards, the employer movement in Kenya made determined efforts to institute workable arrangements whereby management and labour could bargain collectively with one another. The argument advanced is that post-Independence legislation has left these arrangements substantially unchanged and has left Kenya proprietor of wage setting procedures not substantially different from those prevailing in many Western economies.

In the following pages, the qualitative aspects of collective bargaining in Kenya will be primarily assessed, in relation to the problems of equitable income distribution and economic growth. Implicitly, the assessment will question the institution's intrinsic value and that of the somewhat missionary role of international firms in prosletysing its practice and ideology.

Shadow or Substance

In a study entitled *Wage Trends, Wage Policies, and Collective Bargaining: The Problems for Underdeveloped Countries* (to which frequent reference is made in this chapter), Mr. H. A. Turner expresses strong doubts about the genuineness of collective bargaining in underdeveloped countries.[1] However, labour and management in Kenya may discover that what they are now engaging in is nothing other than collective bargaining. Discussion will be directed towards some of Mr. Turner's doubts. To establish the vices and virtues of bargaining, it is necessary first to establish that bargaining exists.

If collective bargaining is orthodoxly conceived as a process whereby employers and trade unions seek to establish employment standards through the free play of bargaining strengths, with ultimate recourse to strikes and lockouts, barring the intervention of the state, third parties, or the law, collective bargaining has not occurred in Kenya since the passage of the Trade Disputes Act.[2] It is arguable, however, that variations of this model resemble collective bargaining. Notably, compulsory arbitration may be substituted for the right to strike and lockout. Under these circumstances, collective bargaining may occur if arbitration awards meet one of two criteria. They have an outcome which is the same as that which would have occurred had the parties been free to strike or lockout. They have an unpredictable outcome and average out to be equally favourable or unfavourable to the negotiating partners. If arbitration awards behave in accordance with either of these criteria, then both parties have as much to gain (or lose) in facing arbitration as in reaching a compromise at the bargaining table. If differences are resolved without resort to an umpire, this may be said to approach collective bargaining although not a facsimile of it wherein the right to strike is operative. For where the right to strike is operative, raw industrial strength will determine the final level of wages and a severe strike may conceivably result in a very radical increase in going rates, if only in the short run. By contrast, it is unlikely that arbitration will upset wage trends to any considerable extent especially where strikes are prohibited and arbitrators are not forced to sue for peace at any price. Thus, the awards of statutory arbitrators frequently fall within a range geared to going norms or a moving average and it is only within this range that the outcome of arbitration awards may prove unpredictable.

So would appear the awards of Kenya's Industrial Court in its short history. Sensitive to overtones of political power and undertones of rebellious strikes and go-slows, the Court has refrained from introducing wage austerity. But neither, seemingly, has it shifted still higher the upward trend of wages, in the belief that growth necessitates wage austerity.[3] More difficult to summarise is the unpredictability (i.e. impartiality) of awards within this compromise zone, which is one presupposition for collective bargaining. The Industrial Court does not typically split the difference in proposals submitted to it. The unions routinely submit demands considered wildly unrealistic by the Court and so awards are closer to the final offers of employers; but such awards are not necessarily more favourable to employers on the average.[4]

Perhaps the best indication of the Court's impartiality rests on empirical evidence, the presuppositions being that:

1. Employers and trade unions have as much to gain (or lose) by going to Court.
2. Both parties might just as well settle at the bargaining table.
3. If one party insists on going to Court the other must agree.
4. Both parties are willing to engage in negotiations.

Whilst the number of cases handled each year by the Court increased steadily from the start, 1967 saw the trend reversed, with the reversal maintained in 1968.[5] Arbitration may be growing less popular in Kenya as it grows less novel. Moreover, whilst the Court settled 50 cases in 1968, FKE members signed a total of at least 200 agreements (many of which embraced a large number of firms) in the same year (and in previous ones). Further, not all Court awards concerned wages. Many involved a point of principle or a subsidiary fringe benefit. Often in cases where the Court settled a wage dispute, agreement had already been reached on a host of minor issues at the bargaining table. A significant number of Court awards related to local government authorities. Others pertained to individual companies. Thus, the bulk of the FKE's membership found it possible to agree voluntarily with the unions on terms of service.

By way of explanation, employers appear to recoil instinctively from abandoning their conditions of employment to regulation by an outsider particularly where fringe benefits are concerned. Employers may give way on wage rates, the yardstick by which union members usually judge their leaders, and negotiate a *quid pro quo* on costly fringe benefits. The FKE emphasises that resort to the Industrial Court is a serious step to take and employers are encouraged to compromise on a package deal without outside help.

The union's behaviour also evinces more than the mere fact that compromise at the bargaining table generally promises benefits as great as those expected from the Court. Quite simply, it is a bother to invoke Court proceedings and to prepare Court cases. Since it is the policy of the Industrial Court to encourage as much collective bargaining as possible, the Court insists that the unions present cogent briefs based on preliminary negotiations. To avoid such preparation, unions may prefer to take what they can get at the bargaining table.

The Government's Influence on Terms of Employment

The incompatibility of collective bargaining with infringements on the right to strike is not the only issue raised by Mr Turner. He argues that collective bargaining amounts to no more than window dressing in economies where the government is the largest single employer and negotiations in private industry merely result in adjustments to government scales. Certainly in Kenya the government exerts a powerful influence with respect to Industrial Court awards, wage determination in the public services, wages councils, and minimum wages. But do negotiations in private industry simply reproduce government administered standards?

The Industrial Court

It may be suggestetd that insofar as most collective agreements are concluded privately, they tend to serve as references for Court awards, rather than *vice versa*. It is not impossible, however, that these terms of trade will alter in the future. Bargaining by two wage leaders, the oil and longshoring industries, has in the last few years terminated in arbitration. But the expressed dissatisfaction of the Dockworkers' Union with at least one Court award makes the future terms of trade uncertain.

The Public Sector

The government in Kenya represents the largest single employer, although it accounts for a much lower ratio of total employment than other African governments. Nearly 50 per cent of the non-agricultural labour force is employed in the public services.[6] This makes it enevitable that government rates will have a marked influence on private ones. But it is arguable that in spite of this, collective bargaining has not been robbed of meaning. The agreements signed by FKE members and the unions do not represent semi-automatic adjustments to government scales.

The Kenya (central) Government (hereinafter referred to as the civil service) accounted in 1965 for almost 50 per cent (85,000 employees) of the reported labour force in the public sector.[7] Yet, two years earlier, it was estimated that only 21,000 unskilled and semi-skilled workers served in the civil service.[8] Given that they are posted throughout the country, the government may be afforded less leverage in any one area than a large firm or FKE association. Because high-level manpower is concentrated in the public sector, its impact on private employment is far greater.

There is little collective bargaining in the civil service. Conditions of employment are determined by commissions which are appointed from time to time when pressure for wage reform can no longer be ignored. The most recent Salaries Review Commission (SRC) reported in July 1967. The recommendations of its immediate predecessor were instituted in April 1964 (its report was published in 1963).[9] Both the 1963 and 1967 Commissions divided the subordinate category within the civil service into three grades. The revised terms proposed for these grades in 1967 were as follows.[10]

Shillings Per Month
(excluding housing)

Grade III	130 $\times$ 15—160
Grade II	185 $\times$ 20—225
Grade I	250 $\times$ 20—275 $\times$ 25—300

The subordinate staff of 12 townships, however, are given cost of living allowances. According to the 1967 SRC recommendations, all unskilled and semi-skilled civil servants in Nairobi and Mombasa should earn at least 215sh. a month (excluding housing). This represents an increase of 15 shillings over the previous SRC award. But in the words of the Commission:

> . . . the effect of minimum wage arrangements [cost of living allowances] is that an employee in Nairobi or Mombasa receives initially no increment until he is advanced to Grade I. In other words, almost all employees in Grades II and III receive the same salary, irrespective of their length of service, and this has caused dissatisfaction among long-service employees. There is a similar effect in other townships. . . .[11]

The infrequency of Salaries Review Commission reports and the fact that subordinate salary scales are often frozen (unless promotion occurs) until still another SRC report is issued have important implications for private bargaining arrangements. For in the interim between SRC reports, almost all agreements in private industry are re-negotiated on an annual (or biennial) basis. Agreed terms do not appear to be tied to the frozen levels in the government. Indeed, it would not be surprising if successive Salaries Review Commissions were influenced by intervening developments in private employment.

In light of this, it is more understandable why SRC awards have not kindled a general fever for wage revisions.[12] This contrasts sharply with common practice in many West African countries. As already noted, the Association of Commercial and Industrial Employers encouraged collective bargaining in Kenya to avoid the conflict predicted to arise in its absence.

In 1965, local government authorities employed approximately 60,000 workers, many of whom were teachers. This constituted roughly 30 per cent of total public employment. Methods of wage determination for local government workers are little less than chaotic. Terms of service are not stipulated by Salaries Review Commissions. Each local government authority bears responsibility for its own conditions.[13] The 1967 SRC had this to say:

> We have been struck by the great diversity as regards both salaries and other conditions of service which exists between the various Councils.[14]

This very diversity implies that whilst private industry may be influenced by general standards in local government, such standards do not constitute rigid guidelines. To introduce a more orderly framework for local government bodies, the 1967 Salaries Review Commission went on to say: We recommend . . . at the first stage . . . negotiation between a body representing the Local Government authorities and the Local Government Workers' Union'.[15] It is not unlikely that the body elected to represent local government authorities will be the Kenya Association of Local Government Employers (KALGE). The KALGE is a loose confederation of 30 or so local councils and is affiliated to the FKE. The chief executive officer of the FKE serves as its Secretary. At present, the KALGE endeavours to co-ordinate informally employment conditions in all local government bodies. If this function is formalised as a result of the 1967 SRC's advice, the FKE may continue to exert a fair amount of influence over them.

The determination of employment conditions in services jointly administered by the three East African Governments appears no less chaotic than in local councils. This sector, generally referred to as EACSO, embraces the East African Railways and Harbours Administration, the East African Posts and Telecommunications, and the East African Common Services Organisation. It employs a total of roughly 30,000 workers in Kenya (or approximately 17 per cent of public employment).

Before 1965, labour disputes in EACSO were handled separately by the three East African Governments but because of the inter-territorial nature of EACSO services, conditions in the three countries had to be made uniform. To systematise dispute settlement procedure, an Act was passed by the three East African Governments in 1965, a railway strike late in 1964 providing the occasion. But the Act was a failure, its procedures for settling disputes more time-consuming than useful, its restrictions on union membership to low-income employees thoroughly objectionable to COTU. With the formation of an East African Common Market, rationalising industrial relations assumed even greater urgency. An East African Labour Court was eventually created. It has not, however, put an end to a confusion of strikes in EACSO, which has made labour standards in the sector unlikely material for close imitation in the private sector. Indeed, private employers appear to have done a better job than the government in rationalising industrial relations along efficient and business-like lines. Since the Trade Disputes Act, most major strikes in Kenya have been waged by public employees, not only in EACSO but also in local government and the civil service. Nor may all the unrest be attributable to the peculiar nature of public employment.

The 1967 Salaries Review Commission also refrained from specifying detailed terms of service for employees in more than 50 para-statal bodies, such as the Kenya Meat Commission and Kenya Maize and Produce Marketing Board. The SRC noted that employment conditions 'vary very substantially from Board to Board'.[16] Many of the Boards are members of the FKE and consult with FKE executives on terms of service.

By way of conclusion, if 1965 is used as an example, monthly wage

scales (including housing) in the lowest grade of the public sector stood
as follows:

Civil Service (Mombasa and Nairobi)	235 sh.
Civil Service (Nanyuki township)	220 sh.
Railways (Mombasa and Nairobi)	210 sh.

Wages in local government varied widely as did terms of service in
the more peripheral public enterprises. In the private sector, terms of
service in several industries far surpassed government rates. In other
private sectors they hovered around those outlined above. For example,
the Distributive and Allied Trades Employers' Association paid its
its ordinary labourers 240sh. a month (including housing) in 1965.[17]
In the same year, the Motor Trade and Allied Industries Employers'
Association paid workers in the lowest grade in Nairobi and Mombasa
250sh. a month (including housing).[18] If the 1967 Salaries Review
Commission report is implemented, civil servants in Grades III and II
in Nairobi will first be getting 250sh. a month (including housing) in
1968. The new consolidated minimum wage for employees covered by
the Engineering and Allied Industries Employers' Association, as of
March 1, 1968, will be 273sh. a month as a result of an agreement
voluntarily concluded. On the other hand, government standards in
1965 were often superior to those effective in many FKE groups and
individual firms.

Whilst wages in the public sector obviously influence those in the
private sector, it is not impossible that the reverse is true as well.
The foregoing discussion, however, did not presume to analyse wage
structures but rather to suggest that collective bargaining is more than
mere window dressing because:

1. Methods of wage determination (and wages themselves) are diverse
   in the public sector, SRC reports are infrequent, and, consequently,
   wages of many subordinate staff in the civil service are frozen;
   meanwhile,
2. Negotiations in private industry occur regularly, often on an annual
   basis.

Such negotiations are pursued vigorously by FKE members in order to
fix wages which may either match or fall above or below those effective
in the government.

Wages Councils

Mr. H. A. Turner argues that whilst wages councils in Britain (and the
colonies) were initially envisaged as precursors to collective bargaining,
once established, they linger and fail to achieve their objective. For
where terms of service are determined under the guidance of an inde-

pendent party, and are applied automatically to unorganised firms, the
essential quality of collective bargaining is lost.

In 1965, there were ten wages councils in Kenya, excluding the one
in mixed farming. They embraced approximately 88,000 workers. Of
this total, however, almost 44,000 workers were concentrated in the
wholesale and retail distributive trades. Another 16,000 were in the
hotel sector. Apart from these two industries, wages councils covered
roughly 10 per cent of private employment.

Wages council orders are determined as a result of negotiations
between trade union representatives and the appropriate FKE body.
The government rarely amends terms of service arrived at in this
fashion. The point, however, is not that collective bargaining is approxi-
mated by this procedure (which characterises the hotel, knitting, tailor-
ing, and building industries). Rather, many FKE members and the
unions with which they deal regard wages council orders as minima
for non-FKE employers only. FKE members covered by wages councils
often negotiate agreements which provide terms of service far in excess
of legal rates, and little detracts from the essence of collective bargaining under these conditions (which apply in the wholesale distribution, baking, footwear, and motor engineering industries).

Minimum Wages

Mr. Turner poses a further argument. He states that one essential pre-
requisite for collective bargaining in underdeveloped countries is:

> . . . that legal minimum wages must be confined to a 'safety net', a broad
> national minimum which should be fixed substantially below the pre-
> vailing level of unskilled wages—or at least 'frozen' so that future
> improvements in such wages depends on the workers' own . . . efforts.
> Otherwise trade union energies will concentrate on political pressure to
> raise the minimum, rather than on sectional economic combination.[19]

These prerequisites appear to be fulfilled in Kenya. Minimum wages
were frozen from December 1963 to July 1967 and there was little, if
any, trade union agitation for an increase in statutory rates. By way
of explanation, few unskilled labourers in trade unions of FKE firms
(in industry and commerce) received the bare minimum and a substantial number received wages far in excess of the statutory floor.[20]
As early as in 1963, the FKE conducted a survey of terms of service
prevailing in 207 member companies of varying size. It discovered
that:

> The median of the minimum rate for unskilled labourers [in Nairobi] was
> Shs. 37/50 above the Statutory Minimum in force in 1963. . . . [This
> median is roughly 28 per cent above the statutory floor.] The percentage

of employers paying the Statutory Minimum Wage as the basic rate to employees . . . has now fallen to an almost negligible proportion, . . . 8·7 per cent in 1963.[21]

Thus, at least with respect to the FKE companies sampled, minimum wages in Kenya are in the nature of a 'safety net'.

Trade Union Membership and the Extent of Collective Bargaining

In a conference on industrial relations and economic growth, Mr. Arthur M. Ross questioned whether collective bargaining is shadow or substance in underdeveloped countries in terms of '. . . ordinary quantitative measures, such as the size of union membership. . . .'[22] In 1964, more than 30 unions in Kenya claimed to have a voting membership of almost 250,000, which represented roughly 40 per cent of the labour force (including public employees).[23] While it is recognised that this figure is overstated, the necessity of a high level of union membership for collective bargaining is immaterial. It is FKE policy and a tenet of the Industrial Relations Charter that a company recognise the appropriate industrial union and negotiate with it regardless of the number of union members. Most FKE affiliates adhere to this rule so that many more workers may be covered by collective agreements than are *bona fide* union affiliates. A better indication of the scope of collective bargaining is the representativeness of the FKE. Commercial agriculture is examined first. It accounts for approximately 34 per cent of total employment in Kenya. Of this percentage, roughly half the number of agricultural workers find employment in mixed farming. The remainder labour in the plantation sector: coffee, tea, sisal and sugar.

FKE Membership and the Extent of Collective Bargaining

There is little collective bargaining in mixed farming. The Agricultural Employers' Association (formerly the Kenya National Farmers' [Employer] Union) represents a small fraction of total mixed farms. Negotiations with the Kenya Plantation and Agricultural Workers' Union are a formality within the context of a wages council. AEA members distinguish themselves from other mixed farmers (both European and African) primarily by paying even the legal minimum.

Collective bargaining is far more widespread in the plantation sector. This is especially the case in sisal and tea. The Sisal Employers' Association (SEA) and the Kenya Tea Growers' Association (KTGA) presently account for 95 and 90 per cent of sisal and tea workers respectively. The SEA has not for the most part found it necessary to resolve a wage dispute in the Industrial Court. This was also true of the KTGA until 1967. Members of the Kenya Coffee Growers' Association (KCGA) account for only 22½ per cent of total coffee acreage. The remainder of coffee is grown on mixed farms and on small non-KCKA African holdings. Nevertheless, the KCGA represents the majority of large coffee estates east of the Rift Valley and employs approximately 30,000 permanent workers.[24] The Kenya Sugar Employers' Union has 49 members located in the Nyanza area. It negotiates one agreement with the Kenya Sugar Plantation Workers' Union. A number of sugar estates near the coast negotiate separately.

In July 1967, the government established a general minimum wage applicable to all rural areas, the plantation industries included. The new order called for a consolidated minimum rate for adult males of only 60shs. a month. The agreements in effect for the four plantation industries in 1966, however, provided adult male minimum rates (if consolidated on a monthly basis) nearly 25 per cent (and in some cases 40 per cent) above 60 shillings.[25] The rural general minimum wage with respect to the plantation sector appears to be as much a 'safety net' as the urban general minimum wage with respect to a large pro- portion of private industry. Thus, it may be argued that the employ- ment conditions of some 80,000 permanent workers in the four plan- tation industries are determined by collective bargaining. Several com- panies in other agricultural pursuits, such as cashew nuts and cotton, also engage in joint negotiations.

In the industrial sector, FKE membership embraces roughly 60 per cent of all employees in firms with at least 10 workers each (domestic servants excluded). In numerical terms, this comprises 100,000 workers at a conservative estimate (excluding the hotel industry), in some 1,200 companies. With the exception of a few pursuits governed by wages councils (principally building and hotels), the 100,000 workers in FKE member firms are covered by collective bargaining arrangements. Many of the FKE's affiliates are large expatriate estab- lishments in the major industries. Collective bargaining, however, is by no means an elitist affair in Kenya. As suggested in Chapter Six, *at least* 400 of the FKE'S members employ fewer than 50 workers each and span almost all the lesser industries. It appears that the 40 per cent of private industry not affiliated to the FKE is concentrated in a few selected pursuits: food manufacturing, wholesale distribution, and transport (although a number of companies and employer associations within these sectors negotiate collective agreements). In the remain- ing industries (or sub-industries), whether high or low paying, large of small, FKE representation, and hence, collective bargaining, is rather extensive.

The term 'collective bargaining' is used advisedly. Restrictions on the right to strike and the presence of the Industrial Court curb the free play of bargaining strengths, an essential element in the strict orthodox view of collective bargaining. The strict orthodox view, however, meets little practical application in any setting and insofar as collective agreements cover some 180,000 workers in Kenya, or roughly 45 per cent of private employment, both in industry and in agriculture, the scope of 'collective bargaining', for want of a better term, is fairly impressive.

Wage Trends and Wage Differentials: The Setting for Collective Bargaining

The economic and social effects of collective bargaining may be less impressive. In terms of industrial peace, the story is one of relative success. Since Independence, there have generally been fewer strikes and man days lost than in the immediate preceding period. But at what price has peace been bought over the years?

Between 1958 and 1965, the *real* earnings of the labour force increased by over 75 per cent. Between 1960 and 1965, average African earnings increased by about 87 per cent. At the same time, recorded employment *declined* by over ten per cent. Wage earnings have risen at a much faster rate than total output. Whilst average wage earnings doubled since 1958, Gross Domestic Product rose by about 40 per cent.[26] This implies that the paid labour force has bettered itself at the expense of the great mass of agricultural peasants; and African wage earners are only a small fraction of the total population.[27] In 1965, it was estimated that:

> the average wage worker earns twice as much total income and ten times as much money income as the average small farmer.[28]

It should be made clear that the rising income of all African workers in Kenya is an imperfect index of the benefits accruing to the lowest paid labourer: for increased Africanisation has pulled up the average. Nevertheless, even when allowance is made for this factor, as the 1967 Salaries Review Commission points out, ordinary labourers appear to have increased their real wages very considerably (both relative to agriculture and absolutely).

It may be questioned whether collective bargaining has acted as a charge or check on wage rates. Although the dynamics of collective bargaining suggest a steady upward spiral, the FKE has built counterweights into the system. The question, however, is inconclusively answered by the data.[29] The inbred relationship between the Industrial Court and private negotiations confounds apportioning responsibility for the rate of money wage increase to either wage setting procedure. True enough, whilst real earnings rose steadily from the mid 'fifties, they rose even faster from the late 'fifties, when collective bargaining was getting underway. But the pace has been faster and the magnitude greater in government employment where there is no collective bargaining but where there is more Africanisation. In 1966, fewer African males earned below £120 in government employment (28·5 per cent) than in private industry (53 per cent).[30] Yet the private figure is not restricted to workers covered by collective agreements.

A brief examination of wages in other African countries also leaves unanswered the question of whether collective bargaining checks or kindles the rate of wage increase. Whilst Mr. H. A. Turner cautions against placing undue reliance on available data, he argues that wage trends are nevertheless clear. He states that in most underdeveloped countries, Kenya included, it is surprising to find wages:

> . . . not merely chasing prices but running ahead of them . . . at rates quite comparable with those in the advanced industrial countries.[31]

The income differential between wage earners and the mass of subsistence peasants has also widened:

> In the African case . . . the whole benefit of economic development during the 1950's was transferred to African wage-earners. . . .[32]

It is generally assumed that the degree of collective bargaining in most underdeveloped countries is marginal. The evidence presented so far indicates that Kenya provides an exception. Therefore, as a very rough test indeed, if wages have risen more in Kenya than elsewhere, it may be presumed that collective bargaining is an important contributory factor; if they have risen less, collective bargaining and the organised efforts of employers pose as restraints. But two illustrations chosen from the raw data afford little insight. Mr. Turner sweeps across Africa with an estimate of real wages of all workers rising at an annual rate of some 4 per cent. Whereas for unskilled urban workers only in Kenya (unadjusted for coverage of the public sector) 'it is clear' to Mr. Dharam Ghai that real income has been rising at an annual rate of 8 per cent (1960–66).[33] Figures collated by the International Institute for Labour Studies tell a different story. Kenya ranked fifth from the top in rate of increase in real wages in manufacturing (1956–64) amongst six African countries. The rates of increase were 3·8 per cent in Kenya, 12·3 per cent in Tanzania, 9·3 per cent in Nigeria, 9·1 per cent in Southern Rhodesia, 8·1 per cent in Zambia, and 1·6 per cent in Ghana.[34]

Given quantitative limitations, the question of whether collective bargaining checks or kindles pressure on wage rates is perhaps best answered with a qualitative assessment of the bargaining apparatus itself. It may be seen whether certain patterns of negotiation favoured by the FKE inherently make for certain patterns of wages. Such an assessment is undertaken after the setting in which collective bargaining operates is more fully described. For the setting poses to collective bargaining more than the challenge of urban wages rising faster than peasant incomes. Other differentials have caused very serious concern as well.

First, it is stressed that the distribution of wages is unsatisfactory and inequitable. Too many workers are bunched together at the lower end of the wage scale without distinction as to skill and ability whilst a very small fraction of workers receive extremely high wages. In 1964, 41,000 professional, managerial, administrative, and technical personnel accounted for roughly 7 per cent of recorded employment and received nearly 44 per cent of the total wage bill.[35]

Second, it is claimed that the spread in wages between labourers and artisans is 'far larger' than that prevailing in developed economies.[36] Such differences 'have no such obviously rational basis as that of skill and responsibility'.[37]

Third, 'it is generally agreed that a relative overvaluation of clerical work as compared with manual work is widespread in Africa'.[38] Whilst there is little reliable evidence for Kenya specifically, in all of Africa south of the Sahara 'such evidence as can be collected suggests that in recent years the average skilled manual differential has been narrowing while the clerical differential has been widening'.[39] This is in spite of the fact that there is often a shortage of skilled manpower in underdeveloped countries and a surplus of clerks and typists.[40]

Fourth, attention has been drawn in Kenya to large differences in pay between workers in commercial agriculture and unskilled labourers in urban industry. If only the rural and urban minimum wages are compared (and most workers in mixed farming receive the minimum whilst many workers in urban industry receive far above the minimum), urban rates are almost three times as great as rural rates. Since there is already a serious unemployment problem in the towns, this differential can only worsen it.

Fifth, payment varies considerably amongst different industries and companies of different size and national origin within the same pursuit. According to a National Wage Policy Advisory Committee, 'These differences are too wide to have any logical justification. . . .'[41] By way of illustration, the Committee noted that in some industries, unskilled operatives in abundant supply earned far more than teachers, who are at a premium.

L

Characteristics of Bargaining

More than 30 trade unions in Kenya negotiate directly or indirectly with some 1,200 companies employing approximately 100,000 workers in industry and commerce. Obviously, any comments on the attitudes which such parties bring to the bargaining table can only be the roughest of generalisations. From discussions with a number of union leaders and employers, however, and from observations drawn from a number of bargaining sessions, a sketchy picture emerges.

Strategy at the Bargaining Table

The union offensive at the bargaining table rests on allegations of the widening profit margins of employers at the expense of exploited and impoverished workers.[42] Industry, COTU states, should not be attracted to Kenya by the cheapness of labour but on the basis of 'our having a skilled, efficient and responsible labour force. . . .'[43] It is never forgotten that the government once pledged itself in favour of a small, decently paid labour force rather than a large hungry one.[44] The unions also argue that their members are the nation's social security system, remitting money to extended families in the reserves and rearing relatives in search of work in the towns. This equilibration of the rural and urban income differential is lent support by the popular journals, such as the *Reporter*:

> A short survey carried out this week tended to confirm suspicions that the man in paid employment is being increasingly battened on by his relatives. . . .
>   His 'in-laws' demand gifts in cash and kind, on the ground that as he is in paid employment, he has a duty to share the proceeds. . . . There is no shame in demanding such tribute. 'This,' claim the relatives, 'is African Socialism.'
>   But is it?[45]

Peter Gutkind claims that it is not. The extended family system is disintegrating in the towns and the unemployed live by their wits in tightly knit isolated communities.[46] As for remittances to the reserves, a recent study on financial behaviour of Africans in Nairobi estimates that remittances become positive only for households whose income exceeds 330sh. a month.[47] In 1966, 53 per cent of Africans in private industry earned less than 200sh. a month; too poor to make remittances, as the unions no doubt also stress during negotiations.

The counter-arguments of employers at the bargaining table preach the need for wage restraint in light of development priorities, invoke the spectre of unemployment and redundancy, and point to the lower wages paid by non-unionised firms. The plantation associations stress that they are at the mercy of international price fluctuations and that any undue wage increase is bound to inflict injury on Kenya's major source of exports. The plantation associations and many of the FKE's small firms or groups seemingly stick to their guns at the bargaining table. Whether the bark of international firms is worse than their bite is best answered through an examination of bargaining structure.

The Structure of Collective Bargaining

An examination of bargaining structure re-opens the question of whether bargaining itself has checked or kindled the rate of money wage increase. The structure of bargaining in Kenya is for all practical purposes two-tiered. At the top is the FKE. It defines the zone within which its members may negotiate, and influences their employment conditions. At the bottom is a diversity of bargaining units. As suggested in Chapter Six, multi-employer bargaining is most popular but company-wide bargaining is not uncommon. Each has important *a priori* implications for wage rates and differentials.

It had long been a policy of the employer movement in Kenya to canalise individual companies into industry-wide associations to effect bargaining along the same lines. At first, this was seen as a preventive measure against whipsawing. With the coming of Independence, it was also considered a preventive of queasiness and irresolution on the part of employers. There is strength in unity and by bargaining together, determination in the new political milieu could be secured. Thus, industry-wide bargaining may serve to hold the line on wage increases. There is also the historical fact that unions in Kenya have tended to strike less against firms bargaining in unison than against firms bargaining alone; with obvious implications for wage rates. Pulling, however, in the opposite direction, firms bargaining in unison may sanction wage increases more readily than otherwise. They enjoy the knowledge that their competitors will share the same fate. Many East African industries have high concentration ratios and cater for the local market; so the safety-valve of higher prices presents itself.

Once the FKE realised that its fears of whipsawing were exaggerated, it ceased to expound uniform rates across-the-board and instead encouraged employers to negotiate according to their own capacity to pay. Hence the existence within one industry of assorted bargaining units (often of the multi-employer variety). Such an arrangement may be seen to give freer rein to large firms to pay high or to introduce distortions between large firms and small ones within the same pursuit. The argument, however, is two-sided. Negotiating sections within the same industry which draft agreements on a geographical basis enable conditions in the local labour markets to be taken into consideration. Also, redundancy is prevented and the small firm aided by agreements tailor made to what wages can be afforded. Otherwise, industry-wide agreements, geared to the wealthiest firm under union pressure, might take their toll in unemployment. (Then again, they might reduce discrepancies in 'willingness' and 'ability' to pay.)

Either for whole or part of an industry, multi-employer bargaining is said to introduce a more rational wage structure:

> Centralised bargaining permits constructive joint attention to such vital matters as wage uniformity, standardisation of job titles, job classification, interplant wage rationalisation (elimination of interplant inequities), and raising productivity levels.[48]

Multi-employer bargaining, however, introduces a measure of inflexibility, particularly where incentive systems of wage payment are concerned.

Negotiable Issues

The issues which are subject to collective bargaining in Kenya far outnumber those which are not.[49] The long list of the Motor Trades' Employers Association includes: job classifications, wages, overtime pay, travelling leave, paid leave allowance, paid sick leave, medical expenses, maternity leave, safari allowances (the expenses paid by a firm when one of its employees is travelling on company business), acting allowances, probation, termination of service, principles of redundancy, redundancy pay, retirement benefits, protective clothing, transfer of union officials, the check-off, and duration of agreement.[50] This list appears to be fairly representative of others governing large employer associations and many individual firms. Fewer issues will appear in the agreements of smaller groups although these are fairly numerous nonetheless.

Categories of Workers Covered by Collective Agreements

If collective agreements cover a wide range of subjects, they also cover a wide range of job categories. The fight for the unions has not been a very easy one. Recently the country was plunged into darkness by a strike in the electricity industry waged to extend the classification of employees eligible for unionisation. By and large, most unions now bargain for all manual workers, including artisans and clerical workers, including those earning relatively high wages. For example, the Kenya

Union of Commercial, Food and Allied Workers concluded an agreement with an insurance company which covered white collar workers earning as much as £1,392 per annum.[51]

The latitude of job categories covered holds important implications for wage differentials. It permits the bargainers to narrow or widen the gap between operatives, artisans, and clerks. To date, however, there has been little uniformity in the rises stipulated (either at the bargaining table or at Court). Sometimes the highest paid are given a higher rise than the man at the bottom. At other times, the same rise is negotiated across the board. There is also the small fact that many increases in Kenya are negotiated on the basis of shillings-per-month rather than straight percentages; and shillings-per-month increments across the board preserve absolute differentials but relatively compress the wage structure. To date, breakaway staff associations have not been a consequence. Nor has the slight relative compression provoked breakaway craft unions; and perhaps to the good. In Kenya, as elsewhere, the differential between the skilled and unskilled is substantial. But in Kenya, unlike what is thought to be the case elsewhere, artisans are frequently rewarded more handsomely than clerks. Separate craft unions might improve the position of artisans unduly. With the example of British labour relations in mind, the FKE has long opposed institutionalising the power of a handful of key skilled men to bring production to a halt.

Wages

It is an established policy of the FKE to prevail on all employers to pay manual workers standard wages, i.e. rates for the job as opposed to incremental time scales. The FKE argues that incremental time scales are appropriate only for certain categories of staff. A fair number of employers have followed the FKE's advice although this has meant abandoning the payment of wages based on length of service, which was popular practice at one time. The FKE argues that there are other options available for rewarding long service, e.g. pension and provident schemes, gratuities, etc. In a survey carried out by the FKE in 1963, 109 firms of the 207 sampled provided their workers with some sort of retirement benefit.[52] With the commencement of a national social security system in 1966, however, many employers are no longer making additional contributions to their own schemes.

The FKE's arguments in favour of rates for the job are as follows:

1. It is unfair to pay a machine operative with, say, five years' service more per day than a newly trained starter who may perform the same job just as well or even better.

2. Incremental time scales tend to operate automatically regardless of performance or vacancies in a higher grade.
3. When incremental time scales exist, negotiations tend to become complicated, difficult, and costly. The same is true of payroll administration.
4. In collective bargaining, a pattern of annual regular reviews has developed and this makes it extremely illogical to operate a system of annual increments.[53]

Firms bargaining jointly set rates for the job at the national level. They are, moreover, applied to the letter, wage drift being of little consequence in an economy marked by critical unemployment. This leaves little room for payment by results, for '. . . when we have any form of payment by results, even straight piece-work, it is impossible to settle the payment completely in national agreements'.[54] The reward for skill, however, is thought to be desirable in an underdeveloped country. According to Mr. Turner.

> . . . payment systems themselves should be strongly 'incentive' . . . there is a great deal to be said for 'progressive' piece-rate systems of the Taylorist or (former) Soviet type.[55]

In fact, it is questionable whether piece-rate systems can be introduced in Kenya on a widespread scale. It is generally recognised that piece-rates are most easily applied to factory labourers who are 'direct' workers. In Kenya, a large proportion of the private labour force (outside agriculture) is employed in commerce and the service industries.[56] It appears that many 'indirect' workers fall within this category. Whilst it is not impossible to tie incentive schemes to 'indirect' workers, it is generally difficult to do so.

Although the FKE has recognised that even firms bargaining on a multi-firm basis may choose to pay production bonuses, the payment of such bonuses and/or piece rates is relatively uncommon. The survey conducted by the FKE in 1963 revealed that only 22 firms out of 207 sampled offered some form of incentive.[57] Those firms which did tended to bargain alone.

Fringe Benefits

Whilst wages continue to be the most important item on the bargaining agenda, fringe benefits are becoming increasingly important (and, according to most employers, an increasing fraction of total labour costs).

It is FKE policy to advise its members to pay both clerical and manual workers 'clean' (i.e. 'all-in') wages. Although 'free' rations and rudimentary housing continue to be the rule in commercial agriculture, the once common practice of providing 'free' housing or a housing allowance in addition to a basic wage shows signs of decline in urban industry. This coincides with rising rentals and costs of construction as well as a more acute shortage of accommodation.

One fringe benefit to which the unions attach great importance is paid annual leave, since many workers have business interests to attend to and families to care for in the reserves. The Boards of Governors of Secondary Schools in Kenya, for example, negotiated an agreement with the Domestic and Hotel Workers' Union in June 1966 which stated:

> After the completion of each period of 12 months' continuous service with the Employer, an employee shall be entitled to Annual Leave of 21 consecutive days with full pay [in addition to paid Gazetted holidays].

These terms appear to be fairly typical of those concluded in most industries, although the bigger firms have begun granting 28 days' paid leave; in the case of commercial agriculture, 14–18 days.

Another important fringe benefit is paid sick leave. An agreement concluded in 1965 between the Minor Engineering Employers' Group of the FKE and the Kenya Engineering Workers' Union stipulated that after completion of a probationary period and subject to proof of incapacity, an employee be entitled to the first 18 days of sick leave on full pay and the next 18 days on half pay: similarly with paid maternity leave, where provided.

The FKE has directed much of its energies and powers of persuasion to ensuring that fringe benefits do not get out of line and do not escalate in new directions. For example, one of its Newsletters states:

> Recently, two members, in negotiation, conceded fringe benefits substantially above established levels. Members are reminded of the need to consult with the Federation before considering the improvement of terms of service which already conform to the established pattern.[58]

Happily for employers, such vigilance can summon up development strategy in its defence. Like higher wages, attractive fringe benefits can only widen the rural-urban income differential and worsen unemployment in town. Improved fringe benefits will also enlarge the fixed component of the wage bill when it is argued that remuneration be made variable with output in underdeveloped countries.

The fringe benefits discussed thus far, however, are those applicable to categories of workers eligible for unionisation. Fringe benefits for the salariat are usually more generous but have elicited less vigilance on the part of the FKE. When Africanisation was first gaining momentum, the FKE prepared a manual on recommended terms of service for local managerial, executive and senior staff.[59] Employers were cautioned against competing with one another for qualified Africans by offering them handsome supernumerary inducements. But the tone of the report was pessimistic, qualified Africans being at a premium and the government calling the tune since it paid the preponderance of senior personnel. Whether any development strategy can be summoned up in defence of liberal fringe benefits and handsome salaries for executives is discussed in the following section.

Wages Policy

All is not well in Kenya. The chronic scarcity of land; the critical level of unemployment; the inequitable distribution of income between peasant and proletarian, between manager and labourer, are ample evidence. The foregoing analysis has conveyed the indecisive effect of collective bargaining on wage trends and certain differentials. The two-tiered bargaining structure may act as a restraint on wage increases although multi-employer bargaining may lend itself to a wage-price spiral. The wide latitude of job categories covered by collective agreements allows the bargainers to improve the blue collar-white collar/unskilled-skilled differential, although such license may not have been put to use in the past. The effect of collective bargaining has been decisively nil, however, on the differential which excites the greatest passion—that dividing those who labour and those who own or control the means of production. The technocrats are outside the jurisdiction of collective bargaining and profits are little more than touched by it. Because all is not well in Kenya and because something more (or less) than collective bargaining is wanted, interest in the West's well-worn essays in wages policy has been awakened.

Nor is Kenya alone in falling back on Western essays in troubled times. Recently a symposium on wages policy in underdeveloped countries was convened under the auspices of the International Institute for Labour Studies. Its detailed report stresses the inequities and development handicaps of typical wage trends and differentials. The report recognises at length that wages policy has its limitations and that optimum economic solutions often tend to be politically untenable. But the report for the most part denies the reader even brief theorising or inspiration on the political economy that might lend itself more to optimum solutions or that might mitigate some of the problems. As Thomas Balogh writes:

> Faced with Cold War, Western (and especially American) economists are unwilling and unable to reconsider their theories because such reconsideration might call in question the merits of the private enterprise economy

while, again especially in America, the moral case for democratic advance
has become inextricably bound up—indeed synonymous—with the case
for private enterprise.[60]

The symposium appears to reach the greatest measure of consensus
on the need to compress the wage structure; from the top downwards.
But even here there is dissent. Mr. Elliot Berg, professor at the University of Michigan, points to the dangers of tampering with the market
by pegging the salaries of executives in short supply. He also defends
the differential they enjoy on the grounds that they mix with the
wealthy. When the income of the African elite is compared not with
that of the peasant but with that of the expatriate, the comparison,
according to Mr. Berg, is 'particularly cruel'.[61] In sharp contrast is the
view of a post-war British commission on the salaries of civil servants
in East Africa. As noted in Chapter One, it stressed 'the disadvantages
of so remunerating any class of Africans [on a par with Europeans] as
to create a mandarin caste. . . .' The contrast is even more striking
when it is realised that Mr. Berg served as an economic consultant to
Kenya's 1967 Salaries Review Commission.

Little wonder that its Report has come in for criticism for its failure
to lower the relative price of high-level manpower. Mr. Emil Rado
writes:

> . . . one is surprised that the possibility of compressing the salary
> structure, by scaling it down at the upper end, is not even raised, much
> less recommended. . . . Though its avoidance of fundamental issues, and
> its reluctance to question implicit assumptions, can be understood, it is
> also to be regretted . . . the basic work of evaluating the colonial
> legacy . . . is yet to be done.[62]

Proposals on wages policy submitted independently by another of
the SRC's economic consultants, Mr. Dharam P. Ghai, go a step further
than most. They concern themselves not only with the 'tremendous'
gap between the incomes of the salariat and the ordinary labourer.
They also concern themselves with the 'enormous' gap between 'the
incomes of capitalists and skilled persons on the one hand, and of unskilled workers and peasant farmers on the other'.[63] The proposals
recommended by Mr. Ghai to contain the capitalist differential, however, are less convincing than those recommended to peg the wages of
ordinary labourers:

> Taking into account the surtax on distributed dividends, . . . the
> effective rate of taxation of business profits probably amounts to more
> than 50 per cent. . . . It is doubtful whether corporate taxes can be
> raised much further without affecting foreign private investment in the
> country.

Mr. Ghai also recognises the 'political and administrative difficulties encountered in devising an appropriately progressive [income] tax structure'. His proposals for clamping down on the capitalists, therefore, are limited to extending tax coverage and to policing the pricing policies of monopolists. These limitations alone make it highly questionable whether an *ad hoc* wages policy can be relied on to effect a fundamental redistribution of income. Yet a fundamental redistribution of income may be the prerequisite for a successful wages policy. The West's well-worn essays in 'guidelines' for prices and incomes are perhaps indicative.

Although the unions in Kenya have repeatedly demanded a wages policy, the government has shied away from the political ordeal of producing one. The FKE has also gone on record countless times as being in favour of wage restraint, but in 1967, Sir Colin Campbell acknowledged:

> All in all, I consider that Kenya has found a reasonably satisfactory compromise between the political and economic realities affecting wages.[64]

The FKE alone may be complacent. The unemployed, the peasant, and the unskilled may be less content.

A Perspective on Collective Bargaining

The large corporation was instrumental in proselytizing the practice and ideology of collective bargaining in Kenya after the outbreak of 'Mau Mau'. A consensus was reached on the institutionalisation of conflict between management and labour through the medium of collective bargaining. Need Kenya have *institutionalised* something as undesirable as conflict as early in its history as it did? Since Independence, both the practice and ideology of collective bargaining have come into question. Need Kenya again find the answer in the West's questionable essays in wages policy? To put income determination on a 'rational' basis it is necessary to put the distribution of income on a 'rational' basis, and here there is much less consensus.

The proselytization of collective bargaining at a turning point in Kenya's history turned attention away from the *sources* of conflict between management and labour, from practices and ideologies other than collective bargaining. Such pre-emption, such foreclosure, is the important starting point for a critique of the influence exerted by the international firm on the labour affairs of an underdeveloped country. Mr. Balogh's point is well taken.

REFERENCES

1 H. A. Turner, *Wage Trends, Wage Policies and Collective Bargaining: The Problems for Underdeveloped Countries*, Occasional Papers 6 (Cambridge: At the University Press for the Department of Applied Economics, 1965). (Hereinafter referred to as *Wage Trends*.)
2 *Ibid.*, p. 34. These are some of the criteria suggested by Mr. Turner for collective bargaining.
3 The difficulties in comparing wage trends stipulated by the Court and those arising out of collective bargaining agreements are recognised. If the Court had stipulated only wage increases of 10 per cent, this may be no greater than increases negotiated privately which cover both wages and fringe benefits. A study of Court awards is presently being undertaken by Dharam P. Ghai, Institute of Development Studies, Nairobi.
4 In 1966, for example, the Court handed down 89 awards. Most embraced more than one issue. In 67 instances, the Court made a nil award. In 68 instances, it introduced a positive increase or improvement. In only three instances was an established benefit actually reduced. (Federation of Kenya Employers, 'Annual Report', 1967, p. 5. [Mimeographed.] [Hereinafter the Federation of Kenya Employers will be referred to as the FKE.].)
5 FKE, 'Annual Report', 1968.
6 I.L.O., *Methods and Principles of Wage Regulation*, Report III, Second African Regional Conference, Addis Ababa, 1964 (Geneva: ILO, 1964), p. 31.
7 Republic of Kenya, *Economic Survey 1966* (Nairobi: Statistics Division, Ministry of Economic Planning and Development, 1966), Table 46, p. 62.
8 Republic of Kenya, *Report of the Salaries Review Commission 1967* (Nairobi, 1967), p. 31. (Hereinafter referred to as *Salaries Review Commission 1967*.)
9 Government of Kenya, *Revised Conditions of Service for the Kenya Civil Service* (Nairobi, 1964).
10 Republic of Kenya, *Salaries Review Commission 1967*, p. 30.
11 *Ibid.*, p. 31.
12 There were considerably fewer strikes in 1963 when an SRC published its report than in 1959, 1960 and 1962 when collective bargaining was getting under way. (Republic of Kenya, *Statistical Abstract*, 1967, Table 178, p. 155.) There was little noticeable unrest following the 1967 SRC report except from the disenchanted Civil Servants' Union.
13 The Minister of Local Government, however, must approve all such conditions. Much against the government's wishes, a large number of local government agreements on terms of service have been settled at the Industrial Court.
14 Republic of Kenya, *Salaries Review Commission 1967*, p. 112.
15 Ibid., p. 112.
16 Ibid., p. 116.
17 Distributive and Allied Trades Employers' Association, 'Handbook', Nairobi, [1966]. (Mimeographed.)
18 Motor Trade and Allied Industries Employers' Association, 'Handbook', Nairobi, [1966]. (Mimeographed.)
19 Turner, *Wage Trends*, p. 51.
20 Between 1958 and 1965, real earnings in Kenya rose by over 75 per cent whilst the statutory minimum in Nairobi rose by only 35 per cent. (Republic of Kenya, *Salaries Review Commission 1967*, p. 16.) The real wages of

ordinary labourers are said to have increased by 8 per cent per annum between 1960 and 1966. (Dharam P. Ghai, 'Incomes Policy in Kenya: Need, Criteria and Machinery', *East African Economic Review*, Vol. 4 [N.S.], No. 1 [June 1968], p. 20.) Even so, statutory minima may still have an influence on going rates. This may be particularly true in non-FKE firms and in FKE-firms which pay above, but close to, the legal floor.

21 FKE, 'Survey Report: Manual Workers, Including Artisans,' 1963, p. 2. (Mimeographed.) (Hereinafter referred to as 'Survey Report 1963'.) In 1963, the FKE had a total industrial membership of 674 firms. The 207 companies sampled ranged from those with less than 50 workers to those with over 1,000 workers each. While the limitations of the FKE's sample are recognised, the information which it contains is nevertheless revealing. In Mombasa, the median minimum wage paid by FKE companies above the statutory minimum was Shs. 30/75 in 1963. The comparable figure for Kisumu, a typical smaller township was Shs. 30/50.

22 Arthur M. Ross, 'Introduction', in *Industrial Relations and Economic Development*, ed. by the same author (London: Macmillan for the International Institute for Labour Studies, 1966), p. xxviii.

23 Republic of Kenya, *Ministry of Labour and Social Services Annual Report 1964* (Nairobi, 1967), Appendix V, Table 9.

24 Republic of Kenya, Industrial Court: 'Cause No. 24 of 1965: The Kenya Plantation and Agricultural Workers' Union and the Kenya Coffee Growers' Association', p. 2. (Mimeographed.)

25 FKE, 'Wage Rates in Agriculture and the Plantations', 1966. (Mimeographed.)

26 Republic of Kenya, *Salaries Review Commission 1967*, pp. 15–16.

27 It was estimated that adult male wage earners represented 28·2 per cent of all able bodied males (aged 15–60) in 1960. (Colony and Protectorate of Kenya, *Reported Employment and Wages in Kenya, 1948–60* [Nairobi, 1961], p. 2.)

28 Republic of Kenya, *Salaries Review Commission 1967*, p. 16.

29 Some of the problems of measuring the impact of unions on wages in the United States are summarised by Neil W. Chamberlain, *The Labor Sector: An Introduction to Labor in the American Economy* (New York: McGraw-Hill, 1965), pp. 468–80.

30 Republic of Kenya, *Statistical Abstract*, 1967, Table 175(a), p. 153.

31 Turner, *Wage Trends*, p. 12.

32 *Ibid.*, pp. 13–14.

33 Ghai, 'Incomes Policy in Kenya: Need, Criteria and Machinery', p. 20.

34 *Wage Policy Issues in Economic Development*, ed. by Anthony D. Smith, The Proceedings of a Symposium held by the International Institute for Labour Studies at Egelund, Denmark, 23–27 October 1967, under the Chairmanship of Clark Kerr (London: Macmillan, 1969), p. 44.

35 R. H. Green, 'Employment, Productivity and Consumption', in *Education, Employment and Rural Development*, ed. by James R. Sheffield (Nairobi: East Africa Publishing House, 1967), Tables I and II. Referred to by Ghai, 'Incomes Policy in Kenya: Need, Criteria and Machinery', p. 21.

36 I.L.O., *Methods and Principles of Wage Regulation*, p. 26.

37 Turner, *Wage Trends*, p. 16.

38 I.L.O., *Methods and Principles of Wage Regulation*, p. 27.

39 Turner, *Wage Trends*, p. 17.

40 One writer argues that it is wishful thinking to expect this differential to narrow by very much. Even with a surplus of clerks, firms will pay high to

keep their current clerical staff since skill and experience are acquired on-the-job. (Koji Taira, 'Wage Differentials in Developing Countries: A Survey of Findings', *International Labour Review*, Vol. 93, No. 6 [March 1966].) Employers in Kenya often complain of the unpreparedness of clerks in the market.

41 [Republic of Kenya], 'Report of the National Wage Policy Advisory Committee', [1965], pp. 3–4. (Mimeographed.)

42 Not infrequently, the larger unions will come armed with facts and figures on cost-of-living and profits. They are, however, at a disadvantage when they bargain with the private subsidiaries of international firms which do not have to publish financial statements.

43 COTU, 'Forward With the Workers: A Statement of Policy', [August 1966], p. 2. (Mimeographed.)

44 Colony and Protectorate of Kenya, *Labour Department Annual Report* (Nairobi, 1962), p. 1.

45 *Reporter*, January 13, 1967.

46 Peter C. W. Gutkind, 'The Energy of Despair: Social Organisation of the Unemployed in Two African Cities: Lagos and Nairobi (2nd Part)', *Civilisations*, Vol. 17, No. 4 (1967), pp. 394–95.

47 C. W. Howe, 'An Analysis of African Household Consumption and Financial Behaviour in Kenya and Uganda', *East African Economic Review*, Vol. 4 (N.S.), No. 1 (June 1968), p. 55.

48 H. W. Davey, *Contemporary Collective Bargaining* (2nd ed.; Englewood Cliffs, New Jersey: Prentice-Hall, 1959), pp. 93–94.

49 Non-bargainable issues typically include: annual bonuses, merit pay, training and trade tests. Sometimes these issues will be raised in works councils.

50 Motor Trade and Allied Industries Employers' Association, 'Handbook', 1966.

51 FKE, 'Newsletter', No. 93, 31 January, 1968, p. 5.

52 FKE, 'Survey Report 1963', p. 22.

53 FKE, 'Report on Recommended Terms of Service for Manual Workers, Including Artisans', 1963, pp. 2–4. (Mimeographed.)

54 Allan Flanders, 'Collective Bargaining', in *The System of Collective Bargaining in Great Britain*, ed. by Allan Flanders and H. A. Clegg (Oxford: Basil Blackwell, 1964), p. 291.

55 Turner, *Wage Trends*, p. 22.

56 Republic of Kenya, *Ministry of Labour and Social Services Annual Report 1964*, Appendix I, Table 1.

57 FKE, 'Survey Report 1963', p. 21.

58 FKE, 'Newsletter', No. 89, August 29, 1967, p. 3.

59 FKE, 'Report on Recommended Terms of Service for Local, Managerial, Executive, and Senior Staff', 1961. (Mimeographed.)

60 T. Balogh, 'The Conventional Wisdom of Kenneth Galbraith', *New Left Review*, No. 26 (Summer 1964).

61 Anthony D. Smith, ed., *Wage Policy Issues in Economic Development*, pp. 326–27.

62 Emil Rado, 'Kenya Salaries Report, A Holding Operation', *East Africa Journal*, Vol. 4, No. 8 (December 1967).

63 Ghai, 'Incomes Policy in Kenya: Need Criteria and Machinery', p. 21.

64 *East African Standard*, April 1, 1967.

CONCLUDING NOTE

I

Little over a year ago, the tribal mood in Kenya was ugly, no less so perhaps than on the eve of 'Mau Mau'. In October 1969, the Opposition Kenya Peoples' Union was banned, its leaders placed under house arrest or detention. This followed a demonstration against President Kenyatta in Kisumu some months after Tom Mboya's death. The demonstration provoked the President's personal bodyguard to open fire on the Luo demonstrators, killing at least thirteen. Earlier, the policy manifesto of the Opposition party was declared prohibited reading, along with the thoughts of Chairman Mao and other subversive material. At about the same time, news broke in Parliament that Kikuyus were being forced to take loyalty oaths to the Kenya African National Union and Kenyatta; one prominent Christian Kikuyu was allegedly murdered for his refusal to do so.

The analogy with 'Mau Mau' is not superficial even if it is inexact. Behind the conflicts of yesterday and today there is grinding poverty and more grating, perhaps, the frustrating ineqitable distribution of wealth, social privilege and political opportunity. The lurid accounts of 'Mau Mau' have been discredited by scholarly accounts of injustice. The unhappiness in Kenya today may reopen examination of who is gaining what from development and what precisely the intrinsic gains from development are. In the hearing, international firms will no doubt be asked to testify for they are an integral part of the economic organisation and the power that it bestows.

The relationship between tribalism and the corporation is thus in-direct and more subtle than of old. The arch colonial powers, so the accusations ran, played on tribalism with a strategy of divide and rule. The newer institutions, exemplified by big business after 'Mau Mau', strove to reconcile the tribes and races to improve the climate for investment. The belief seems to have been that collective bargain-ing would legitimise confrontation between white man and black man in the more convential cross of management and labour. The fruits of collective bargaining would reduce strains amongst all Africans, the intention never being to excite them. Certainly the industry-wide unions which subsequently developed managed to pre-sent a united front in the fight for higher wages.

The latter day strategy to distribute discreetly the corporation's surplus gained renewed appeal as Independence approached and with it, the 'Communist menace'. But since then, incidentally, army coups rather than socialist revolutions have been the rule in Africa. Martial law is itself less threatening to big business than socialism or tribal bloodshed. If martial law is assured on the heels of unrest, it, too, is less threatening. To look ahead, it is not impossible that personnel policy will change in nuance slightly and grow less seductive in years to come. An editorial in the London *Times* à propos of the Somali coup was hardly critical of army takeovers in Africa. It suggested that they allowed for a breathing spell and restored law and order under civilian government usually without undue delay.[1]

II

From the 'fifties onwards, employer policy in Kenya deliberately encouraged the growth of a bread and butter trade union movement to pre-empt radical political change. The complexity of the situation is not to be belittled, for other forces at play ceaselessly laboured for the same trade union model. The corporations, however, handed the workers a system with tangible pay-offs. Not that it was unnatural after 'Mau Mau' that management followed the course that it did. The question is not why it did so but whether it should have been allowed to continue doing so unimpeded: particularly after Independence and particularly since it was done so well.

It was all done so well because eventually the trade unions and international firms reached a consensus on the rules and hierarchical rights of industrial life: and not unlike the case in other countries where the corporation thrives,

> . . . negotiation and conflict between management and labor have been essentially on ground chosen by management: within the business rather than political arena.[2]

Over thirty industry-wide unions have concentrated their energies adroitly on collective bargaining. Bargaining itself has reached impressive proportions. By the criterion of industrial peace it is orderly. By the criterion of the corporations it is well ordered. The centralised locus of authority within the employer movement has empowered the FKE to build counterweights into the bargaining apparatus. The era of the modern corporation began in Kenya with a concerted effort to reinforce the mettle of management in the post-'Mau Mau' political milieu: to hold the line against the unions' wage demands externally and to prevent a competitive play for political points through wage concessions internally.

When a small effort is made to peer behind the scenes, however, the picture of success becomes forbidding. There are very serious tensions at play which make not so much for dynamism as alarm. Whilst no industrial setting is free of them, the uneasy conclusion drawn from the preceding chapters is that tensions have been magnified in Kenya by employer policy.

On his return from a business trip to the United States in 1967, the President of the FKE was at pains to panegyrise the American way of life. Sir Colin Campbell stated in the Press:

What impressed me above all else was the general attitude towards achievement and wealth, its outward symbol.

The man at the lower end of the scales is not saying: 'He's got more than I have, let's take it off him.' He regards the man who is richer than he, or who has been more successful than he, as an example, as someone to copy. In effect he is saying: 'Let me get where he is.'

The trade unions there understand that all good things in life come from profits. . . .

It is significant that trade union leaders there earn as much and sometimes more than leaders of industry.

. . . the fundamental I wish to make . . . is that for the community to get the best it can from a free enterprise system the individuals who make up that society must mentally recognise and support its basic philosophies.[3]

The ideological imperialism of the ICFTU in Kenya has been bitterly attacked both within the country and without. The FKE, however, is also wedded to a doctrine. It is also richer than the ICFTU and more intimately involved in the diurnal affairs of management and labour. The pro-Western activities of the internationals, however important, may emerge in perspective as little more than frosting on the cake. But if the unions have driven the internationals out from within their midst, they have been kinder to the FKE with an ultimatum that it Africanise. Rumours of corruption and pay off were central to the ICFTU's downfall in Kenya. It is interesting how few innuendos there are of a flow of cash between the big corporations and union chiefs. FKE members have seemingly succeeded through formal arrangements in putting across their views. These pay lip service to Gomper's pithy philosophy of 'more'.

There are grave implications in teasing trade union leaders in Kenya with the prospect of salaries equal to those of their American counterparts. The hardcore unemployed are said to number one-third of recorded employment. There have also been warnings that

wage earners have very markedly improved their position relative to small farmers, that the income differential between the two groups is large and growing.[4]

M

All was born of 'Mau Mau' but 'Mau Mau' showed signs of a peasant revolt. For the most part, the surplus of the corporations has not filtered down to the mass of subsistence peasants. There are grounds for concern that the FKE's insular policy to ward off unrest in the small industrial sector may prove self-defeating in the long run and defeatist for Kenya at large.

The creation of trade unions in Africa, first the inspiration of the Colonial Office, has been criticised as 'one of its most unimaginative decisions'.[5] Trade unions, the criticism runs, embody the 'idea of necessary conflict in working relationships . . . the most defeatist and destructive which the West exported to the developing world'. The critique, widely read, is that of Mr. Guy Hunter. With more feeling than form he proposes a humane approach to working relationships: through the medium of joint consultation in works councils and through a loosening of the enslaving bonds born of the factory system. These suggestions were explored in Chapter Three. The conclusion reached was that the presence of private enterprise makes inevitable the presence of institutions designed for conflict, however institutionalised the conflict may be. Without a political transformation of the economic order, schemes invented by personnel management schools for worker participation may be as unconvincing as de Gaulle's rhetoric of participation after the French general strike of 1968.

Analysis transcends FKE policy *per se* when it admits the discordance created by the very presence of the corporations that make up the FKE. Employers have been instrumental in encouraging the growth of business unions in a very poor country. But this hardly justifies moralising on the need for wage restraint on the part of the unskilled labourer. The income differential between wage earners and small farmers in Kenya has been described as 'large'. Part of the blame is suspected to lie with collective bargaining. But the income differential between salaried personnel and the unskilled has been described as 'tremendous' and that of the differential between capitalists and the unskilled as 'enormous', in spite of collective bargaining. Tanzanian socialists aim to minimise class conflict in the short run rather than sacrifice all to the tyranny of growth targets in the long run (not that private enterprise guarantees the easy attainment of growth targets). By contrast, the Kenya Government seemingly aims to check the 'socialism' of some trade union leaders with detention, licence to bargain 'hard', and other *quid pro quo*, perhaps. This is no growth strategy at all, short or long run. Neither is it equitable. The tensions crystallising in Africa today may necessitate a strategy which places equity first if wage restraint necessary for growth is to be forthcoming at all.

If many have seconded socialism as both a solution to class conflict and as a realistic growth strategy, others have fallen back on a wages policy in a troubled economic and political setting. The problems attendant upon such a policy, however, were raised briefly in Chapter Nine. They are likely to be considerable if the Western countries are any index. Nor is such an index wholly inappropriate for purposes of comparison. For income controls to be effective at the bottom, it is recognised that they must also be effective at the top. Here almost total reliance is placed on fiscal measures. The corporation tax in Kenya is roughly 50 per cent: about equal to that in the United States. But it is also recognised that any tax above 50 per cent will put Kenya at a disadvantage in the international capital market. A Kenya worker with little thought to international capital may be no more disposed to accept wage restraint than an American worker; and the FKE has exhorted the one to think like the other.

To date, Kenya does not have a wages policy. The government's position, a political sore point, was artfully summed up by the late Tom Mboya, a product of the labour relations of the 'fifties:

> Some 'levelling downwards' is, of course necessary in any policy of income distribution . . . but it would defeat its purpose in the long-run if all the emphasis is laid on 'levelling downwards'. We do not believe in the theory of equitable distribution of poverty.[6]

The FKE has gone on record countless times as being in favour of a wages policy for the country's good. But a remark of the FKE's President suggests that employers are satisfied with the bargain struck between 'the political and economic realities affecting wages'. The international firms have encouraged a bread and butter system of industrial relations. If the bread and butter are rationed, the system is unarmed. We are back to square one.

III

In a study on African Socialism, Friedland and Rosberg put forth the following proposition, not at all an unfavourable one to industry in their home country:

> There appear to be many advantages in permitting and encouraging foreign private investment while inhibiting the development of indigenous capitalists. This facilitates the importation of much-needed capital and at the same time acts to prevent a local group from . . . developing a degree of economic independence that may have social and political ramifications in the future.[7]

If Kenya is any guide, such a proposition is unduly compartmentalised. The expatriate employer community has not stayed aloof. Along with its capital it has brought its institutions and ideology, the one impossible to isolate from the other. The FKE has had tremendous influence on the personality of an African trade union movement. The FKE is also likely to provide a fillip to African enterprise. This is in spite of the fact that big corporations have acquired something of a reputation for stifling cut-throat competition amongst themselves whilst cutting the throats of small entrepreneurs. True enough, the FKE has in the past supported a rise in the statutory minimum wage to protect its members from small non-unionised competitors. It has gently bullied Asian (or European) family establishments to bring their standards of employment up to par—lest the image of private enterprise in Kenya become tarnished. It has also turned the tables on pre-'Mau Mau' days with demands for equal pay for equal work: that is, infant African companies and giant European ones should be treated equally under the labour law. Nevertheless, the FKE may emerge as a high priest in the initiation of the novice African firm into the ways of modern capitalism. Novitiates are invited into bargaining units tailored to their ability to pay. They are educated in the secrets of the managerial revolution and the rites of scientific personnel administration. Through contact with other employers, they are afforded the chance to gauge the scope of their competition and the state of the market. Although this accords with official government policy, the dangers of eking out an African middle class on the remains of the Asian shopkeeper have not gone unrecognised. Nor have the other areas in which the corporation makes its influence felt.

IV

Disingenuousness has a habit of creeping into the most scholarly of works. In a symposium on wages policy and economic growth, for example, the following remarks are recorded:

> . . . there is one very important argument in favour of profit-sharing schemes in underdeveloped countries. It seems to be almost essential that, given the present stage of their political development, the formulation of an incomes policy for such a country must provide for something which appears to hurt the employers. Nationalisation, action against monopolies, taxation, etc., never convince the workers. . . . But profit-sharing schemes can fulfil this role.[8]

That nationalisation never convinces the workers may be false. That profit sharing *appears* to hurt the employers seems deliberately misleading. Given the present stage of their political development and given the formative stage of industrialisation, it is crucial that workers in underdeveloped countries understand precisely the nature of the system under which they labour. Such was one aim of this study, intended for Kenyans and, by way of abstraction, those interested in the fate of other underdeveloped countries.

REFERENCES

1 *The Times*, October 22, 1969.
2 Edward S. Mason, ed., *The Corporation in Modern Society* (Cambridge, Mass.: Harvard University Press, 1960), p. 21.
3 *East African Standards*, April 1, 1967.
4 Republic of Kenya, *Salaries Review Commission 1967*, p. 23.
5 Guy Hunter, *The Best of Both Worlds?*, pp. 88 and 90.
6 T. J. Mboya, 'The Development Progress in Kenya', *East Africa Journal* (October 1965).
7 William H. Friedland and Carl G. Rosberg, Jr., 'The Anatomy of African Socialism', in *African Socialism*, ed. by the same authors (Stanford: Stanford University Press, 1964), p. 6.
8 *Wage Policy Issues in Economic Development*, ed. by Anthony D. Smith, The Proceedings of a Symposium held by the International Institute for Labour Studies at Egelund, Denmark, 23–27 October 1967, under the Chairmanship of Clark Kerr (London: Macmillan, 1969), p. 108. The remarks are those of Professor H. A. Turner.

BIBLIOGRAPHY

I. Books, Pamphlets, and Dissertations

Aaronovitch, S., and Aaronovitch, K. *Crisis in Kenya*. London: Lawrence and Wishart, 1947.

Arrighi, G. 'International Corporations, Labour Aristocracies and Economic Development in Tropical Africa', *The Corporations and the Cold War*. Edited by D. Horowitz. London, forthcoming.

Attwood, William. *The Reds and the Blacks: A Personal Adventure*. London: Hutchinson, 1967.

Baran, Paul A., and Sweezy, Paul M. *Monopoly Capital: An Essay on the American Economic and Social Order*. Penguin Books, 1966.

Barber, William. *The Economy of British Central Africa*. London: Oxford University Press, 1961.

Barnett, Donald L., and Njama, Karari. *Mau Mau From Within: Autobiography and an Analysis of Kenya's Peasant Revolt*. London: Macgibbon and Kee, 1966.

Baryaruha, Azarias. *Factors Affecting Industrial Employment: A Study of Ugandan Experience, 1954–64*. Occasional Paper I. Nairobi: Oxford University Press for the East African Institute of Social Research, 1967.

Bennett, George. *Kenya: A Political History: The Colonial Period*. London: Oxford University Press, 1963.

————, and Rosberg, Carl G. Jr. *The Kenyatta Election: Kenya, 1960–61*. London: Oxford University Press, 1961.

Berg, Elliot J. The Economics of the Migrant Labor System', *Urbanization and Migration in West Africa*. Edited by Hilda Kuper. Berkeley: University of California Press, 1965.

————. 'French West Africa', *Labor and Economic Development*. Edited by Walter Galenson. New York: John Wiley, 1959.

————. 'Major Issues of Wage Policy in Africa', *Industrial Relations and Economic Development*. Edited by Arthur M. Eoss London: Macmillan for the International Institute for Labour Studies, 1966.

————. 'Real Income Trends in West Africa, 1939–50', *Economic Transition in Africa*. Edited by Melville J. Herskovits and Mitchell Harwitz. London: Routledge and Kegan Paul, 1964.

————, and Butler, Jeffrey. 'Trade Unions', *Political Parties and National Integration in Tropical Africa*. Edited by James S. Coleman and Carl G. Rosberg, Jr. Berkeley: University of California Press, 1964.

Blumberg, Paul. *Industrial Democracy: The Sociology of Participation*. London: Constable, 1968.

Bowen, Walter. *Colonial Trade Unions*. Research Series No. 167. London: Fabian Society, 1954.

British Labour Party. *The Colonies: The Labour Party's Post-War Policy for the African and Pacific Colonies*. London: Transport House, 1943.

Brockway, Fenner. *African Journeys*. London: Victor Gollancz, 1955.

Butler, Jeffrey and Castagno, A. A. eds. *African Transition in African Politics.* Vol. 3 of Boston University Papers on Africa. New York: Praeger for the African Studies Centre of Boston University, 1966.

Buxton, Mary Aline, *Kenya Days.* London: E. Arnold, 1927.

Clark, Paul Gordon. *Development Planning in East Africa.* East African Studies No. 21. Nairobi: East Africa Publishing House for the East African Institute for Social Research, 1965.

Clegg, H. A. 'Employers', *The System of Industrial Relations in Great Britain.* Edited by Allan Flanders and H. A. Clegg. Oxford: Basil Blackwell, 1964.

Davey, Harold W. *Contemporary Collective Bargaining.* 2nd ed. Englewood Cliffs, New Jersey: Prentice-Hall, 1959.

Davies, Ioan. *African Trade Unions.* Penguin Books, 1966.

Dilley, Ruth. *British Policy in Kenya Colony.* New York: Thomas Nelson, 1937; 2nd ed., with a new bibliography by Dr. Marion E. Doro, Frank Cass, London, 1966.

Due, J. F. 'The Reform of East African Taxation', Vol. 2 of *Readings in the Applied Economics of Africa.* Edited by Edith H. Whethan and Jean I. Currie. Cambridge: University Press, 1967.

Dumont, Rene. *False Start in Africa.* London: André Deutsch, 1966.

Ehrmann, Henry W. *Organised Business in France.* Princeton, New Jersey: Princeton University Press, 1957.

Elkan, Walter. *An African Labour Force.* East African Studies No. 7. Uganda: East African Institute of Social Research, 1956.

————. *Migrants and Proletarians.* London: Oxford University Press for the East African Institute of Social Research, 1960.

Engholm, O. F. 'African Elections in Kenya', *Five Elections in Africa.* Edited by W. J. M. Mackenzie and Kenneth E. Robinson. Oxford: Clarendon Press, 1960.

Epstein, Arnold L. *Politics in an Urban African Community.* Manchester: Manchester University Press, 1958.

Ewing, A. F. *Industry in Africa.* London: Oxford University Press, 1968.

Fabian Colonial Bureau. *Kenya, White Man's Country?* Research Series No. 7. London, 1944.

Farson, Negley. *Last Chance in Africa.* London: Victor Gollancz, 1949.

Fearn, Hugh. *An African Economy: A Study of the Economic Development of the Nyanza Province of Kenya, 1903–53.* London: Oxford University Press for the East African Institute of Social Research, 1961.

Friedland, William H., and Rosberg, Carl G. Jr., eds. *African Socialism.* Stanford, California: Stanford University Press, 1964.

Galbraith, John Kenneth. *The New Industrial State.* London: Hamish Hamilton, 1967.

Galenson, Walter, ed. *Comparative Labor Movements.* New York: Prentice-Hall, 1952.

————. *Labor in Developing Economies.* Berkeley: University of California Press, 1962.

Geiger, Theodore and Armstrong, Winifred. *The Development of African Private Enterprise.* Planning Pamphlet 120. Washington, D.D.: National Planning Association, 1964.

Ghai, Dharam P., ed. *Portrait of a Minority: Asians in East Africa*. Nairobi: Oxford University Press, 1965.

Greaves, I. C. *Modern Production Among Backward Peoples*. London: G. Allen and Unwin, 1935.

Hailey, Lord. *An African Survey*. Rev. ed. London: Oxford University Press, 1957.

————. *Native Administration in the British African Territories*. Part I: East Africa. London: HMSO, 1950.

Hammond, Peter B. 'Management in Transition', *Labor Commitment and Social Change in Developing Areas*. Edited by Wilber E. Moore and Arnold S. Feldman. New York: Social Science Research Council, 1960.

Hance, William A. *The Geography of Modern Africa*. New York: Columbia University Press, 1964.

Hodgkin, Thomas. *Nationalism in Colonial Africa*. London: Frederick Muller, 1956.

Hunter, Guy. *The Best of Both Worlds?: A Challenge on Development Policies in Africa*. London: Oxford University Press for the Institute of Race Relations, London, 1967.

————. *Education for a Developing Region: A Study of East Africa*. London: George Allen and Unwin, 1963.

————. *The New Societies of Tropical Africa*. London: Oxford University Press for the Institute of Race Relations, London, 1962.

Huxley, Elspeth, and Perham, Margery. *Race and Politics in Kenya: A Correspondence Between Elspeth Huxley and Margery Perham*. Rev. ed. London: Faber and Faber, 1956.

Hymer, Stephen. 'The Multinational Corporation and Uneven Development', *Economics and World Order*. New York: World Law Fund, 1970.

———— & Rowthorn, Robert. 'Multinational Corporations and International Oligopoly: the Non-American Challenge', *The International Corporation*. Edited by C. P. Kindleberger. Cambridge, Mass.: M.I.T. Press, 1970.

Ingham, Kenneth. *A History of East Africa*. London: Longmans, 1962.

Inter-African Labour Institute. *Absenteeism and Labour Turnover*. Publication No. 69. Abidjan: Commission for Technical Co-operation in Africa South of the Sahara, 1961.

————. *The Human Factors of Productivity in Africa*. 2nd ed. London: Inter-African Labour Institute, 1960.

International African Institute. *Social Implications of Industrialization and Urbanization in Africa South of the Sahara*. Paris: UNESCO, 1956.

International Bank for Reconstruction and Development. *Economic Development of Kenya*. Baltimore: Johns Hopkins Press, 1963.

International Labour Office. *Social Policy in Dependent Territories*. Studies and Reports, Series B (Economic Conditions), No. 38. Montreal, 1944.

————. *African Labour Survey*. Studies and Reports, New Series, No. 48. Geneva, 1958.

————. *Industrial Relations in Certain African Countries*. Labour-Management Relations Series: No. 22, Documentation and Summary of Proceedings of a Seminar in Industrial Relations, Abidjan, 15–26 October. Geneva, 1964. (Mimeographed.)

N

————. *Methods and Principles of Wage Regulation*. Second African Regional Conference, Report III, Addis Ababa, 1964. Geneva, 1964.

————. *Report to the Government of Kenya on the Development of Vocational Training*. Expanded Programme of Technical Assistance. Geneva, 1965.

————. *The Report to the Government of the United Republic of Tanzania on Wages, Incomes and Prices Policy*. Dar es Salaam: Government Printer, 1967.

Johnston, T. L. *Collective Bargaining in Sweden: A Study of the Labour Market and Its Institutions*. London: George Allen and Unwin, 1962.

Joint East and Central African Board. *Race Relations in Industry and Commerce*. London: Joint East and Central African Board, 1959.

Kariuki, Josiah Mwangi. *'Mau Mau' Detainee: The Account by a Kenya African of His Experiences in Detention Camps, 1953–60*. Penguin Books, 1963.

Kenyatta, Jomo. *Facing Mount Kenya: The Tribal Life of the Gikuyu*. London: Secker and Warburg, 1953.

————. *Harambee!: The Prime Minister of Kenya's Speeches, 1963–64*. Nairobi: Oxford University Press, 1964.

Mair, Lucy. *Primitive Government*. Penguin Books, 1962.

Mandel, Ernest. 'International Capitalism and Supra-Nationality', *The Socialist Register 1967*. Edited by Ralph Milliband. London: The Merlin Press, 1967.

Marris, Robin. *The Economic Theory of 'Managerial' Capitalism*. London: Macmillan, 1964.

Mason, Edward S., ed. *The Corporation in Modern Society*. Cambridge: Harvard University Press, 1960.

Mbotela, Tom. 'An African Comments', *Kenya Controversy*. Controversy Series No. 4. London: Fabian Colonial Bureau, 1947.

Mboya, Tom. *Freedom and After*. London: André Deutsch, 1963.

————. *The Kenya Question: An African Answer*. London: Fabian Colonial Bureau, 1956.

Meynaud, Jean and Salah Bey, Anisse. *Trade Unionism in Africa: A Study of Its Growth and Orientation*. Trans. by Angela Brench. London: Methuen, 1967.

Middleton, John. 'Kenya: Changes in African Life, 1912–45', Vol. 2 of *History of East Africa*. Edited by Vincent Harlow and E. M. Chilver. Oxford: Clarendon Press, 1965.

Mitchell, Philip E. *African Afterthoughts*. London: Hutchinson, 1954.

Moore, Wilbert E. *Industrialization and Labor*. Ithaca, New York: Cornell University Press, 1951.

————, and Feldman, Arnold S., eds. *Labor Commitment and Social Change in Developing Areas*. New York: Social Science Research Council, 1960.

Morgan, D. J. *British Private Investment in East Africa*. Report of a Survey and Conference. London: Overseas Development Institute, 1965.

Morris, George. *CIA and American Labor: The Subversion of the AFL-CIO's Foreign Policy*. New York: International Publishers, 1967.

Northcott, C. H., ed. *African Labour Efficiency Survey*. Colonial Office Research Publication No. 3. London: HMSO, 1949.

November, Andras. *L'évolution du mouvement Syndical en Afrique Occidental*. Paris: Editions Mouton et Cie, 1965.

Nyerere, Julius. *Freedom and Unity/Uhuru na Umoja: A Selection From Writings and Speeches, 1952–65.* London: Oxford University Press, 1967.

OEF [Organisation of Employers' Federations and Employers in Developing Countries]. *Localisation in Developing Countries: International Conference.* [London: OEF], November 1967.

O'Connor, A. M. *An Economic Geography of East Africa.* London: G. Bell for the London School of Economics and Political Science, 1966.

Odinga, Oginga. *Not Yet Uhuru.* London: Heinemann, 1967.

Ogot, B. A. 'Migration and Settlement Among the Southern Luo Peoples'. Unpublished Ph.D. Dissertation, University of London, 1965.

Oliver, Roland, and Mathew, Gervase, eds. *History of East Africa.* Vol. 1. Oxford: Clarendon Press, 1963.

Orde Browne, G. St. J. *The African Labourer.* London: Oxford University Press for the International Institute of African Languages and Cultures, 1933; reprinted Frank Cass, London, 1967.

————. *Labour Conditions in East Africa.* Colonial Office Publication No. 193. London: HMSO, 1946.

Organisation of Employers' Federations and Employers in Developing Countries. *The Co-operation of Employers in Overseas Territories.* Occasional Papers. Rev. ed. London, 1965.

Overseas Employers' Federation. 'Industrial Organisation: Kenya', London, 1956. (Mimeographed.)

Palekar, S. A. *Problems of Wage Policy for Economic Development.* London: Asia Publishing House, 1962.

Parker, Mary. *Political and Social Aspects of the Development of Municipal Government in Kenya With Special Reference to Nairobi.* London: Colonial Office, [1949]. (Mimeographed.)

Powesland, P. G. *Economic Policy and Labour: A Study in Uganda's Economic History.* East African Studies No. 10. Edited by Walter Elkan. Kampala: East African Institute of Social Research, 1957.

Presence Africaine, *Le Travail en Afrique Noire.* Paris: Editions du Seuil, 1952.

Reynolds, Lloyd G., and Gregory, Peter. *Wages, Productivity, and Industrialisation in Puerto Rico.* Homewood, Illinois: Richard D. Irwin, 1965.

Roberts, B. C. *Labour in the Tropical Territories of the Commonwealth.* London: G. Bell for the London School of Economics and Political Science, 1964.

Rosberg, Carl G. Jr. 'Political Conflict and Change in Kenya', *Transition in Africa.* Edited by Gwendolyn Carter and Robert Brown. Boston: Boston University Press, 1958.

————, and Nottingham, John. *The Myth of 'Mau Mau': Nationalism in Kenya.* New York: Praeger for the Hoover Institution on War, Revolution, and Peace, Stanford University, Stanford, California, 1966.

Ross, Arthur M., ed. *Industrial Relations and Economic Development.* London: Macmillan for the International Institute for Labour Studies, 1966.

Ross, W. McGregor. *Kenya From Within: A Short Political History.* London: George Allen and Unwin, 1927; reprinted Frank Cass, London, 1968.

Scott, Roger. *The Development of Trade Unions in Uganda.* Nairobi: East Africa Publishing House for the East African Institute of Social Research, 1966.

Sheffield, James R., ed. *Education, Employment, and Rural Development*. The Proceedings of a Conference held at Kericho, Kenya, in September 1966. Nairobi: East Africa Publishing House, 1967.

Singh, Makham. *History of Kenya's Trade Union Movement to 1952*. Nairobi: East African Publishing House, 1969.

Smith, Anthony D., ed. *Wage Policy Issues in Economic Development*. Proceedings of a Symposium held by the International Institute for Labour Studies at Egelund, Denmark, 23–27 October, 1967, under the Chairmanship of Clark Kerr. London: Macmillan, 1969.

Sorrenson, M. P. K. *Land Reform in the Kikuyu Country*. London: Oxford University Press, 1967.

Sturmthal, Adolf., ed. *Contemporary Collective Bargaining in Seven Countries*. Ithaca, New York: Institute of International Industrial and Labor Relations, 1957.

Turner, H. A. *Wage Trends, Wage Policies and Collective Bargaining: The Problems for Underdeveloped Countries*. Occasional Papers 6. Cambridge: University Press for the Department of Applied Economics, 1965.

United Nations. Economic Commission for Africa. *Social Factors Affecting Labour Stability in Uganda*. New York, 1963.

Warmington, W. A. *A West African Trade Union. A Case Study of the Cameroons Development Corporation Workers' Union and its Relations With the Employers*. London: Oxford University Press for the Nigerian Institute of Social and Economic Research, 1960.

Weber, Arnold R. 'Stability and Change in the Structure of Collective Bargaining', *Challenges to Collective Bargaining*. The American Assembly, 30th Assembly, October 1966. Edited by Lloyd Ulman. Englewood Cliffs, New Jersey: Prentice-Hall, 1967.

Wells, F. A., and Warmington, W. A. *Studies in Industrialization: Nigeria and the Cameroons*. London: Oxford University Press for the Nigerian Institute of Social and Economic Research, 1962.

Who Controls Industry in Kenya?: Report of a Working Party [National Christian Council of Kenya]. Nairobi: East Africa Publishing House, 1968.

Who's Who in East Africa, 1965–66. Edited by E. G. Wilson. 2nd ed. Nairobi: Marco Publishers (Africa), 1966.

Wilson, Gordon. 'Mombasa: A Modern Colonial Municipality.' *Social Change in Modern Africa*. Edited by Aidan Southall. London: Oxford University Press, 1961.

Woddis, Jack. *Africa: The Lion Awakes*. London: Lawrence and Wishart, 1961.

Yesufu, T. M. *An Introduction to Industrial Relations in Nigeria*. London: Oxford University Press for the Nigerian Institute of Social and Economic Research, 1962.

II.   Periodicals, Papers, and Proceedings

Barber, William. 'Some Questions About Labour Force Analysis in Agrarian Economies with Particular Reference to Kenya', *East African Economics Review*, (N.S.), Vol. 2, No. 1 (June 1966).

Bavin, Tom. 'Organising the Plantation Workers', International Confederation of Free Trade Unions. *Free Labour World*, 118 (April 1960).

Belknap, R. J. 'The Role of Private Enterprise in a Developing Nation', *East African Management Journal*, Vol. 1, No. 1 (October 1966).

Berg, Elliot J. 'Backward Sloping Labor Supply Functions in Dual Economies: The African Case'. *Quarterly Journal of Economics*, Vol. 75, No. 3 (August 1961).

Chesworth, D. 'Statutory Minimum Wage Fixing in Tanganyika', *International Labour Review*, Vol. 96, No. 1 (July 1967).

Davies, D. I. 'The Politics of the TUC's Colonial Policy', *Political Quarterly*, Vol. 35, No. 1 (January–March 1964).

Elkan, Walter. 'Circular Migration and the Growth of Towns in East Africa', *International Labour Review*, Vol. 96, No. 6 (December 1967).

————. 'Migrant Labour in Africa: An Economist's Approach', *American Economic Review*, Vol. 49, No. 2 (May 1959).

Etherington, D. M. 'Projected Changes in Urban and Rural Population in Kenya and the Implications for Development Policy', *East African Economics Review*, (N.S.), Vol. 1, No. 2 (June 1965).

Fischer, Georges. 'Syndicats et décolonisation', *Présence Africaine*, Vol. 34, No. 35 (October 1960–January 1961).

Fox, Alan. 'Managerial Ideology and Labour Relations', *British Journal of Industrial Relations*, Vol. 4, No. 3 (November 1966).

Francis, E. Carey. 'Kenya's Problems', *African Affairs*, Vol. 54, No. 216 (July 1955).

Frankel, S. H. 'The Tyranny of Economic Paternalism in Africa', *Optima* (Supplement) (October 1960).

Ghai, Dharam P. 'Incomes Policy in Kenya: Need, Criteria, and Machinery', *East African Economic Review*, Vol. 4 (N.S.) No. 2 (December 1968).

Gonidec, P. F. 'The Evolution of Unions in Black Africa', Inter-African Labour Institute. *Bulletin* (May 1963).

Gutkind, P. C. W. 'African Responses to Urban Wage Employment', *International Labour Review*, Vol. 97, No. 2 (February 1968).

————. 'The Energy of Despair: Social Organisation of the Unemployed in Two African Cities: Lagos and Nairobi', *Civilisations*, Vol. 17, Nos. 3 and 4 (1967).

Heyer, Judith. 'Kenya's Agricultural Development Policy', *East African Economics Review*, (N.S.), Vol. 2, No. 2 (December 1966).

————. 'Kenya's Cautious Development Plan', *East Africa Journal*, Vol. 3, No. 5 (August 1966).

Howe, C. W. 'An Analysis of African Household Consumption and Financial Behaviour in Kenya and Uganda', *East African Economic Review*, Vol. 4 (N.S.) No. 2 (December 1968).

Husband, J. I. 'Wages Councils', *East African Economics Review*, Vol. 2, No. 5 (January 1955).

'KPU's Programme for a Socialist Kenya', *Africa and the World*, Vol. 5, Nos. 47 and 48 (May and June 1969).

Kamau, J. 'Problems of African Business Enterprise', *Proceedings of the Conference of the East African Institute of Social Research*. (August 1965). (Mimeographed.)

Kannappan, Subbiah. 'The Economics of Structuring an Industrial Labour Force', *British Journal of Industrial Relations*, Vol. 4, No. 3 (November 1966).

Kilby, Peter. 'African Labour Productivity Reconsidered', *Economic Journal*, Vol 17 (June 1961).

176   BIBLIOGRAPHY

Kilson, Martin Jr. 'Land and the Kikuyu: A Study of the Relationship Between Land and Kikuyu Political Movements', *Journal of Negro History*, Vol. 40, No. 2 (April 1955).

—————. 'Land and Politics in Kenya: An Analysis of African Politics in a Plural Society', *Western Political Quarterly*, Vol. 10, No. 3 (September 1957).

Knight, J. B. 'The Determination of Wages and Salaries in Uganda', *Bulletin of the Oxford University Institute of Economics and Statistics*, Vol. 29, No. 3 (1967).

'Labour Compulsion in Kenya', *International Labour Review*, Vol. 45 (June 1942).

Lauterbach, A. 'Managerial Attitudes and Economic Development', *Kyklos* (1962).

Leakey, L. S. B. 'The Economics of Kikuyu Tribal Life', *East African Economics Review*, Vol. 3, No. 1 (July 1956).

Marris, Peter. 'The Social Barriers to African Enterprise', Institute of Development Studies, Conference at Bellagio, Italy, Private Overseas Investment, October 1967. (Mimeographed.)

—————. 'Economics is Not Enough'. *East Africa Journal*, Vol. 3, No. 2 (February 1967).

Marris, R. 'Galbraith, Solow and the Truth about Corporations', *The Public Interest* (Spring 1968).

Mazumdar, H. 'Underemployment in Agriculture and the Industrial Wage Rate', *Economica* (November 1959).

Mboya, Tom. 'African Socialism', *Transition*, Vol. 8 (March 1963).

—————. 'The Development Progress in Kenya', *East Africa Journal* (October 1965).

—————. 'Incomes Policies for Developing Countries?', International Institute for Labour Studies. *Bulletin*, 3 (November 1967).

—————. 'Trade Unionism in Kenya', *Africa South*, Vol. 1, No. 22 (1957).

McCaffree, Kenneth M. 'A Theory of the Origin and Development of Employer Associations', *Proceedings of the Fifteenth Annual Meeting of the Industrial Relations Research Association*. Publication No. 30. Edited by Gerald G. Somers. Pittsburgh, December 1962. Madison, Wisconsin: Industrial Relations Research Association, 1963.

Mohiddin, Ahmed. 'Sessional Paper No. 10 Revisited', *East Africa Journal*, Vol. 6, No. 3 (March 1969).

Ord, H. Wilson. 'Private Ownership of Physical Assets in Kenya', *South African Journal of Economics*, Vol. 30, No. 4 (December 1962).

Perroux, F. and Demonts, R. 'Large Firms Small Nations', *Présence Africaine*, Vol. 10, No. 38.

Rado, Emil. 'Kenya's Salaries Report, A Holding Operation: A Review Article on Kenya's Salaries Commission Report, 1967', *East Africa Journal*, Vol. 4, No. 8 (December 1967).

—————. 'Manpower Planning in East Africa', *East African Economics Review*, (N.S.), Vol. 3, No. 1 (June 1967).

—————. 'A Review of Walter Elkan, *Migrants and Proletarians: Urban Labour in the Economic Development of Uganda*', *East African Economics Review*, (N.S.), No. 1 (1964).

Rayner, J. 'The Economic Problem and Colonial Policy in an East African Reserve', *Economica*, Vol. 1, No. 4 (1952).

'Reconstruction in Kenya', *Round Table Quarterly Review of British Commonwealth Affairs*, No. 175 (June 1954).

Reynolds, L. G. 'Wages and Employment in the Labour Surplus Economy', *American Economic Review*, Vol. 45, No. 1 (March 1965).

Riddell, David. 'Social Self-Government: Theory and Practice in Yugoslavia', *Anarchy*, 95 (January 1969).

Rotberg, Robert. 'The Rise of African Nationalism: The Case of East and Central Africa', *World Politics*, Vol 15, No. 4 (October 1962).

Sanger, Clyde and Nottingham, John. 'The Kenya General Election of 1963', *Journal of Modern African Studies*, Vol. 2, No. 1 (1964).

Savage, Donald C. 'Labour Protest in Kenya, the Early Phase: 1914–39', *Proceedings of the East African Institute of Social Research Conference*, June 1963. (Mimeographed.)

Schecter, Dan, Ansara, Michael, & Kolodney, David. 'The CIA is an Equal Opportunity Employer', *Ramparts* (July 1969).

Smith, A. D. 'Minimum Wages and the Distribution of Income with Special Reference to Developing Countries', *International Labour Review*, Vol. 96, No. 2 (August 1967).

Sofer, S., and Ross, R. 'Some Characteristics of an European Population', *British Journal of Sociology*, Vol. 2, No. 4 (December 1951).

Taira, Koji. 'Wage Differentials in Developing Countries: A Survey of Findings', *International Labour Review*, Vol. 9, No. 3 (March 1966).

Tordoff, William. 'Trade Unionism in Tanzania', *Journal of Development Studies*, Vol. 2, No. 4 (July 1966).

Vernon, Raymond. 'The Multinational Enterprise and National Sovereignty', *Harvard Business Review* (March/April 1967).

Warren, W. M. 'Urban Real Wages and the Nigerian Trade Union Movement, 1939–60', *Economic Development and Cultural Change*, Vol. 15, No. 1 (October 1966).

Wortman, Max S. Jr. 'Influences of Employer Bargaining Associations in Manufacturing Firms', *Proceedings of the Fifteenth Annual Meeting of the Industrial Relations Research Association*. Publication No. 30. Edited by Gerald G. Somers. Pittsburgh, December 1962. Madison, Wisconsin: Industrial Relations Research Association, 1963.

Yale University Economic Growth Center. *The Multinational Corporation and the Nation State: Outline and Reference Bibliography*. New Haven, Conn.: January 1968. (Mimeographed.)

III. Government Documents: Great Britain

(Arranged Chronologically)

Statement of Policy on Colonial Development and Welfare. Cmd. 6175. 1940.

Labour Supervision in the Colonial Empire, 1937–43. Colonial No. 185. 1943.

Labour Conditions in East Africa. Colonial No. 193. By G. St. J. Orde Browne. 1946.

Report of the Commission on the Civil Services of Kenya, Tanganyika, Uganda, and Zanzibar, 1947–48. Colonial No. 223. 1948.

African Labour Efficiency Survey. Colonial Research No. 3. Edited by C. H. Northcott. 1949.

Labour Administration in the Colonial Territories, 1944–50. Colonial No. 275. 1951.

Report to the Secretary of State for the Colonies by the Parliamentary Delegation to Kenya, January 1954. Cmd. 9081. 1954.

East Africa Royal Commission Report, 1953–55. Cmd. 9475. 1955.

Despatches from the Governors of Kenya, Uganda, and Tanganyika, and from the Administrator, East Africa High Commission, Commenting on the East Africa Royal Commission Report, 1953–55. Cmd. 9801, 1956.

The Colonial Territories, 1955–56. Cmd. 9769. 1956.

Labour in the United Kingdom Dependencies. Central Office of Information, 1957.

Historical Survey of the Origins and Growth of Mau Mau. By. F. D. Corfield. Cmd. 1030. 1960.

Annual Report of the Colony and Protectorate of Kenya. 1945–62.

IV.   Government Documents: Kenya and the East Africa High Commission

(Arranged Chronologically)

Native Labour Commission, 1912–13; Evidence and Report. 1913.

Report of the Commission of Inquiry appointed to Examine the Labour Conditions in Mombasa. 1939.

Sessional Paper No. 8 of 1945: Land Utilization and Settlement: A Statement of Government Policy. 1945.

Manpower, Demobilisation, and Reabsorption Report, 1945–46. 1946.

Report of the Development Committee. 2 Vols. 1946.

Analysis of Wages Paid to African Employees in Kenya for the Month of November 1946. 1947.

Report on the Economic and Social Background of Mombasa Labour Disputes. By H. S. Booker and N. M. Deverell. 1947. (Mimeographed.)

Report on African Labour Census, 1947. 1948.

Report of the Cost of Living Commission. 1950.

The Pattern of Income and Consumption of African Labourers in Nairobi, October–November 1950. 1951.

Estimates of the Geographical Income and Net Output for the Years 1947–51. No. 17, East African Statistical Department. 1952.

Some Aspects of the Development of Kenya Government Services for the Benefit of Africans from 1946 Onwards. 1953.

Report of the Committee on African Wages. 1954.

Sessional Paper No. 21 of 1954: Implementation of the Recommendations of the Report of the Committee on African Wages. 1954.

Commission on the Civil Services of the East African Territories and the East Africa High Commission Report, 1953–54. 2 Vols. 1954.

Sessional Paper No. 17 of 1954: Proposals for the Implementation of the Recommendations contained in the Report of the Commission on the Civil

Services of the East African Territories, and the East Africa High Commission, 1953–54. 1954.

A Plan to Intensify the Development of African Agriculture in Kenya. 1954.

Report of the Cost of Living Committee. 1954.

Sessional Paper No. 51 of 1955: The Development Programme, 1954–57. 1955.

Reported Employment and Wages in Kenya, 1954. 1955.

'Report and Recommendations of the Board of Inquiry Appointed by the Minister of Labour on 4th April, 1955, under Section 13 to Inquire into a trade dispute between the Kenya Local Government Workers' Union and the Nairobi City Council,' 1955. (Mimeographed.)

Sessional Paper No. 1 of 1958/59: Statement of Government Policy. 1958.

Sample Population Census of Nairobi, 1957/58. 1958.

Commerce and Industry in Kenya. 1959.

The Pattern of Income, Expenditure and Consumption of Africans in Nairobi, 1957/58. 1959.

Report of a Board of Inquiry Appointed to Inquire into Employment in the Port of Mombasa. 1959.

Report of a Board of Inquiry Appointed to Inquire into a Trade Dispute at the Athi River Premises of the Kenya Meat Commission. 1960.

Survey of Unemployment. By. A. G. Dalgleish. 1960.

Sessional Paper No. 10 of 1959/60: Unemployment. 1960.

Reported Employment and wages in Kenya, 1948–60. 1961.

Report of the Board of Inquiry into The Causes and Circumstances of the Strike in the Grain Milling Industry, April 1961. 1961.

Report of the Board of Inquiry Appointed to Inquire into the Questions of the Sisal and Coffee Plantation Workers' Union being afforded by the Kenya Coffee Growers' Association Recognition for the purposes of voluntary collective bargaining on Terms and Conditions of Employment in the Coffee Industry, and Rights of Access to its Members and Potential Members Residing on Coffee Plantations. 1962. (Mimeographed.)

Report of the Fiscal Commission. 1963.

The Growth of the Economy, 1954–62. 1963.

In the Matter of an Arbitration of a Trade Dispute between The Sisal and Coffee Plantation Workers' Union and The Kenya Coffee Growers' Association: Award of Jimmy Verjee, Esq. 1963. (Mimeographed.)

Report of the Board of Inquiry Appointed to Inquire into Labour Unrest at the Macalder-Nyanza Mines and into the Machinery for Negotiation with the Kenya Quarry and Mine Workers' Union. 1963. Mimeographed.)

Report of the Board of Inquiry Appointed to Inquire into a Trade Dispute between certain Employers as represented by the Distributive and Allied Trades Association and certain Employees as represented by the Kenya Distributive and Commercial Workers' Union. 1963. (Mimeographed.)

Abridged Texts of 1961 Trade Dispute Arbitration Awards. [1963] (Mimeographed.)

Abridged Texts of Arbitration Awards Made During 1962. 1963. (Mimeographed.)

Development Plan, 1964–70. 1964.

Revised Conditions of Service for the Kenya Civil Service. 1964.

'A Note on Unemployment in Kenya.' 1964. (Mimeographed.)

The Pattern of Income, Expenditure and Consumption of African Middle Income Workers in Nairobi, July 1963. 1964.

Abridged Texts of Arbitration Awards Made During 1963. 1964. (Mimeographed.)

Sessional Paper No. 10 of 1963/65: African Socialism and its Application to Planning in Kenya. 1965.

'Report of the National Wages Policy Advisory Committee.' [1965.] (Mimeographed.)

The Policy of Trade Union Organisation in Kenya. 1965.

High-Level Manpower: Requirements and Resources in Kenya, 1964–70. 1965.

Report of a Board of Inquiry into (i) the claim by the Dockworkers' Union to represent certain categories of worker in Mombasa, and (ii) industrial unrest in Mombasa in the year 1964. 1965. (Mimeographed.)

Ministry of Labour and Social Services Annual Report 1963. 1965.

Kenya Population Census, 1962 Vol. 3: African Population. 1966.

Development Plan, 1966–70. 1966.

Report of the Salaries Review Commission, 1967. 1967.

Ministry of Labour and Social Services Annual Report 1964. 1967.

Labour Department Annual Report. 1945–62.

Statistical Abstract.

Statistical Digest

Economic Survey

Trade Report.

Gazette and Supplements.

Legislative Council Debates.

East Africa High Commission. *Quarterly Economic and Statistical Bulletin.*

V.   Documents: Federation of Kenya Employers and Member Bodies

(Arranged Chronologically)

'Joint Consultation Report.' 1957. (Mimeographed.)

'Statement of Purpose Appended to the Joint Consultation Report.' 1957. (Mimeographed.)

'Notes on the First ACIE/KFL Meeting.' 1957. (Mimeographed.)

'Memorandum on the Essential Services (Arbitration) Ordinance From the Employer's Point of View.' 1958. (Mimeographed.)

'Memorandum on Industrial (Vertical), Craft (Horizontal) and General (Horizontal) Unions.' [1958.] (Mimeographed.)

'Notes on the Demarcation Agreement.' 1958. (Mimeographed.)

'Memorandum on the Organisation of Employers for Industrial Negotiations (The Two-tier Structure).' 1959. (Mimeographed.)

'Report on Terms of Service.' 1959. (Mimeographed.)

'Africanisation.' 1961. (Mimeographed.)

'Report on Recommended Terms of Service for Local Managerial, Executive and Senior Staff.' 1961. (Mimeographed.)

'Code of Conduct.' 1963. (Mimeographed.)

'Recommended Terms of Service for Manual Workers, Including Artisans.' 1963. (Mimeographed.)

'Survey Report: Manual Workers, Including Artisans.' 1963. (Mimeographed.)

'Copy of Agreement on Measures for the Immediate Relief of Unemployment, 10 February, 1964.' 1964. (Mimeographed.)

'Press Release: Private Provident Funds and Pension Schemes.' 1966. (Mimeographed.)

'Investment of Provident Fund Contributions: Survey Results at June 21, 1966.' 1966. (Mimeographed.)

'Copy of Statement Issued Following Meetings Between Government and COTU(K) [on Private Provident Funds].' 1966. (Mimeographed.)

'Wage Rates in Agriculture and the Plantations.' 1966. (Mimeographed.)

Engineering and Allied Industries Employers' Association. 'Handbook for Employers.' [1966.]

Motor Trade and Allied Industries Employers' Association. 'Handbook.' [1966.]

Distributive and Allied Trades Employers' Association. 'Handbook.' [1966.]

'Annual Report.' 1958–68. (Mimeographed.)

'Newsletter.' 1956–68. (Mimeographed.)

'Constitution.' 1965. (Mimeographed.)

Minutes of Meetings. 1956–66. (Typewritten.)

VI. Documents: Kenya Trade Unions

Kenya Federation of Labour. 'Reorganisation Report for February, 1962.' By Fred Kubai. (Mimeographed.)

————. 'Memorandum to the Trade Union Ministerial Committee Appointed by his Excellency the President to Consider Trade Union Developments in Kenya.' 1965. (Mimeographed.)

Central Organisation of Trade Unions. 'Forward with the Workers!: A Statement of Policy.' [1966.] (Mimeographed.)

Minutes of Meetings. COTU Governing Council.

VII. Newspapers and Magazines

East African Standard (Nairobi).
Daily Nation (Nairobi).
Kenya Weekly News (Nakuru).
The Times (London).
Financial Times (London).
Reporter (Nairobi).
Le Monde (Paris).

INDEX

African enterprise, 87, 97–8, 131, 166
Africanisation, 128–33; and employers, 54, 115, 116, 128–9, 130, 131, 132, 145, 146; ideology, 83, 131–2, 133
African Socialism, 34, 36, 37, 85, 148, 164, 165; *see also* Democratic African Socialism
African Workers' Federation, 31
Agriculture: collective bargaining, 143–4; employer association, 75, 85, 87, 88–9; workers and trade unions, 18, 70–1, 74, 75–6, 85, 88, 89, 114
Akumu, Dennis, 108, 109, 110–11, 112, 113, 114, 115–16, 117
All African Trade Union Federation, 108, 109
American Federation of Labour-Congress of Industrial Organisation, 30, 115
Amin, S., 21–2, 23
Arbitration, 33, 55–6, 64–5, 72–3, 79, 85, 122–4, 125–6, 135–7; *see also* Collective bargaining, Industrial Court
Asian community, 42, 87, 129, 130, 166
Associated Chambers of Commerce and Industry of East Africa, 48, 49, 57
Association of Commercial and Industrial Employers, 47, 54, 125, 139; founding, 49, 54–7; early trade union policy, 54–7, 63–8, 69, 70–1; *see also* Employers, Federation of Kenya Employers, International Firms

Balogh, Thomas, 154–5, 156
Banking industry, 86, 91–2
Baran, Paul A., 52, 55
Bavin, Tom, 70
Berg, Elliot, 22, 23, 29n., 155
Blumberg, Paul, 38, 39
British Government: *see* Colonial Office, Government: Colony and

Protectorate of Kenya, Labour Department
British Trade Union Congress, 30, 31, 34, 54, 104
Building industry, 86, 91, 142

Campbell, Sir Colin, 98–9, 101–2, 156, 163
Carpenter Report (Kenya Committee on African Wages), 12, 17–18, 19, 21, 22, 23, 24–5
Central Organisation of Trade Unions, 105, 111–12, 113, 114, 115, 116, 117, 118, 119, 126, 131, 132, 133, 140, 148
Check-off, 65, 66, 76, 150
Chemical industry, 86, 93
Collective bargaining, 87, 92–3, 94, 156, 162; early employer influence, 55–7, 64, 72–4; employer strategy, 148–9, 161; fringe benefits, 152–3; Government influence on terms of service, 138–41, 146; immediate post-war, 26; job categories covered, 150–1, 154; legislation, 122–5, 135; negotiable issues, 150; shadow or substance, 135–45; structure, 149, 154; *see also* Arbitration, Federation of Kenya Employers, Wages
Colonial Development and Welfare Act, 3, 12, 30
Colonial Office: trade unions, 3–5, 30, 34, 35, 104; *see also* Government: Colony and Protectorate of Kenya, Labour Department

Democratic African Socialism, xii, 129, 131
Dispute settlement procedures, 79–80, 132–3; *see also* Arbitration, Collective bargaining, Industrial Court
Distributive trades, 86, 92, 141, 142

Joint consultation, 34, 35–6, 164

Kannappan, S., 21
Kebachia, Chege, 31, 32
Kenya African Democratic Union, xii, 106, 108, 109
Kenya African National Union, xii, 106, 107, 108, 109, 110, 112, 113, 115, 116, 117, 118, 161; see also Government: Kenyatta Administration
Kenya African Union, 31, 32, 33
Kenya African Workers' Congress, 109–11, 112, 116
Kenya Committee on African Wages, 12; see also Carpenter Report
Kenya Distributive and Commercial Workers' Union (later Kenya Commercial, Food and Allied Workers' Union), 68, 69, 111, 114, 150–1
Kenya Federation of Labour, 33, 34, 65, 67, 70, 71, 75, 79–80, 85, 106, 107, 108, 109, 110, 111, 112, 114–15, 116
Kenya Local Government Workers' Union, 43, 93, 113
Kenya Peoples' Union, xii, 107, 112, 113, 114, 117, 162
Kenya Quarry and Mineworkers' Union, 78
Kenya Trades Union Congress, 107–8
Kenyatta, Jomo, xi, xii, 31, 83, 106, 107, 108, 111, 115, 116, 117, 161
Kikuyu tribe, xii, 32, 106, 112, 114, 116; see also Tribalism
Kipande, 8, 32
Kubai, Fred, 31, 32, 40, 119
Kutahi, Adam, 96

Labour: migrant, 15, 20–4; stability and turnover, 17–18, 20–2, 101
Labour Department, 12, 13, 16–17, 20, 30–1, 33, 34, 49, 53, 65, 75, 77, 79, 86, 101; see also Government
Lidbury, Sir David, 9–10
Local government, 86, 93, 139–40, 141
Longshoring industry, 85, 93, 115
Lubembe, Clement, 109, 110, 112, 113, 114–15, 116, 132
Luo tribe, xii, 41, 112, 114, 161; see also Tribalism

Mak'Anyengo, O. O., 108, 109, 110, 112, 113, 116, 117

Managerial capitalism, 51–2, 55; see also Association of Commercial and Industrial Employers, Employers, Federation of Kenya Employers, International firms
Mathu, Eliud, 8
Mau Mau, ix–x, 8, 9, 13, 14, 17, 40, 42–3, 49, 57, 106, 157, 161, 162, 164
Mboya, Tom, xii, 33, 37, 43, 66, 69, 79–80, 96, 106, 107, 108, 109, 113, 115, 161, 165
Mitchell, Philip, 14
Mohiddin, Ahmed, 131, 132
Mombasa Coast Province Employers' Association, 56, 71
Motor trades, 86n., 90–1, 141, 142
Muhanji, Sammy, 68–9

Nigeria, ix, 56, 146

Ochwada, Arthur, 107–8
Odinga, Oginga, xii, 107, 108, 112
Oil industry, 57, 85, 92, 108
Overseas Employers' Federation (later the Organisation of Employers' Federations and Employers in Developing Countries), 53–4, 94, 128–9, 131, 132

Perham, Margery, 53
Press reports, 32, 74, 115, 116
Productivity, 19–20, 24–5, 35–6
Profit sharing, 35–6, 166
Prices and Incomes Policy, see Wages

Racial discrimination: wages, 8–9, 32, 42, 130
Rado, Emil, 155
Richmond, David, 96, 99

Settler community, 15, 30, 47–8, 49, 53
Shop stewards, 76
Singh, Makham, 31, 32, 40, 119
Sweezy, Paul M., 52, 55
Strikes, 5, 16, 30, 31, 32, 37, 43, 55–6, 74–9, 91, 105, 106, 114, 117, 125, 126–7, 133, 145, 149; legislation, 33, 42, 80, 122–5, 132–3; political, 31–3, 105, 106, 107, 110–11, 114, 117, 118; public sector, 140; unofficial, 76–8, see also East African Trade Unions' Congress